KNITTING
IN PLAIN ENGLISH

Knitting
in
Plain
English

MAGGIE RIGHETTI

St. Martin's Press / New York

Design by Laura Hough

Original drawings by Maggie Righetti
Redrawn by Michael Brown

Library of Congress Cataloging in Publication Data
Righetti, Maggie.
    Knitting in plain English.
    1. Knitting.   I. Title.
TT820.R54   1986   746.9'2   86-1800
ISBN 0-312-45853-3 (pbk.)

10 9 8 7 6 5

CONTENTS

PREFACE

Whether the reader is a beginner, a casual knitter, or an experienced enthusiast, this book offers an easily understood and complete course in knitting. It begins with basic concepts and simple but useful ideas to make the project go quickly and smoothly and works up to the fine and intricate detailings that individualize a handknit. All along the way, common misunderstandings and stumbling blocks are cleared up.

Using common sense, plain English, and a sense of humor, I try to make clear the workings of the fine and ancient art of handknitting. I believe that knitting is an easy, relaxing, rewarding, creative, and exciting craft. If in the past there has been frustration and confusion, it's because no one has written about knitting in clear, direct, and vigorous language.

In addition to explaining everything from how to choose which project to make, all the way to finishing off and adding eye-catching details, this book will build the reader's confidence as each chapter is worked through. Once the knitter has mastered a basic step, I show how to create variations and think through to other possible applications. The more aware the knitter becomes, the more personal judgment will be trusted.

Knitting can be creative, thought provoking, and delightful. This book can take the knitter from "I did everything just as the instructions said and the garment doesn't fit and looks terrible" to "I did what Maggie's book said and my handknit fits and looks terrific, and I'm so proud of myself."

I want to acknowledge and give special thanks to: Debbie Allen, a treasured and dear friend, who kept me going and pushed me through the rough places; Ron Fisher, who encouraged me to do what I do best; Uncle George, who always told me to tend to my knitting; and Marilyn Barnes, a fine knitter, who read the manuscript and made suggestions.

INTRODUCTION

A KNITTING INSTRUCTOR SHARES HER EXPERIENCE

There simply isn't time for a knitting instructor to tell each and every pupil all he or she needs to know to select, knit, finish, alter, or salvage every project. Whether or not you were ever lucky enough to have a knitting instructor, there are subjects covered in this book that will make your craft more enjoyable. I've seen and solved the whole range of problems, from a beginning knitter's overly ambitious and difficult lace pattern to an experienced knitter's struggle with two-color knitting. This book is filled with many of the things I've learned.

The book is divided into four parts. The first part covers all of the things a knitter needs to be aware of before another stitch is knitted. Part 2 covers all those pesky details of working and shaping the knitted fabric into a marvelous creation. Part 3 explains the finishing touches that can transform the fabric into a useful article.

Part 4 is Learning Lessons for the beginner or intermediate knitter. These projects may be done alone or in class with a knitting instructor. They are cunningly devised to cover every possible knitting detail situation that the average knitter will encounter. Every step of the instructions is written three ways so that, later on, the knitter will recognize all styles of pattern direction-writing.

Because of the four divisions, this book can be used in many ways. Beginning and experienced knitters can start with chapter 1 and go straight through to the book's end. Advanced knitters can start with later chapters and pick up intricate and new techniques, or jog their memories for half-remembered ones. This book can be used as a text and reference by knitting instructors.

The emphasis in this book is on making knitting a creative, delightful, and joyous endeavor and thing to do.

I

BEFORE YOU
BEGIN TO KNIT

1

YOU CAN ALWAYS TELL WHAT'S WRONG WITH THE GARMENT BY THE WAY THE MODEL IS POSED

or

SLENDER FIVE-FOOT-TEN-INCH-TALL MODELS CAN LOOK GOOD IN ANYTHING

It happens every June and it happens every January. It happens so regularly you can count on it.

Every June and January, starry-eyed and eager craftspeople invade their friendly local yarn supplier bearing fresh-off-the-press copies of the needlework periodicals that are blossoming with elegant and enchanting visions of projects to make, sweaters to create—and potential disasters.

A part of the knitting instructor's job is to help people understand the techniques and details necessary for them to complete the project they have chosen to make. An equal and perhaps even greater part of the instructor's job is gently but firmly to steer people away from projects with problems, sweaters that will sag, and demoralizing disasters.

Simply the fact that we knitting instructors see hundreds of garments both in progress and completed means we also become painfully aware of what the knitted fabric will and will not do. And after the fitting and adjusting of hundreds of garments on hundreds of different kinds, sizes, and shapes of people, we have become absolutely certain of what shapes knitting will take and what shapes the human body will not.

So every June and January (and often in between) I gather these starry-eyed and eager knitters around the work table, and using their new periodicals as texts, I hold an impromptu class called "You Can Always Tell What Is Wrong with the Garment by the Way the Model Is Posed." It's a fun class with lots of giggles, "ah-ha"'s, and exclamations like "So that's why it never looked right!"

Listen in and join the class. I'll assign you your homework before we begin. Pick up your newest periodical that is filled with knitting designs and look at the photos. That's all. Just look—and then think about them. Your homework is to *look* for yourself, *think* for yourself, and *learn* to recognize for yourself when something is not quite right.

With as many patrons around me as I can gather, the lesson starts. Beginning with the cover, I say:

Be aware—beware—of any garment whose model is not standing in a normal relaxed position.

1

A good-looking, well-designed, properly proportioned garment can easily stand scrutiny. It looks good straight on and on straight. The model could just stand there and you'd want to make the garment, sure in the knowledge of what the finished project would look like. A sweater worth making has nothing to hide.

But what if the model is posed in an exaggerated way so you can't see the neckline or the wrists or both shoulders? The model on the cover of your first impromptu text is a perfect example. *(See drawing # 1.)* You can only see one shoulder. The neckline is covered up with a very attractive blouse. But you are not making the blouse— you are making the sweater and you haven't the foggiest idea of how the neck is finished or where it is supposed to sit on the human body. One wrist is covered by a bracelet; the other is hidden in shadow.

The model is posed as if she were stretched out in front of a roaring fire all cuddly and warm and enjoying her wonderful sweater. Heaven help her, though, if she tried to get up and walk to a window to look out. Her sweater would probably drop to her knees, judging by the way the bottom of it is hidden in folds. You'd have no idea whether it was just a case of a tiny model and a sweater too big for her, or if the waistline was intended to be the hemline.

You really need to know what you're making and what it's supposed to look like and how it's intended to fit before you begin. If you don't know these things, how will you know if you are doing it right?

If you can't see the whole garment in the photo, don't make it!

Next is a picture of a striking handbag, we all agree. The model is posed in a knit dress, of course, Yet this large handsome shoulder bag is the focal point of the photo. If this is a knitting book whose instructions are trying to sell the yarn for a knit dress, why cover it up with a luscious handbag? *(See drawing # 2.)*

A veteran of misleading photos of knitting projects, whom my class calls Grandma, immediately spots the inconsistencies. "She carries that handbag because the shoulders don't fit. Just look at the picture—you can't see the left shoulder at all, it's turned away and out of the picture. The right shoulder is covered up with the strap of the bag. What's more, the bag covers her waistline. If the dress looked good, they wouldn't have to hide it. Now, if it had raglan sleeves and if the waist were brought in somehow, it'd be good looking. They can't fool an old lady like me with a huge handbag." She has learned to separate the fiction from the reality.

Younger, more inexperienced knitters quickly learn how to detect the inconsistencies between the photograph and the finished product. One points out that the dress is vertically striped and that all the stripes are the same width from top to bottom. "So where did the extra width at the waist and bust go?"

2

A retired salesclerk explains with a laugh. "Well, honey, in the old days when I was selling dresses, if it was too big around the waist or in the bust, we'd just hold it together in the back while the customer was looking in the mirror. That's the old clothespin-in-the-back trick."

The knitters in the class know that they can't walk around with a clothespin-in-the-back, and they won't make a "cannot work" project.

On the next page of the magazine is a study of a sweet young thing in marvelous golden tones. Her hair is spun gold, the sweater tawny gold, and the chair golden brown. We can't tell where one begins and the other ends. It is all one golden glow. *(See drawing # 3.)*

The class "ooh"'s at the lovely illusion. It is great mood photography. But as far as information about the sweater pattern it is trying to sell, it is a big loss.

I ask the class, "Honestly now, can you visualize yourself in the sweater? Where will the neckline fit around your neck? Where do the shoulders rest? Does it have shoulders at all? How long are the sleeves? How will they fit around your arms? Where and how does the garment end? If you make it, you may find out—to your dismay!"

3

The class "ah-ha"'s. We flip over the page.

From the next photo, you could mail-order the jewelry and know exactly what you would be getting. The sweater, however, is another matter. (*See drawing # 4.*)

The class has caught on and learned the lesson well. They ask me to forget the jewelry and tell them about the sweater.

I begin, "It has a collar."

"What kind?" they ask.

"I can't tell, but it has sleeves."

"What kind?"

"I can't tell."

"How long are they?" they ask.

"I can't tell, but I don't think that they are long," I answer.

"How long is the sweater? Where does it end?"

"I can't tell, but I can tell you that if I try to tuck a sweater into a gathered skirt, I look like a barrel."

"Why don't they show the shoulders?"

"I don't know. I don't want to make the sweater, but I do want to know how I can order the jewelry."

Because we can't order the jewelry, we turn the page. (*See drawing # 5.*) Listen in again.

"That's cute."

"Which one, the sweater or the hat?"

"Both!"

"How can you tell that the sweater's 'cute'?"

"What is it made of?"

"I can't see. Get a magnifying glass."

"It's made of some sort of fuzzy stuff."

"I'd rather make the hat."

"Well, you've got to admit the hat is a real show stopper."

"Are there instructions for it?"

"Look on page seventy-eight."

"No hat instructions."

"How about the sweater?"

"It has instructions."

No one can tell anything about the sweater; there isn't even a graphic drawing. Granny says, "If the sweater was worth making they'd show it to us. It's called 'attraction by association.' Because the hat is pretty, you just naturally think the sweater is pretty, too."

We turn to yet another page, still looking for something to make. (*See drawing # 6.*)

"A coat—I need a short car coat."

"I've always wanted a knitted car coat."

"Too bad they didn't put that one on a slender model—she looks dumpy."

"She *is* skinny. Look at the cheek bones and neck. It's the coat that's dumpy and huge."

We look at the instructions. They say "small, medium, and large." There is no indication of how small "small" is, nor how large "large" is. There are no drawings, charts, or measurements included in the instructions.

We don't know if it was merely that there was only a slender model available for a large coat when the photo was taken or if the garment was planned to be huge and dumpy. Since we don't know what size to make, we can't make the car coat either.

In the same way we go through the whole periodical, the students getting wiser all the time. Never again will they make a garment that they cannot clearly see. Never a garment that has places covered up. Nor will these students be taken in by set-in sleeves made according to the "book," for God was not consulted about the variety of human shoulders to be covered. Set-in sleeves, particularly in a horizontally striped garment, lose a great deal aesthetically. To fit in the armhole opening properly, a sleeve cap should be one and one half inches shorter than the armhole depth. The stripes, however, must be the same number of rows wide. The problem becomes where to lose the extra one and one half inches and still make the stripes of the two pieces match. It's not easy, but if you recognize the problem, it can be solved.

Any other type of sleeve rather than set-in sleeves—for instance, raglan, dropped shoulder, or saddle sleeves—look better *on* the wearer (which is where they should be, rather than left in the bottom of a drawer somewhere). In pictures, the problem of poorly fitting shoulders and sleeves can be solved by hiding at least one shoulder and "adjusting" the other. You can't do that when you are wearing the garment. *If the shoulders fit, they would be shown.* Those smart-looking pictures of men's sweaters frequently show the models with hands on hips and chest out in order to straighten the armhole wrinkles. Outstretched arms are often used to camouflage the saggy-baggy look.

The picture-book lesson concludes with the realization that the proper fit for the proper person can be achieved. Eyes have been opened; minds have been awakened; knitters have become aware. Even if you couldn't attend my class, you can become aware also.

Look at old, as well as new, knitting pattern books and magazines. Try to avoid the projects where the model is in an exaggerated pose. Look for a pattern that may be adapted to your special way of life, quite unlike the model in the phony setting. See for yourself the good and bad ways the design is shown and choose the project most suited for the personality of the wearer.

Look at current high-fashion magazines to spot classic good looks and high style. This is how many handknitters steer away from faddy projects. On the other hand many fast and prodigious knitters make a whole wardrobe of "fads." It is best to "know thyself." Don't start something that will obviously be out of style by the time you finish it. Do indulge in smaller fun things if someone will wear them when you get them finished.

Don't get into a khaki-colored K 1, P 1 rut. Do try a new bouquet of knit patterns. Know the person who will wear what you knit because, if it is liked and worn, it makes the knitting more fun.

Look for knitting ideas, not just in knit shops, but in fashion stores and on the street. Observe strangers and friends. Try on garments to test their feel and the way they are made. Ask other knitters what they are doing or have done and if they would do it again. Most knitters are friendly people who will happily share their projects, their past glories, and sometimes even their disasters. To study other people's knits is better than copying the adjusted photographed model.

Don't fault the magazine editors who select these photos. They are journalists and they may or may not be knitters. Most probably they are not knitting instructors. They do not necessarily understand the limitations of either knitted fabric or the human body. They have to create magazines that will sell.

And don't fault the photographers, either. Photographers are artists. Rarely are they knitters. They simply do the best they can with what they are given to create an attractive picture.

Look for yourself. Think for yourself. Learn to recognize for yourself when something is not right, and trust the judgment of the knitting instructor at your helpful yarn supplier.

2
GAUGE CAN GET YOU

When I was a beginning knitter, I worried about a lot of things, but I never worried about gauge. I worried about having exactly the right yarn called for in the instructions. I worried about having precisely the right needles. I worried about following the instructions exactly as they were written. But I never even thought about gauge.

I didn't understand it, so I never bothered to consider it; I just knitted merrily away. Sometimes things were too big. Sometimes they were too small. Once in a while they were just the right size.

When things were too small or too large I gave them away. It was always the knitting of the thing that I loved, not the knitted thing. The few things, the very few things, that were just right were enough to keep me knitting.

I did wonder though, even back in those early days, just why some things came out to be the size I had hoped for and why most did not. The yarn was right, the needles were right, I followed the directions exactly. Everything was perfect except the garment didn't fit.

Then I went to Mexico, and those beautiful women told me about gauge. That

Stitches per inch times the desired number of inches will determine the size.

Sure enough, it was right there: "Gauge: 9 sts = 2 in" and it began to develop some meaning for me.

I started to look at the instructions for how to measure gauge. Some said to place pins in the work an inch apart and then count the stitches in between the pins. Some said to use a window in cardboard or a metal check guide and then count the stitches in the window.

I got out a ruler and tried to count the number of stitches I was getting in one inch. It was hard to count those funny wiggly things, but count I did. I did not count them accurately, but I did count them. Still, my projects didn't come out the size that they should have.

I bought every book on knitting that I could find and finally stumbled across a method of making a four-inch-wide swatch with two colors of yarn so you could measure in between the color changes. And try to measure I did. It wasn't always accurate.

MEASURING GAUGE

It wasn't until I went to work for Ruth at the local knit shop that I really learned how to accurately measure gauge.

A gauge swatch must be made on the needles and the yarn that you will be using for the project. A gauge swatch must be in the pattern stitch specified. A gauge swatch must be made when the knitter is comfortable and at ease. A gauge swatch must be at least 4 inches wide. Don't try to count the stitches within the swatch. Divide the total number of stitches in the swatch by the width of the piece.

Let's take that previous paragraph apart sentence by sentence and see what it means. Because gauge is so all important to successful knitting, it is vital that we understand all the facets of it.

To make an accurate test piece, *you must use the same needles and yarn that you will use in making the garment itself.* There can be a huge difference in the circumference of one manufacturer's size 8 needle and another manufacturer's. There can be a difference in circumference of the same manufacturer's aluminum size 8 needle and his nylon size 8. All size 8 needles are not created equal. Neither do all needles allow the yarn to "float" over them with equal ease. Different needles of the same size can give you a different gauge with the same yarn. Sometimes the differences in needles will amount to nothing. Sometimes it will significantly affect your gauge.

Different colors of the same kind of yarn may have different weights. Usually white and very light-colored yarns will be thinner than the same yarn in deep and dark colors. The dyes used to achieve the darker hues cause the differences. You may get a different gauge on the same needles with navy blue than you do with white. There may be no difference at all, but the one time you try to make a gauge swatch with a different color is the one time that it *will* make a difference. If you get three and a half stitches to the inch instead of four, your garment may be huge.

Pattern stitches will affect your gauge. My laces and seed stitch are much, much looser than my stockinette stitch with the same yarn and needles. If you were to make a test swatch in stockinette stitch, would it be the same width as when you were working in cables or lace? Not necessarily!

(There is another advantage to making the test swatch in the pattern stitch of the garment. If the pattern drives you up the wall on the sample, you can change your mind before you start the garment and choose a different pattern stitch.)

PROBLEMS WITH GAUGE

When I was first working as a knitting instructor, I *forced* my patrons to make a gauge swatch in the store under my very eyes before I sent them home with their instructions. I soon found that that was a mistake. "In the store under my very eyes" many knitters were under pressure and strained to do a perfect, but hurried piece. When they got home and relaxed their gauge changed. The fault was not theirs, it was mine. *An accurate gauge swatch needs to be made in a comfortable environment.*

Don't you notice a difference in your work when you are feeling good and all is going well, and when you are nervous and tense and worried? Sure you do! Your gauge swatch needs to reflect your "most of the time" attitude.

It is also true that room temperature and humidity can affect your gauge, but if we were going to worry about that, we are going to worry ourselves out of knitting altogether.

Any swatch less than 4 inches wide just doesn't tell the story. It is too hard to account for half and quarter stitches per inch in a smaller piece. To make a 4-inch-wide gauge swatch, look at your instructions. Usually just below the suggested yarn and needles and before the directions themselves there is a note about gauge. Sometimes the word "tension" will be used instead of gauge. Both words mean the same thing. The note about gauge or tension should tell you how many stitches you ought to get in one or two inches. Multiply that to get 4 inches of stitches if directions to make a swatch are not given.

If the instructions say, GAUGE: 5 stitches = 1", multiply by 4 to get the number of stitches for a 4-inch-wide swatch. If you find, GAUGE/TENSION: 9 sts = 2 ins, multiply by 2 to get the number of stitches that you will need to make a 4-inch-wide swatch.

In a comfy place at a quiet time, cast on 4 inches worth of stitches with the yarn and the needles that you intend to use for the project. Work even in the pattern stitch for 4 inches. Stop. With the side the public will see face down, lay the swatch on a flat surface. In the middle, measure across the whole width of the piece, gently uncurling the side edges if necessary. If the piece is less than 4 inches wide, get some larger needles. If the piece is more than 4 inches wide, get some smaller needles. Make a purl ridge row across your swatch so that you can see where you changed to different needles. Work even on the new needles for 4 inches. Stop and measure again. If it still is not 4 inches wide, try another set of needles. Work however many times it takes until your piece is 4 inches wide. Always divide the total number of stitches by the width of the piece. That is your gauge.

Placing pins one inch apart in your work and then counting the stitches between the pins doesn't work. The pins themselves distort the knitted fabric and throw the count off.

Flagging stitches with a different color and measuring between the flagged stitches does not always tell the truth. The changing of colors to flag the stitches can distort the fabric.

Using a "window" in cardboard or in a metal device is an invitation to disaster. It is too easy to flatten the fabric and stretch it apart or to scooch it together to "prove" that your gauge is correct. I have cheated on myself more times than I care to tell using the "window" technique.

Gauge determines size. A difference in stitches per inch can be the difference between too large, too small, and just right. Check it out for yourself. At five stitches to the inch, one hundred stitches will be twenty inches wide. At four stitches to the inch, one hundred stitches will be twenty-five inches wide. That five-inch difference is the difference between fit and failure.

Please don't just make a gauge swatch once and think that forever after your gauge will be fine, and remain the same throughout the garment. That was the mistake I made as a beginning knitting instructor. Rather, *stop and check your work for total width as you go along.*

After you have knitted on your piece for about 2 inches in pattern stitch, spread it out and measure the total width. If your needles are not long enough to spread the work, slip a portion of the stitches onto an extra-smaller-size circular needle so that the article can lay flat.

If the width is correct, you can continue on in confidence, having spent only a few moments to make sure that you are accomplishing what you set out to do.

If it is not the width that you want it to be, stop working on it. Switch to different needles, follow the directions for a larger or smaller size, or ask your yarn dealer what to do. Please don't continue working on something that is not right! Life gives all of us enough problems to cope with. We don't need to manufacture our own.

Any time during the making of a project you can spread it out and check it for width. The Bible says that God checked out Creation and saw that ". . . it was good, it was very good." You should do the same with the stitches that you are creating.

Please worry about gauge before worrying about anything else.

3

DON'T GET ALL
BALLED UP IN YARN

Before you start another knit, crochet, weaving, or craft project, let's talk about the materials you'll use, in this instance the yarns themselves. There is no reason to get all balled up in yarns. They are simple enough to understand if you unravel their parts strand by strand.

Books—whole textbooks and encyclopedias, in fact—have been written about yarns: the histories of how they have been made in the past, the types and shapes of the fibers that compose them, how they are carded and spun, and how they are dyed. I don't deny the importance of this type of information, but that is not what I want to talk about.

What I want to discuss is the yarn most of us usually use—commercially spun, standardized stuff that we purchase from our friendly local yarn supplier.

My eyes dance and my fingers tingle when I begin to write about the glorious array of colors and textures that are available for purchase today. We are very fortunate indeed to have such a variety to choose from. It is about making a wise choice that this chapter is written.

Recently, I went to a regional needlework trade show and there, in the vendors' booths, laid out before me, were incredibly lovely color combinations, enchanting mixtures of fibers and textures, glossy yarns and fluffy yarns, tweeds and heathers. My hands wanted to stop and play with them all.

And *play* with the yarns we must, in order to make an intelligent choice from the more than 1,500 possible selections available in the marketplace today. Only by taking them in our hands, manipulating them, and testing them out, will we know what to purchase.

Always buy the best quality yarn you can afford. There are as many stitches and hours in an article of poor-quality yarn that will not last through half a dozen wearings as there are in an heirloom quality creation.

Fine quality and high price do not always go together. Good workable yarn is not always expensive, and expensive yarn is not always good and workable. There are a few quick and easy tests that you can make to find out if a yarn is of good quality and knittability.

TESTS FOR YARN

Poor yarns will ball or pill at points of wear. An easy way to check out whether a yarn has a tendency toward this is to rub it between your fingers. Hold the ball, skein, or hank in your left hand. Place about three or four strands of yarn between your right thumb and forefinger and rub them together eight or ten times. See what happens to the yarn. This is what will happen to the yarn between the sleeve and the body at the underarm if you make it up into a sweater. Do you like what is happening to those strands of yarn? If they ball or pill before they are ever worked up with just a few rubs of your fingers, that yarn is not worth your time, effort, or energy. Some yarns are notorious for this behavior. Cashmere and certain acrylic yarns are good examples of it, one very expensive and the other very cheap. Neither has good wearing qualities, though both have other advantages. Cashmere is deliciously soft, while acrylics can be used and abused, machine washed and dried.

When you do the "rub test," also check to see if the yarn comes apart. Do the threads that are "plyed" together to form the finished yarn separate? Will it come apart as you are working with it and possibly slow down your progress and hasten your frustration? Quality yarns do not separate.

After you have finished the "rub test," do the "stretch and snap back" test. "Test the yarn for resilience" is the fancy way to say it. Position your hands about three inches apart. Hold a single strand of yarn between the thumb and forefinger of each of your hands. Pull firmly on the yarn and then quickly release the tension. Is the yarn elastic? Does it pop back or does it stay stretched out? Good resilience is a characteristic of fine wool yarn. Some synthetic yarns have been specially treated so that they, too, have great resilience. Cotton, linen, and silk all have poor elasticity. This is the reason that so many of today's yarns are blends of different fibers—to get the best characteristics of each.

Next time you are in a yarn shop, "stretch and snap back" half a dozen different yarns and note the results. Experienced knitters can knit successfully with yarns that have no resilience. Beginners and intermediate knitters will be happier working with yarns that "stretch and snap back."

Quality in yarns can also refer to the yarn only having a few "bad" spots. All yarns will have some "bad" spots: places where the strands that make up the yarn were joined, drops of oil that soil the fiber, bits of foreign matter in the yarn, or areas that are frayed or simply not twisted together. One or two "bad" spots per ball or skein is okay. More than that and the yarn is poorly manufactured.

Quality also refers to the evenness of dye and color fastness of the yarn. For these two factors you should trust the experience of your dealer, who will not knowingly stock an inferior yarn; he or she can't afford to. Your retailer depends on your repeat purchases to stay in business. His or her experience in selling and working with the yarn is your guide to assuring yourself fine quality.

Just because a yarn looks luscious and inviting sitting on the shelf or displayed attractively in a basket doesn't mean that it will be fun to work with. Not all yarns are easily knittable. Some yarns split and fracture no matter how careful the knitter is. Regardless of the price, or lack of it, no yarn is worth working with if it drives you up the wall just to make simple stitches.

Some "novelty" and "specialty" yarns that have lots of extraneous threads and loops are the dickens to knit with. At times my needle has a hard time telling which is the yarn strand and which is just a fancy loop. Don't be angry with your local shop if the proprietor refuses to order some yarn you saw written up in a magazine. The owner probably saw it at the last trade show and decided not to subject customers to such torment.

APPROVING THE YARN

After you have decided whether or not a yarn is of sufficiently good quality to deserve your time, and that it is knittable enough to deserve your effort, you still have another test to make.

It is impossible to tell how a yarn will look without making a swatch. Color flecks that dance before your eyes in a skein may get absorbed and lost in the knitted fabric. The brilliant baubles may all fall on the purl side of stockinette stitch. Yarns that look dull and uninviting on the shelf may come to life in your hands as you knit them.

There is no substitute for making a swatch before you buy. Look at the label for an indication of needle size and gauge. Then cast on four inches of stitches and play with your intended. You'll not only find out what happens to the color, but you'll soon know whether or not your fingers approve of your selection.

Most yarn shop owners love yarns and will allow you to play with them before you buy. (They love to play with them, too!) Don't allow yourself to be pressured into buying a yarn that you are not familiar with and cannot experiment with.

CLASSES OF YARNS

I used the word *ply* a few paragraphs back to describe the individual threads that are twisted or worsted together to make a strand of yarn. Now I want to dispel some ideas about "plyed" yarns, as in three-ply, four-ply, eight-ply, and twelve-ply yarns.

Ply has nothing to do with the weight or class of the yarn.

It means how many strands are twisted together. Modern manufacturing methods can give us very heavy two-ply yarns and very thin twelve-ply yarns. Don't depend on the word *ply* to determine which kind of yarn to buy for a particular pattern.

Today yarns are divided into classes, and directions will often call for a certain class of yarn:

- *Class A* is fingering-weight yarn. It is usually worked at a gauge of 7 or more stitches per inch on very small needles (U.S.A. sizes 1, 2, and 3). Class A yarn is used to make socks and gloves, fine neck scarves, and beautiful blouses. Machine knitters are fond of it.

- *Class B* is sport-weight yarn. It is usually worked at around 6 stitches to the inch on medium-size needles (U.S.A. sizes 5 and 6). Class B yarn is used to make sweaters, dresses, skirts and suits, scarves, shawls, hats, mittens, baby things, and such. Machine knitters use lots of it.

- *Class C* is heavy-weight yarn. It is usually worked at around 4 to 5½ stitches per inch on large-size needles (U.S.A. sizes 8 or 9). Class C is the most widely used weight of yarn. Sweaters, mittens, vests, leg warmers, hats, jackets, scarves, and afghans are made of it.

- *Class D* is bulky-weight yarn. It is usually worked at 4 or less stitches to the inch on rather large needles. Class D yarns vary greatly in thickness and are used to make heavy sweaters, coats, jackets, parkas, afghans, and specialty items.

- *Class E* is extra-bulky yarn. It requires huge needles and works up in a gauge of less than 3 stitches to the inch. Please don't be seduced into making a whole wearable garment of this stuff, thinking that because of the gauge it will be quick to knit. It may also be quick to lose its shape and form.

From the beginning of time, trade, and barter, wool and yarns have been sold by weight. Unfortunately nobody uses them that way. We use yarn by the inch, meter, and yard, as the stuff runs through our fingers to become lovely fabrics. In order to use yarns, we need to know how many yards there are in a ball, skein, hank, or cone of yarn and compare it to how many yards are required to make an article.

A two-ounce ball of yarn can contain anywhere between 28 and 285 yards of material. To say that an article will require twelve grams of yarn is to give no help at all. We need more specific information than that.

In the United States in 1984, there were more than 175 companies selling more than 2,000 different yarns. I don't know of a retailer who can keep in her head all of the details about all of the yarns that are available. Some way had to be found to make sense and order out of how much yarn is needed to make what out of which kind of yarn.

I compile and publish Maggie Righetti's *Universal Yarn Finder*™ to be a guide through the tangled maze of yarns so that you can easily tell how much yarn you will need for specific projects. It is on sale at your local yarn retailer's shop. Because new yarns are continually being added and old unsuccessful ones are deleted from manufacturers' lines, I update the *Universal Yarn Finder* about every 18 months.

Use the *Yarn Finder* as a guideline and depend upon the experience of your yarn supplier to determine how much yarn you will need to make the object of your heart's desire. Never be afraid to buy too much yarn. Too little yarn is an invitation to dismay, discouragement, and uncompleted projects.

When you purchase yarn, you yourself should check the dye-lot marking on each and every skein. It is possible for a slight variation of color to occur each time a batch of threads are dyed to make up a yarn. It is almost impossible to procure the identical color time after time. Therefore yarn manufacturers mark each skein or ball with a "dye-lot" or "color batch" number.

> Make sure that all the yarn of one color that you buy for a project is from the same dye lot and that you buy enough to complete the article.

It is not the responsibility of the yarn manufacturer or seller to make sure that you have enough yarn of the correct dye lot to complete *your project.* I hope that you care enough about yourself to make sure.

THE NAP

After you have conjured up in your mind how the completed garment will look, selected your yarn and your needles, decided on what instructions to follow, there is another factor to contend with. That concerns the "nap" or "grain" of the yarn itself.

In the spinning or manufacturing process, individual hairs of the fiber are laid on top of one another and then twisted together. It is inevitable that the yarn will feel smoother in one direction than in the other. Corduroy or velvet flattens under your hands when you run them in one direction, and stiffens and bristles when you run your hands in the other. The same thing happens with yarns. Try it and see. On some yarns there will be a very definite "nap" or "grain." On others you will be hard pressed to tell the difference.

Place your hands close together. Hold a single strand of yarn between your thumbs and forefingers. Slowly and gently move your right hand to the right. Place your hands close together again. Now slowly and gently move your left hand to the left.

Did you feel any difference? Did the yarn feel hairier going in one direction than in the other? You may not be able to feel any difference on smooth classic worsted or cabled yarns, but you will certainly feel a difference on fuzzy and mohair yarns.

Life was meant to be easy and fun. Don't make knitting hard for yourself by fighting with the way the yarn was meant to flow. Use the yarn from either the inside or the outside of a pull skein according to the "grain" or "nap" of the yarn so that it moves through your fingers with the least resistance. Look at the label. Some manufacturers are kind enough to tell you which way to use the yarn. Others are not, and then it is up to you to make life easier.

Yarns can be purchased in balls, skeins, hanks, or cones. Balled, skeined, or coned yarns can be used directly as they come from the store if the flow is with the grain of the yarn. Hanked yarn must be wound into balls before it is used or you will end up with a tangled mess.

If you find it necessary to make a ball of your yarn, please do it lovingly. Consider yarn as a vital, resilient, almost living entity. Treat it gently and with special care, and it will reward you. Never let me catch you with a hard lifeless baseball-like ball of yarn more ready for the Little League field than for your knitting basket.

Determine which way you want the yarn to flow through your fingers as you knit. Wind the yarn into a ball the opposite way against the grain because you will be using it from the outside in. Wind the yarn around your thumb and first two fingers as a cushion so that the ball will be as soft and yielding as fresh homemade ice cream.

If you use lots of hanked yarns you may want to invest in a swift or skein holder, as it is sometimes called, and a yarn baller. Because no one ever seems to be handy (and clean) at the time I need a skein held for balling, and because as a designer I find myself ripping back sometimes to get just the effect I want, I find them both invaluable tools.

YARN LABELS

We have discussed yarns, their characteristics and tests to determine quality, and I've given hints to avoid frustration and annoyance. Let us now take a moment to examine yarn labels and the valuable information we can glean from them. Not all spinners put all of the following facts on their labels, but let us suppose that one of them did. From the label we might be able to learn the following:

- *Name of the manufacturer or distributor and the mailing address.* Useful if you should ever want to contact them, ask if they still make the stuff, inquire where it can be purchased in your area. (If it is not on the label, the address of many manufacturers can be gotten from the *Universal Yarn Finder* or from your local library's reference department.)

- *Name (or quality) of the yarn.* "Floppy" or "Glop-Glop" for instance—and sometimes the article number of the yarn for reordering or reference. Some spinners outside the USA use the term "quality" instead of "name."

- *Color name and/or number.* "Blue" or "Bright Blue Medium" or "Azure" or "Heavenly" or "Brt Blu Med # 36." (Some companies show a great deal of imagination and image suggestion with their yarn names; some companies are simple and matter-of-fact.)

- *Dye lot or batch number.* I hope I have made clear the importance of buying enough yarn of the same dye lot to complete your project.

- *Weight of the ball, skein, hank, or cone.* The weight may be given in ounces or grams. There are lots of conversion or equivalency charts around if you need to change ounces to grams or grams to ounces.

- *Length of the yarn.* That is, the *approximate* number of yards or meters in the "put-up" amount. Length will vary slightly with color and dye lot.

- *Fiber content.* What the stuff is made of. Usually it is given in percentages. Knowing the fiber content gives you some indication of what the stretch or shrinkage factor of the finished thing will be, if any.

- *Suggested gauge or tension.* Both words mean the same thing.

- *Suggested needle size.* A suggestion, *just* a suggestion, as to what size needle or hook to try first to see if you can work to the recommended gauge/tension to attain the desired fabric.

- *Suggested uses.* A little nicety where the spinner may suggest "specially for baby things," or "not recommended for small children's garments," or "ideal for socks."

- *Direction from which to use the yarn.* The spinner may tell you which way to use the skein, from the inside out or from the outside in.

Many yarn labels include the international completed garment cleaning and care symbols as well as pictographs about usage. More and more we are a community of the world, and trade extends everywhere. To overcome translation difficulties, things and processes that are alike all over the globe have been tagged with nonlanguage symbols. People all over the world wash their clothes. Words may vary, but a picture of a wash tub is a picture of a wash tub wherever yarns are sold. These, then, are some of the nonlanguage symbols that may appear on commercial yarn labels.

- A single diagonal slash or a superimposed "X" means *don't* in any language!

- A basin or wash tub means *hand washable.* Sometimes water temperature is indicted in Fahrenheit or Celsius or both.

- An automatic washing machine means just that, *machine washable.* Again, sometimes water temperature as well as type of cycle, such as gentle, is indicated.

- An isosceles triangle with the letters "Cl" inscribed in it stands for *chlorine bleach.*

- A circle with the capital letter "A", "P", or "F" in it symbolizes *dry cleaning* and the type of fluids used.

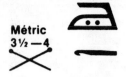

Métric
3½ — 4

- A steam iron means the finished article can be *steam blocked.*

- Knitting needles or a crochet hook indicate the *suggested size* to try. Unfortunately, we don't always know whether it is U.S., U.K., or metric.

- A 4-inch (or 10 cm) gauge swatch gives the manufacturer's recommended *gauge/tension.*

Life is always a compromise, a balancing act. It is impossible to do everything. And so with the labels on the yarns we use. They must be attractive to the eye. They must be compatible with the yarn they wrap. They must be large enough to allow the yarns to be visible and intriguing in their own right. By the nature of the thing, labels are small. What we want and need to know is great. It is not always possible for the manufacturer to put everything on all labels, so he must sometimes compromise. The information we do get is better than no information at all.

Yarn is the material we use to perform our knitting. Without it we could make only "the emperor's new clothes." Understanding it allows us to create marvelous works of art. Now that we've unraveled it strand by strand, you never have to get "all balled up" in yarn.

4

SOME POINTED REMARKS ABOUT KNITTING NEEDLES

It is true that we *could* knit with anything, with cobwebs or cables, with toothpicks or telephone poles. In fact, we usually knit with commercially spun, standardized yarns and factory-made, uniformly sized knitting needles.

In this chapter we are going to consider modern knitting needles, and we need to be aware of three things:

1. The *shape* of the needles—straight or circular, single or double pointed

2. the *form of the tips* of the needles—blunt or sharp

3. the *surface finish* of the needles—that is, how they allow the yarn to float over them.

To begin, let's see if we can reconstruct a bit of the history of knitting needles and how we arrived at the products we now use so we might understand what will best serve our purposes today.

Knitting is old. Knitting is portable. It is an easily learned way of making fabric to keep bodies warm and protected from the elements. Before recorded history and the written word, most nomadic peoples who herded fur-bearing animals had figured out how to do it.

In all probability, early man used the sharpened slender bones of animals for knitting needles. Can you imagine some shepherd twisting together the strands of fur he found clinging to a thorn bush along a trail to make yarn? Can you imagine him picking up from around the campfire the discarded small leg bone of a deer or antelope and looping the yarn over the bone? Now imagine him picking up another similar bone and moving the loops from one bone to the other, adding another row. Think of this person being annoyed at the knobs at the end of the bone. It is an easy step to envision him grinding off one of the knobs and making a point on the end of the bone.

As time went on and as people moved into enclaves and cities and away from primitive campfires and the nomadic life, the art of knitting improved, and so did the needles.

THE CIRCULAR NEEDLE

Early on, knitters realized that, very basically, human bodies were shaped tubes and that knitted tubes fitted bodies very well, with little wasted fabric. Long stockings and sleeves and hats and tunics are tubular shapes made to fit tubular body parts. Flat-knitted pieces had to be bent into tubes in order to be useful.

After the Stone (bone) Age and probably during the Bronze Age, metal workers learned to make wire. Ah ha! Wire could be bent around to form a circle and those tubes could now be worked in the round to form leggings and sleeves that wouldn't have to be lashed on or whipstitched together. Besides, if one is knitting round and round and hardly ever stopping, one is working all the same stitch and never has to take time to turn around, to go back, or to form the loops backwards and opposite to achieve the flat jersey knitting that is commonly called "stockinette stitch."

The Industrial Revolution came along after the sixteenth century, and machines were built by humans to knit thin, fine yarns for them. Though the making of socks and stockings by hand has never ceased and is still done today by some, more and more fine yarns are worked by machines clicking along at incredible speeds.

Many people found that it didn't make much sense to hand-work with fine yarns anymore, yet the technology was not available (or not applied) to make thicker-than-wire circular needles that were pliable enough to form a circle for use with heavier yarns. Thicker-than-wire needles were necessary to work thicker-than-fine-thread yarns, so people went back to knitting with straight needles. Sometimes they used straight single-pointed knitting needles à la caveman, working back and forth, and sometimes they used four double-pointed needles to form a round tube.

True, myriad improvements were made over the animal bones of the ancients. Ivory was used. Steel, celluloid, bamboo, plastic, and aluminum were formed into single-pointed needles. All had advantages and disadvantages, but none could bend enough to form a circle and still be thick enough in diameter to properly shape the stitches for thicker yarns.

Attempts must have been made during the time span between the sixteenth and twentieth centuries to make pliable, large-diameter circular needles, but I am not aware of them. I do have in my collection some flexible steel cable needles from the 1920s.

As I look at these steel-cable needles and try to work with them, I can understand their inherent problems. The cables frayed, and the joinings to the rigid tips were faulty; nevertheless, they were an attempt to return to a better way of knitting—in the round.

I remember sometime in my childhood or early youth the appearance of plastic- and nylon-cabled circular needles. These, too, had inherent problems with a joining that made too fast a jump in size from cable to tip. But, more important, these needles had surface friction on the tips that slowed down the flow of yarn and hence the knitting process.

Today we have the technology and the engineering skills that have produced good, dependable, workable circular needles that allow us to rapidly knit in the round—and *I use circular needles exclusively.*

STRAIGHT VS. CIRCULAR

Why should we use straight needles just because cavemen had only straight bones to work with? That is as silly as insisting that tanning leather should be done by women chewing the raw hides because that's the way our ancestors did it. If you want to use straight needles, that is your privilege; it is also your privilege to chew your animal hides to make leather.

There is nothing you can do with straight needles that you cannot do with circulars. There are things you can do with circular needles that you cannot do with straights.

With circular needles

- you can go back and forth
- you can go round and round (and going round and round stockinette stitch is all knit stitches—no purl)
- you can almost eliminate finish-work because you can go round and round and have no seams to sew

- you can make a sweater all in one piece, trying it on as you go, and discontinue making it any wider when it is wide enough, and bind it off when it is the desired length

- you can go faster because you don't continually have to turn the piece around

- you don't have to stop and pick the needles up off the floor when they accidentally slide out

- your needles won't bump the arms of chairs or get in the way in tight airplane seats

Getting technical about it, when you knit with circular needles the center of gravity of your work is always at the center of your lap. That means it is easier for you, and less tiresome, because the weight of the piece is never on the far end of a single long, straight needle.

Circular needles do have three disadvantages, and I must, in honesty, forewarn you about them.

1. As they come new from the package the nylon cables will be tightly curled and kinky. (But if you place a new circular needle in a bowl or basin of very hot tap water for a few minutes, it will magically uncurl and straighten out.)

2. The next disadvantage is that, because they are smooth from tip to tip, size is not usually marked on the needles themselves. If you decide to use circular needles you will want to make a very small investment in a small metal "size checker" into which you will insert the tips of the needles to determine their size.

3. The only other problem I know of that you will encounter with circular needles when knitting in the round concerns gauge in stockinette stitch. Until you go round and round you can't tell exactly how many stitches you will get per inch. Inasmuch as all the stitches will be knit stitches without any purls, you may find that you get a slightly tighter gauge working in the round than you get working flat. But you can't tell until you do it. (Elizabeth Zimmermann, a knitting authority, suggests that you check for round and round stockinette stitch gauge by beginning to make a stocking cap. I suggest that you just begin at the neck of the garment and work down. Neck measurements for all people—including children—are about the same. The differences in sizes are in the chest width and armhole depth. By starting at the neck and working down a few inches, increasing as you go, no harm can be done

until you can get an accurate gauge measurement and double-check it by trying the garment on.)

There is a place for straight needles, though. Remember how we talked about the caveman and his slender animal bones? Remember how we said that he probably ground off the knob at one end to make a better point? I'm sure that somewhere along the way he figured out that he could make points at both ends of the bone and then using four or five similar sized bones he could knit small diameter tubes. Straight double-pointed needles are still the ideal tools for narrow diametered things like wrist cuffs, socks, and mittens. My beloved circular needles just do not lend themselves well to making small tubes. Our hands need about 3½ to 4 inches of straight tips to hang on to, and that simply doesn't leave enough remaining inches to make the curve to form the circle.

GETTING THE POINT

Regardless of whether you choose to use circular or straight needles, you need to consider the shape of the points in relation to the project you are working on. The shape of the points can vary greatly from manufacturer to manufacturer and from aluminum to steel to plastic to nylon.

There is no "all-purpose" or "one-size-fits-all" kind of tip shape. The tip shape you choose for a particular project will depend upon what yarn you are using and what you are doing with it. There is no "good" and no "bad" kind of tip.

If you are using a yarn that easily splits and shreds, you will want to use needles with blunt shaped tips to prevent injury to the yarn. If you are making a lace with lots of knit-two-togethers and slip-knit-passovers, you will want to use needles with sharply pointed tips to prevent injury to your disposition.

MATCHING NEEDLES AND YARN

Don't hesitate to purchase a special needle for just one particular project. When you stop to add up the total number of hours you will expend in making that project and then divide those hours by the cost of a new special needle, the dollar cost per hour will amount to zilch, but the accumulated gained ease in working will be tremendous.

Today, with modern technology and engineering, good knitting needles can be and are made out of many kinds of different materials. Again, there is no "good" and no "bad" material from which to make needles. Nor is there an "all-purpose" or "one-size-fits-all" material. Again, there are some materials that work better with some yarns and not well at all with others.

One time, many years ago, I was working with a good-quality acrylic yarn on nylon needles. The stitches just wouldn't slide along. I thought that there was something wrong with me; I thought that I had forgotten how to knit, I was having so much trouble. Then by chance I ran across an article in a *Scientific American* magazine that was lying around the house about the "surface tension" of different types of materials. I deduced that the acrylic yarn that I was using was adhering to the nylon needles. I trotted over to my local knit store and bought myself needles made of a different material. What a difference! The stitches fairly floated.

Many yarn stores will let you sit down and try out different needles with the yarns you purchase from them. It's a good idea to do so, because the blunt-tipped needle that worked so well with the Glop-Glop wool may not work well at all with the Gooey-Gooey yarn for the diamond lace pattern blouse. And the sleek, smooth needles over which classic worsted just flew may allow the mercerized cotton to slide off without any provocation.

In our contemporary world of international trade, you may encounter three different sets of needle sizing—United States numbering (U.S.), metric diameter sizing (mm), and Great Britain or United Kingdom (U.K. or G.B.) sizes, which run in the opposite direction from U.S. If your local yarn supplier does not have a size conversion chart, one is found in the *Universal Yarn Finder*.

The size and the material of the needles you choose to use are important to no one but yourself. Don't fight with inappropriate products and struggle to make every stitch. The right needle for the right project can make a difference.

5

SOME WORDS ABOUT PATTERNS AND INSTRUCTIONS

Many years ago, long before my hair turned gray, I visited friends in Mexico. My Spanish was and still is not the greatest, but I could understand enough to be a part of the daily goings-on. A part of those goings-on was the visits between women of the community after siesta when the children had returned to school. As they sat relaxing and knitting, the women talked about everyday housewife and mother-type things; the terrible quality of the onions available in the market or the difficulties a child was having with a teacher in school. Though their talk was ordinary, their knitting was extraordinary.

As an American "book-trained" knitter, I was fascinated. Everything about their knitting was different; their way of holding the yarn in the left hand, their understanding and know-how of what they were doing, their courage in the size and scope of the projects they tackled, but most of all their lack of printed instructions and directions.

They began with pictures clipped from European fashion magazines, yarn and needles, a few measurements, and a pencil and *blank* paper. They finished with glorious, beautiful, well-fitted creations. I thought they were crazy to begin without printed or written instructions. They thought I was crazy to think that it was necessary to have directions.

How could they so easily figure out what to do with how many stitches when? All my American books, which never mentioned holding the yarn in the left hand at all, said not to try to figure out anything on your own. No one had ever told me that stitches times inches equals finished width!

One of the books that I used early on in my knitting career was, unfortunately, one of the most influential. It was *Knitting, Creative Use of Leisure Time* from the Cooperative Extension Service, Kansas State University. On page 7 it said, *"Always read directions step by step. Never read ahead when you are following directions."* The italics are theirs, not mine. The book also admonished knitters, "Follow the instructions exactly," "Do not attempt to make changes," "Work line by line." I faithfully followed and actually believed all that garbage. And I knitted garbage before I went to Mexico and let those lovely women open my eyes and my mind.

After the trip to Mexico, I either purchased or checked out of the library every book on knitting that was in print. Some were helpful; some were gardens of misinformation.

> *I learned that knitting patterns and instructions are based on nothing more than common sense, attention to detail, fourth-grade arithmetic, and a basic knowledge of the human form.*

I have accumulated a shelf of knitting pattern books. My collection includes pattern and instruction books not only from the U.S., but from Europe, the Orient, and South America, as well as Asia. Whenever I see old American pattern leaflets on my antiquing jaunts, I pick them up, too. After studying all of these, I have come to the conclusion that current American and English directions are by far the worst of the lot.

I do not understand either the German or Japanese languages, but I can nearly always understand their handwork instructions. They use not only words, but diagrams and charts as well. I can *see* what I am supposed to be doing. I can *see* where I am supposed to be. I can *see* what the next step is all about and change it if necessary to suit my purposes. Simple charts describe even the most elaborate knit and crochet stitches so that even a child could not get lost in a maze of *P 1, * *[yo K 2 tog] twice SKP rpt from * * K 3*.

BEWARE BAD INSTRUCTIONS

Pre-World War I American knitting books are a delight, full of statements like, "Work even to the wearer's elbow length before decreasing evenly to the wrist," or "Diminish width appropriately to suit the wearer's waist."

Many contemporary American and English patterns are just a bunch of words. They give us no credit for being able to think. They allow us no control of our own knitting. They could be better. You can help to make them better by demanding of the yarn companies that they spend a little more money on pattern writers, typesetters, paper, and ink, and publish more detailed and thoughtful instructions before you will buy their yarns.

The National Knit and Crochet Standards Simplified Instructions guidelines spearheaded by the DuPont Company were a giant leap toward better understandability, but still these fail to allow for individual needs and variations.

I am not saying that you do not need a guide to follow. Most of us do. I am saying that if you understand the medium, it will work for you. Moses, when he was in the wilderness, taught the children of Israel to protect themselves. When they were being besieged by a plague of snakes, he made a model of one of the vipers. He held it up to his people saying, "Look at it. Understand the problem. Study the nature of it. Learn how it functions. Then it will work for you instead of against you." Good old Moses would have banned from his camp all knitting books that said, "Do not attempt to make changes," "Follow line by line," or "Do not read ahead."

Now, in all honesty, I must make a confession, that although for a long time I was vaguely aware that many patterns and instructions were not the best possible, I did not really understand why they were so bad until I began to teach knitting, to design patterns for my patrons, and to try to write out both individual instructions and printed pattern instructions. There are inherent problems in producing commercial printed instructions that are free of ambiguous language and allow for variation without being overly long.

The great majority of the knitted garments for which commercial patterns are available today were designed and made on knitting machines, not by hand. An experienced designer can spot them every time. There are logical reasons why these garments are designed for machines:

1. It is easier to plan, draft, and chart a pattern for a flat, two-dimensional garment made in pieces with sewn-later seams than it is to conceive and describe a circular three-dimensional knitted work.

2. It is easier to write out word for word what to do on flat pieces.

3. It is much quicker and less time consuming for experienced professionals to machine-knit the garment in order to "prove it out" and have photographs taken of it than it is to hand-knit it.

4. Designers and yarn companies often feel that in order to achieve the greatest possible distribution of their pattern books, and hence the highest sales of their yarn, they must limit the instructions to the least

number of words possible. Fine details of design, construction, and finishing are usually omitted.

All these are logical facts, but nonetheless it is a sad situation. The Good Lord in Her infinite wisdom did not make people out of flat pieces with sewn-later seams. Most people are more or less rounded, with bumps here and there. Thank goodness even flat-made hand-knit fabrics are pliable and forgiving, but circular knit garments can conform even better to the human body.

Moreover, many, many knitters, if given the basic fundamental knowledge and understanding of what the medium of knitting itself and figure fitting is all about, would understand what they were attempting to create, and why and how to adjust it. "How to knit" primers, of necessity, leave much unsaid, and individual pattern instructions cannot possible say it all in half a page.

INSTRUCTION GUIDELINES

In addition to these above-mentioned problems, time and again I have run across commercial instructions for garments that could not possibly produce the same garment as pictured. Usually the instructions were "simplified," occasionally they were "augmented," but the end result is that they were *bad*. Ideally, "good" knitting patterns or instructions should consist of the following:

1. An honest photograph showing the entire garment with no covered-up areas and the model in a natural position. No hunched shoulders or scarves at the neck to hide a poorly fitting sweater.

2. A clear diagram with notations of the number of stitches and inches at appropriate locations. "Underarm width of sleeve = 13 inches and 78 stitches" so that a knowledgeable knitter could make it 14 inches and 84 stitches if she wanted to.

3. More plain English words to explain what is happening. "Decrease 6 stitches evenly across the row to narrow for wrist cuff" so that a person with fat wrists can decide not to decrease.

4. Refresher details written right into the instructions at appropriate places. Don't just say, "Increase." Say, "Increase by knitting into the front and back of the next stitch", or whatever type of increase the designer intended to get the desired results.

There is no mystery or magic about knitting instructions. They are fourth-grade arithmetic of stitches × inches × common sense. Don't let them daunt you.

Do read ahead! Read the pattern step by step before you start. Draw a picture of what it says to do.

- Do change instructions to suit you own needs!
- Do try to understand what it is you are creating and how!
- Believe in your own good common sense!

I alone cannot change the yarn industries' concept of "good" knitting instructions. Your help is needed. Insist on clear, detailed instructions. The knitting projects that you save from the rubbish heap could well be your own.

6

ON TYPES OF CONSTRUCTION

An egg can be served sunny side up, over easy, or scrambled, and it is still an egg. We all have our preferences about how eggs are served. I used to hate fixing breakfasts. Timmy wanted his egg scrambled firm. Chris demanded his sunny side up and still gooey. Randy insisted on his over hard. John didn't care how they were cooked, just so long as he got two!

And so it is with the construction of sweaters. We all have our favorite ways of making them, bottom up, top down, crosswise. Each way has its distinct advantages and serious drawbacks. Still they are all sweaters, just like eggs are eggs.

Some of us designers and teachers get downright testy, insisting that our method of making sweaters is the only right and proper way of making them. Sometimes we get like this from learning through bad experiences. At other times we are guilty of doing things only the way in which we first learned them and our prejudice comes from lack of knowledge. But then, isn't that the definition of pejorative judgments, that we refuse to look at other situations?

Once a piece of fabric is knitted, it takes an expert to determine from which direction it was started. And it doesn't matter whether you knit a sweater from the bottom up or from the top down. It can be a joy and a pleasure either way. It makes no difference if you make that garment in lots of small pieces that are seamed together or all in one piece without any seams at all. It can be fun to make and fun to wear. It is simply a matter of preference.

English, German, and French knitters prefer to make garments in lots of different pieces and then sew the pieces together when they are all finished. The advantage is that the pieces are lightweight, easily handled, and soon completed. The disadvantages are that you can't try the thing on to check for fit until it is all done and that you can run out of yarn on the final piece and be unable to complete the project.

While we are discussing sweaters made in pieces, it is a good time to discuss making more than one piece at a time. I stumbled on to this idea when I made one sleeve of a sweater several inches longer than the other sleeve. Make two sleeves, or two fronts, or two patch pockets on the same needles at the same time using separate balls of yarn. (That way you only have to measure once for both pieces.)

Traditionally, American designed patterns begin with the back of a garment. French designed garments begin with the sleeves.

Scandinavian knitters work in the round from the bottom up. The advantage is that you can stop and try on frequently as you work, and working in the round is usually all knit stitches, which is faster and easier. The disadvantage is that the work can get pretty cumbersome and heavy before it is completed, and you can still run out of yarn just before the end. (Did you ever wonder why neck ribbing is often a different color?)

Some designers like to make batwing and dolman-sleeved sweaters crosswise. They begin at the wrist end of one sleeve, cast on extra stitches for the body when the sleeves are completed, bind off those same stitches when the body is completed, and finish by making the other sleeve. The advantage is that a spectacular fashion effect can be achieved and stripes that will appear vertical in the completed garment are a breeze to put in. The disadvantage is that many of these garments are charted in rows instead of inches, and if your row gauge is off your sweater won't fit. The garment can become heavy and awkward as it nears completion. Also, you can't try it on as you go and you can run out of yarn.

Where the idea of making sweaters all in one piece from the neck down came from, I don't know, but it is my favorite method. You can't run out of yarn. You can try on and fit and change your mind as you go along. *And your gauge is not critical:* when the garment is wide enough you just stop making it any wider, and when it is long enough you just quit. The disadvantage, again, is the cumbersomeness.

I stumbled onto making sweaters all in one piece from the neck down when I was an instructor doing lots of original custom designing for my patrons. If a sweater has never been made before, you cannot know how much yarn it will take to make it.

I think, though, that the deciding factor that converted me to the neck-down one-piece garments was the problems people had in getting and maintaining gauge. Gauge, of course, is the determining factor in the width of any piece of knitting. And I would, of course, have my customers make a test gauge swatch before I charted sweaters for them, telling them to come in to have the work checked again before they went very far with it.

When the work was checked in progress, I discovered that more than half of the knitters would be working at a different gauge, which would throw off all of the carefully made plans and charting. Because there is very little difference in the number of stitches that are allowed for a neck opening, and necklines can be tightened or loosened according to how they are trimmed, if one wanders off the starting gauge when making a sweater beginning at the neck, it doesn't matter. Moreover, there is never a problem with ill-fitting set-in sleeves because the sleeves are knitted all in one piece.

I guess that it is obvious that I am biased and opinionated in my preference for knit-from-the-top-down garments. I got that way honestly and with a lot of trial and error.

The object of knitting is to have fun while making fabric. The joy of knitting is the wonderful variety and design interest that you can conjure up. Fulfill the object of knitting and increase the joy of doing it by making garments in whichever way you are most comfortable.

7
MARKERS MAKE LIFE EASIER

The builders of our expressways do a good job of informing us of our location as we speed along the highway. There are markers to let us know that we are on the right road. There are signs to let us know what is available at a particular exit, and there are mile markers that help us figure out how far we have come.

Markers in your knitting can do the same kinds of things for you. They can let you know how far you have come and how far you have yet to go. They can make you aware of the passing stitches and keep you on the straight and narrow road to rich and lovely pattern stitches.

I use lots of markers: horizontal markers, vertical markers, row counters, and "idiot tags." Some are absolutely vital to achieving a well-fitting garment. Some are simply helpers and reminders of where I am. I would rather speed along the highway of stitches with gentle reminders of where I am than to have to plod along counting every stitch/step I take.

HORIZONTAL MARKERS

Horizontal markers are short pieces of thread worked into the fabric of your knitting to give you a reference point from which to measure.

Knitting instructions will often say, "When back measures 7 inches beyond bind-off, shape shoulders." Or "When sleeve measures 5 inches from underarm. . . ." That is all well and good, but from *what* spot do you measure? If you measure along the curve of the armhole, you are getting a distorted measurement—a curved line.

Yet the designer wants you to have a certain number of inches *straight* above the bind-off. If you measure in the middle of the piece you can't always tell where to put the end of your tape measure.

You need to work in a horizontal thread marker in the middle of a piece any time you bind off or begin to shape the edges.

That way you will have a milestone or reference point to go back to when you need to measure.

Also use horizontal markers to measure other lengths. It is easier to see a well-placed horizontal marker and to know, for instance, that you need to make a sleeve two inches longer than it is to constantly get out your tape measure and remeasure the total length over and over.

What you use to make that horizontal marker is of great importance. You want to use a piece of something that will not enlarge the stitches over which it is laid. You want something that will not leave any fleck of color. You want to use something that can be removed easily and without a trace from the fabric after it has fulfilled its purpose.

Do not, therefore, use a contrasting color of yarn for a horizontal marker. It may leave a fleck of color in the center back of a garment that can never be removed. Do not use yarn at all, because it may enlarge the stitches over which it is laid. Horizontal markers made of yarn can also be difficult to remove.

Heavy crochet cotton makes an ideal horizontal marker. A bobbin of it in the goodie pouch of your work basket will take up very little space and will always be handy to use at a moment's notice.

Putting a horizontal marker in place is quick and easy:

Snip off a 12-inch piece of the cotton crochet thread. Leaving about a 4-inch tail-end piece, lay the cotton thread over your working yarn and make about four to six stitches with the 2 strands together. Then drop the thread and continue with the yarn.

Tie the 2 short ends of the crochet thread together just to keep them out of your way. On the next row, be sure to work the yarn and crochet thread together as if they were one so you don't accidentally increase any stitches.

That's all there is to it. You have an easily visible, permanent reference point from which to measure when you need it. The marker can be removed by clipping off the knot and simply giving the thread a strong tug. No one but you will ever know it was there.

VERTICAL MARKERS

Vertical markers are extra loops of a different material that you put upon the working needles between stitches to make your fingers aware that something different is supposed to happen.

Early on in my career as a knitting instructor, I had a delightful customer who very much wanted to make a lace blouse for her daughter-in-law. She selected an attractive fishtail lace, a simple boat-necked pattern, and a delicate-colored sport-weight yarn. After her purchase, she went off excited at the thought of surprising her daughter-in-law and began to knit. She came back a few days later in tears. The pattern was a complete mess. I straightened her out and sent her on her way again.

A few days later she returned, once more in tears. She was off pattern again, and was ready to abandon the project or at least change it to stockinette stitch, crying, "I get just one stitch off and the whole thing goes to hell." I handed her a handkerchief and sold her a couple of packages of thin plastic ring markers. While she dried her tears, I ripped back and placed a ring marker at every multiple of the lace pattern for her. I explained to her what the ring markers were for.

"The ring markers match the asterisks in the pattern stitch instructions. For instance, on row four you must make a 'yarn-over, knit one' just before every marker. If you don't, there is something wrong. Stop and fix it now. If your pattern is correct as you get to each marker, the whole thing will stay on pattern."

The customer brought me a loaf of homemade banana bread the next time she came into the store. I ordered grosses of ring markers and sold them to everyone who wanted to make complicated pattern stitches. Thereafter I set every knitter up with ring markers at pattern stitch repeats before the frustration began and the tears started.

Vertical markers never affect the knitting, they only affect the knitter. They alert your fingers to the fact that something needs to be noticed here. I use gobs of them. I use them when setting up patterns like pleats in a skirt. I keep them in place until I can see what I am supposed to be doing, and then I remove them.

In making raglan garments from the neck down, ring markers are a necessity. They tell your fingers when and where to make the increases.

I have gotten so attached to ring markers that I will not make a lace pattern in which I cannot use them. I avoid lace patterns that have an overlapping stitch at the end of the multiple because the markers have to be reset too often. There are enough pretty laces that allow me to keep my markers in place so that I never have to bother to make those that don't.

It is possible to use little bits of yarn tied with a knot to form a circle rather than the commercially made thin plastic rings. It is true that they are free. However, I find that my needles move the yarn loops more slowly than they do the commercial rings. I knit fast, and I resent anything that slows me down, so I use the plastic rings. They are not expensive at all, and they let me finish the project faster.

For the safest and speediest transfer, slip the plastic ring markers from one needle to the other as if to purl. If you slip them as if to knit, there is always a chance that they will fly off and land on the floor.

Row counters and pegging boards are not markers as such, but they are also reminders of where you are. They are discussed in the chapter about your knitting supplies.

IDIOT TAGS

"Idiot tags" are an invention I stumbled onto as a knitting instructor. Now don't get me wrong! They were invented for smart knitters, not dumb ones. Idiot tags are just little cardboard inventory tags with a string attached to them that any stationery or office supply store sells.

One day a lady who was a very fine and creative knitter came into the store where I was working with little bits of paper pinned all over her work. When I asked her what they were for she said, "Oh, they're just little notes to myself. Like, 'When resuming work on sleeve begin with row five of pattern.' Or, 'Work even two inches beyond the horizontal marker.' Or, 'Make buttonhole on next row.' It is so much easier to write it down when I think about it than to try to remember it later. I feel like an idiot with them pinned all over, but they help me. The only trouble with my notes to myself is that they are not very tidy, and they do tear off."

The store was getting ready for inventory, and there were some tags beside the cash register. I spied them and we substituted them for the more fragile notes she was using. That is how idiot tags were born. I hope they never die.

Don't be afraid to use whatever devices you can come up with to speed you along your way. Markers make sense. They let us know where we are and where we are going. Only an idiot wouldn't use them.

8

YOUR KNITTING BAG

Since you have decided to make knitting your bag, you will have to have a real bag to keep your knitting in. I mean it—a good-looking one. I have a personal thing about people who carry their work around in a worn-out grocery bag as if they were looking for the nearest trash can to dump the garbage.

Honestly, if you enjoy the personal pleasure of making something out of nothing, tote your work in a proud way that suits your personality and your lifestyle. I don't care if you haul your paraphernalia in a standard X-legged knitting stand, a handsome imported basket, a small suitcase, an oversized handbag, a picnic hamper, or a drawstring sea bag. It has to be suitable for the project, handy to move about, convenient to work from, and, above all, good looking. Knitting supply stores are not necessarily the best source of such "knitting bags."

Look around. Use your imagination. Using the unexpected for the obvious is rewarding in itself. Before making your purchase, check to see that the bag you have selected has no sharp edges to catch on clothing or scratch your legs when carrying it from place to place. Make sure it is not too fragile if, like me, you have a tendency to fling your work in the back of the car on your way to the airport to meet Aunt Ruth's plane—which could be two hours late. Those two hours could be spent in happy, relaxed knitting instead of anxious waiting—if you have the proper knitting bag.

Also make sure of your bag's closeability if you have little beings around your house like children or puppies or kittens. Small children, cats, and yarn have a special affinity for one another.

You might even consider purchasing *two* bags. I believe in keeping two knitting projects going at the same time, and this necessitates having two bags.

Whatever you choose to tote your work in, I never want to catch you working out of a worn-out grocery bag. Tired, crumpled paper or plastic sacks demean a fine and ancient craft and its craftsperson.

EQUIPMENT FOR THE BAG

Now that you have selected this handsome container, what should you carry in it?

YARN

Some, not all, of the *yarn* needed for your project. There is no point in overworking your arms by carrying around yarn that will not be called for until later. Keep the as-yet-unneeded skeins in the original package, *together with the receipt,* in a safe corner at home.

NEEDLES

Naturally, you are going to carry the necessary *needles.* Take only those that you will use. I remember a time long ago when I carried superfluous needles with me. I ended up with the right front of a pretty pink sweater worked on a size 4 and the left front worked on a size 5 needle. After finishing the ribbing on the second front, I had reached in my bag and taken out the blue needles. Later I discovered that both sets were blue—the same color blue. I ripped. I learned. Now I carry with me only the size needles that I need for the work at hand.

There are some exceptions about including only working needles.

1. When visiting your neighborhood knit shop to select something new to knit, take along all possible needles in order to play with the yarn on *your* needles before you decide. These can be carried in a paper bag if you promise to leave it at home after the yarn decision has been made.

2. I always carry a size 1 or 2 circular needle to use for ripping back.

3. The final exception applies also to small-size circular needles. I sometimes toss in enough of them to use for holders (as described later) *if* I think I will get to the place where I will need them before I get home again.

INSTRUCTIONS

You will need your *instructions*. Here, a word to the would-be-wise. I have rewritten enough lost instructions, sold enough duplicate books, and given away enough second copies of patterns to tell you to run—do not walk, do not pass Go, do not collect $200—run to the nearest duplicating machine. Invest ten, twenty-five, or fifty cents to make an extra copy to carry with you for your own personal use. Then leave the original at home safely tucked into the box with the remainder of the yarn and the sales receipt in that safe corner of yours. Slide the instructions you carry with you into a plastic page sleeve to protect them from coffee stains or water marks. A smidgeon of forethought can save a bucket of grief and maybe even a whole project.

OTHER NECESSITIES

In this handsome container of yours you have yarn, needles, and a copy of the instructions. Now you need to acquire the other necessities and a separate *little pouch* or *bag* to put them in that will fit into the larger bag. I like students' zippered see-thru containers available at stationery counters.

- A *tape measure*, accurate and non-stretchy, if you please. You cannot depend on anything fitting when it is finished without one. Steel tapes and twelve-inch rulers or guessing will get you into trouble. Even though a steel tape measure in a self-winding case sounds ideal, it isn't. In the first place it's too heavy. There will be enough weight to lug around as it is without that extra pound or so. Secondly, a steel tape is just not flexible enough to use to stop and double-check your own wrist measurement against the cuff ribbing you have just completed. A twelve-inch ruler cannot accurately tell you when you have completed a sixteen-inch body length. A wooden yardstick won't fit into any carry-all knit bag that I know of.

- *Small, sharp scissors* that will cut, not chew, yarn. Some yarns are practically unbreakable, and all yarns, good or poor, cheap or dear, have knots and imperfect spots that *must* be removed neatly. Good scissors are a must for good finishing work. I used to carry my scissors inside the little pouch in my bag until my children discovered that when they needed scissors they could always find a pair in my knitting bag to borrow. Now I tie my scissors with a twisted monk's cord made of scrap yarn to one handle of my bag. Somehow, having to cut the cord to borrow the scissors seems to deter theft.

- A *crochet hook* appropriate to the size yarn you are using in this particular project will be used to pick up dropped stitches or correct imperfect ones. When you are ready to do the finishing work, you may wish to add any other, different-size crochet hooks that may be necessary to do a neat job.

- A *steel tapestry* or *blunt-pointed yarn needle*, as small as can be used on the yarn you are currently using. Plastic yarn needles have a surface finish that tends to "hang up" in the yarn and slow one down as well as stretch the stitches. Oversized needles do more damage than good. The needle should be small enough to slip into a stitch without stretching it or splitting the yarn. Needles with a sharp pointed tip, such as darning or crewel needles, are a definite no-no. They are made to split yarn, and will do so.

- A container of *ring markers*. Different kinds of markers serve different purposes. Use all kinds—plastic circles, hook-on plastic rings, chicken leg rings, even small round paper clips on various occasions to fill certain needs. Slip-on markers are especially nice to set in place after the work has begun. By and large, my favorite working markers are the small, quite thin steel rings sold at good knitting shops, because they do not leave a gap mark. Fat "bone" rings are not satisfactory, for no matter how careful the knitter is, they always leave a gap mark.

- A container of *safety pins*, assorted sizes for assorted needs. Be sure to include at least twenty tiny "gold" safety pins, or better yet, those little no-loop-at-the-end button or knitting pins, when you can find them, which isn't often. Just as I could not cook or bake without a handy-dandy minute timer, I would hate to have to knit without handy-dandy little "gold" safety pins to keep track of increases, decreases, pattern repeats, tag ends of yarn, and such. The discovery of those little pins changed my attitude toward knitting from constant worry to relaxation. Large-size safety pins make great mini-stitch holders, provided the user is careful not to split the yarn.

- a spool or bobbin of *white # 8 crochet thread or ⅛-inch wide polyester ribbon,* not to knit with, but to use to make horizontal markers. They are perfect horizontal marking materials, and I also use them frequently to check on size. I don't know why nobody tells knitters that at any point in knitting, the stitches can be carefully slipped off the needles, as if to purl, onto smooth, strong thread or ⅛-inch knitting ribbon with the aforementioned tapestry needle so that the piece can be checked for size or even tried on.

    Because sometimes, despite the best and most careful intentions, measurements lie. Sometimes we change our minds as we see how a project progresses. Sometimes a better idea occurs part way through. There is no reason why you cannot stop, write yourself a note to tell yourself which row you are on, put the stitches on a long strand of thread secured firmly at both ends to avoid having them slide off, and *try the thing on.* Why go on with a project that you feel in your bones is not quite right?

• A couple of *Band-aids* and an *emery board* tucked ever so quietly in that handsome knit bag can save sanity, too. They do not really have anything to do with the knitting procedures themselves, but rather with being able to knit.

If you have never nicked your fingernail as you closed (slammed is a better word) the car door while running into the hospital emergency room to wait four hours while a loved one is being X-rayed and were not able to work off your anxieties by knitting while you waited because the yarn snagged on that —— broken fingernail, then you don't understand the frustrations and the joys of knitting.

Emery boards also come in very handy to smooth a rough spot on a knitting needle or a crochet hook.

Band-aids were added to my knitting necessities the day I scratched a finger (not dangerously, just bloodily) entering an auditorium to hear a lecture. Because my finger was bleeding, I couldn't knit during the lecture, and because the lecture turned out to be a bore, it was a totally miserable afternoon. I had to sit there motionless, but now I carry Band-aids, and though I may not be able to avoid being bored, I can stop the flow of my own blood and at least engage my hands in constructive, creative, and ingenious handwork.

• A *small-size circular needle* is a must in a kit of goodies. Nobody ever told me I needed it. I have never seen it listed anywhere among knitting supplies, but it certainly makes life easier for me. When I have to rip back, I find that if I rip onto small needles I make less errors. (See chapter 24 on mistakes.)

Moreover, since I much prefer circular needles for almost everything I knit because they are flexible, it seems stupid to me to use a long rigid safety pin type of stitch holder that is always slowing me down or jabbing me. A small short circular needle stoppered with rubber tip protectors at each end is so much more convenient and flexible, both physically and otherwise. It is impossible to ever end up on the wrong end of a stitch holder that has two ends when ready again to work those stitches that had to wait.

• *Stitch holders* are usually necessary. I wish someone would invent some decent ones. Ones that are flexible, that will not snag, on which the stitches will not shrink, and that can be so firmly secured that the stitches will not slip off when you hurriedly jam the work into your bag when the dentist's receptionist finally calls you after an hour's wait.

Until someone invents something better, you will have to make do as best you can. The yarn itself is not usually a satisfactory stitch holder. Neither is crochet thread for a long period of time if you intend to continue working those stitches again. The stitches held either on yarn or thread have a tendency to shrink, and a definite line may be left across the piece. Yarn has the added disadvantage of sometimes leaving flecks. However, either is a good solution for the underarm "bind-off" stitches that you may choose *not* to bind off. (See chapter 25 on finishing.)

Large safety pins work well for a small number of stitches *if* one is careful not to split the yarn as the stitches are removed from the working needle.

Again, a short smaller-sized circular needle secured at both ends works well to hold the front of a garment while the back is being finished, or to hold the back shoulder stitches after they have been short-rowed while completing the front. (See chapter 13 on binding off.)

I do not like the four- or six-inch safety pin type commercial stitch holders, but sometimes I have to resort to using them. Rather than waste my money on those monstrosities, nine- or twelve-inch stitch holders, I would invest in more sizes and lengths of circular needles to add to my collection.

• A *row counter* or *pegging board,* when working a difficult, multi-row pattern, can be a big help, although I rarely use the row counters as the manufacturer intended. He intended me to stick it on the end of a straight needle. Moreover, he intended me to remember to turn the row counter dial every time I turn the work, but I don't have much luck doing either.

As I said, I like to work circular tubes whenever I can (and I usually can). A row counter cannot be stuck in amongst the stitches at the beginning of a round without causing a disturbingly open spot. If I am working flat and have placed the counter at the end of a row, I invariably turn the work without turning the row counter dial. This leaves me the problem of which row I am supposed to work next, the problem that was supposed to be solved by the row counter in the first place.

After lots of bumbling attempts, I discovered a way to successfully use and be helped by a row counter. As I begin a project, I use my handy tapestry needle to thread a piece of my crochet thread through the center of the row counter—the space intended for the knitting needle. I tie a strong knot to form a loop and then tie it to a ring marker. Then I begin knitting and make two stitches on the work in pattern. Now I stop and slip the ring marker onto my right-hand knitting needle. I turn the row counter dial to "1" and proceed across the row or round in pattern stitch.

In using the gadget in this unintended way, since I must hand move it one time on each row or round, it is difficult to forget to turn the dial to the next number as it is moved. It is a natural for my preferred circular knits as well.

- A *pencil* and a small *pad of paper* or *inventory tags* are found in my little pouch. I am forever writing myself notes, and I need something handy on which to write them. Sometimes I scribble directly on my pattern instructions, "Make sleeve 1½" longer." Sometimes the note is attached to the work itself. "When resuming work on front start on row 6." Sometimes I take time out from knitting while waiting for Aunt Ruth's plane to make a grocery list. I have too much going on in my mind to have instant recall of all my good intentions. So notes prod me into remembering.

- *Point protectors* and/or *rubber bands* are necessities for your knitting bag. In an emergency, rubber bands can be used as point protectors, but only for a short period of time because they may leave a mark on the needle. Check to make sure the rubber point protectors you select fit securely on the particular needles that you are using for this project. If they slip off easily and unintentionally, they are worthless.

- *Cable needles* will be necessary for some projects. Various special gadgets are made solely for this purpose. Horseshoe and flattened "U" types have been invented to help you and the manufacturer's sales. I have tried them both. They invariably slow me down, so I go back to a good old-fashioned double pointed sock needle one size *larger* than my working needle. The small difference in size keeps the needle from slipping out of the stitches and makes no perceptible difference in the finished work. (That double-pointed sock needle comes in handy for "evening up" stitches, too. See chapter 24 on mistakes.)

  Although I have included the double-pointed sock needle in this list of things to carry in your little pouch, I do not usually carry it there. Ordinarily when working a pattern stitch that requires a cable needle, it is easier to stick it in the piece of work itself so that it is always handy, instead of having to hunt for it in the bag when needed.

Please notice that I have *not* included a plastic or metal 2-inch-square "gauge check" device. I personally do not like them. They allow me to lie to myself. Once a project is begun there are better ways to continually check your gauge. (See chapter 2 on gauge.)

If I have succeeded in converting you to working with circular needles, there is one more little goodie that will be necessary for you to own. It is a metal or plastic *needle size indicator*. Most circular needles are not marked as to size on the needles themselves, although they are usually sold in packets that are size marked. Mine never seem to get returned to their original packets, and I am left wondering what size is which. Do tie one of these size indicators to your cache of needles that you are not currently using. You do not usually need to carry it with you.

It won't be necessary for you to spend a fortune to prepare yourself handsomely and well for your next undertaking. But let me warn you that poor preparation can send you to the undertaker instead of on a fun-filled spree.

9
DELIVER US FROM DISASTER

Consisting of an open letter to God from a woman who knitted without forethought and purled to no purpose asking for guidance in making sweaters that her men will love to wear:

Dear Lord,

Is there anything that grieves a handknitter more than the realization that the beautiful sweater she so lovingly labored over for that special man of hers lies unused, never worn, and almost forgotten in the back of the bottom drawer of his bureau?

Difficulties in following instructions, problems with making pattern stitches work, dropped stitches, and tangled yarns are adversities I can usually surmount. But the lingering sorrow of knowing that for some mysterious reason he just won't wear that handsome, handmade garment is something else again.

Lord, I love those four men in my family. I love to knit for them. Why don't they love the things I love to make especially for them?

How long, Lord, Oh how long, will it take me to adjust my way of thinking to their likes and dislikes?

Why is common sense so uncommon?

Teach me, Lord, to think as my stubborn sons think. Grant me better than 30 percent success in getting them to wear their birthday and Christmas presents, that my efforts may be fulfilled and my sanity preserved.

It's not that I don't appreciate the loving acceptance in their eyes or the kiss, the hug, or the "Thank you, Mama," when they see the finished sweater. I do, I do. But I just wish they would take the thing out of the back of the bottom drawer once in a while.

I have come a long way, Father. I have learned lots of "make nots" from previous mistakes. Just please keep me from making new mistakes.

I'm not asking for guidance in making the absolutely perfect cheese soufflé, Lord. My fast food freaks would rather have grilled cheese sandwiches anyway. All I ask is for some sweaters that will be worn as a pleasure, not as a duty to Mama.

Oh God, I really hate to confess the error of my ways and list the umpteen fiascos in order to gain guidance, but if admission and repentence is the only way to more profitable knitting, I'll recount them to You even though You already know my sorrows.

First there was the red sweater for Oldest Son Tim. He must have been in junior high at the time, very shy yet very vain about his blossoming manhood. You remember, Lord, how he stood in front of the mirror for hours on end admiring his broadening shoulders, not noticing his unbrushed teeth.

It was to be his birthday present. A bright red, 4-ply worsted classic cardigan with set-in sleeves. Oh, the nights on end that You helped me keep my eyes open till the end of the late-late show to get it finished on time—and it was! But pride blinded my eyes, never anticipating the finished-on-the-man appearance.

Though he said, "Thank you, Mama; I love you," he never wore it.

I learned, Lord. I learned two things. Never again will I knit a gaudy-colored garment for a shy person. Quiet personalities just will not wear flamboyant colors. Never again will I knit a tight sweater of stiff 4-ply yarn with set-in sleeves. They just don't fit. They just don't enhance the appearance of a man who has broad shoulders. When, after several years of being unworn, I tried to pawn it off on his shoulderless cousin, I discovered it just didn't fit him either and certainly didn't enhance his slight figure.

So I made a mistake. I admit it. I have never knitted set-in sleeves again. I just made other mistakes, Father.

Like the next sweater. It was an exquisitely lovely, frightfully expensive, ruddy tweed, thick and thin wool for Number Two Son Chris, again a growing teenager at the time.

I thought I was profiting by the previous disaster. It wasn't a gaudy color and it had raglan sleeves instead of set-in ones. I even thought, "The shawl collar will keep him warm at the football games and the tweedy texture won't show the Coke stains."

Lord, the problem with that sweater was that by the time it was finished it was spring, the football games were over for the year, and Chris had grown six inches.

Why do I keep on making new mistakes, Father? Like the brown saddle-sleeve classic cardigan for Mr. Impeccably-Dressed-High-School-Football-Playing-Number-Three-Son Randy. I know now that I should have cast on fewer stitches at the bottom for his narrow hips and increased to gain the necessary width at his he-man-sized chest, but even so it did fit, sort of.

He did love it though, and he did look as handsome, Lord, as Joseph did in his coat of many colors. He did wear it—for a month. Then it drifted to the back of the bottom drawer with nothing being said till Mama had the temerity to ask why it wasn't worn.

His explanation was typical of a teenager. "It just doesn't look neat."

I'm sorry that I must have sounded like the Grand Inquisitor, God, when I responded, "Neat! What do you mean neat?"

He was honest. "All this fuzziness and all these little balls just don't look neat." And he was right. I had purchased cheap, poor-quality yarn, on sale at that, and it lost its neat look after just a few wearings.

I know that You love a cheerful giver, Lord, and I haven't ever scrimped on money spent for yarn since.

God, I was really trying hard for my youngest son, John; I really was. I didn't want his Christmas sweater to be a fiasco, too.

I had learned—cross my heart I had.

It wasn't too bright.

It wasn't too cheap.

It wasn't late.

It wasn't poorly fitting.

It just wasn't fitting at all.

The design was glorious and classic. The colors were muted and natural. The multicolored yoke broadened his shoulders and the waist tapered perfectly. John looked like Thor himself.

Oh, it was wonderful and warm. Much too warm for Southern California's balmy breezes. That Norwegian ski sweater was much more suited for forty-degree-below-zero blizzards in the frozen north. But, after I'd spent the money for the yarn (and for new bifocals to read the charts in the pattern), I couldn't afford to send John to where he could wear it!

So it is with all my knitting, Lord, I still am lacking wisdom.

Please grant me the ability to change from what I like to make to making what they will like to wear and the serenity to accept the fact that some of the sweaters will end up at the back of the bottom drawer anyway.

Just help me to help myself make my percentage of successes a little better, Lord.

Amen and love,

Maggie

II

DETAILS, DETAILS, DETAILS

10
CASTING ON

Getting started is the hardest part of doing anything. I think that it was Alice in Wonderland who said that life would be ever so much easier if we could start things in the middle and then go back to the beginning when we knew what we were doing.

But life doesn't allow us that option. Neither does knitting. We have to start at the beginning, and the way in which we start can determine how the finished project looks and wears.

Casting on is the term we knitters use to describe how we throw the first row of loops onto the needle in order to get started knitting. There are as many ways for knitters to put that first row on the needle as there are for a major league baseball pitcher to throw a winning game. Just as he can throw sliders, sinkers, and knuckleballs, we can cast on with one or two strands, knitwise or purlwise, firmly or loosely.

Each kind of cast-on has its advantages and disadvantages. No one cast-on works well in all situations, so you will want to master several different styles.

Before I discuss any of them, however, I need to tell you about a simple rule of thumb that applies to all knitting. It is the *rule of thumb of three*. I'm sorry that I never heard of it in my beginning years of knitting. It wasn't until I began to work with knitting machines in a knit shop that I became aware of it. I find it so helpful that now I teach it to all my beginning knitters.

The rule of thumb of three is simply that it takes three times the width of a piece to knit across it once.

For example, if you are working across a piece that is twenty inches wide, you will use up a sixty-inch-long length of yarn in working across one row. It will take a length of yarn fifteen inches long to knit across a piece five inches wide.

Remember that this is a rule of thumb. It is not exactly accurate. It will vary with the knitter and the pattern stitch. I don't want to hear any howls of outrage that you used only fifty-eight inches on a twenty-inch-wide piece or that you needed sixteen inches to work across five. What I do want you to be aware of is that it is a handy-dandy way of "guesstimating" whether or not you have enough yarn to complete one row and, as in the case of casting on with two strands, where you should place the slip loop to start with.

Before you can cast on that first stitch, you will want to make a slip loop on the needle. All knitting, and crocheting too, begins with a *slip loop*, which is just a way of fastening the yarn on the needle so it will appear to look like all the rest of the stitches. To make it

7

Hold your left hand in front of you with your index finger extended. Hold the yarn in your right hand. With your right hand wrap the yarn completely around that left finger, from front to back to the front and back again. (See drawing # 7.)

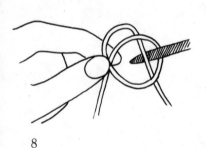

8

With your left thumb, scooch the crossover point of the yarn to the end of the extended forefinger. With the needle in your right hand, scoop up the shorter end of the yarn, and pull it part way through the circle you have formed. (See drawing # 8.)

Gently pull down on both ends of the yarn to firm up the loop on the needle. The loop needs to be secure, but still able to slide on the needle. (See drawing # 9.)

In knitting, the slip loop always counts as the first stitch. (In crocheting it does not.)

9

DOUBLE-STRAND KNITTING ON

The first type of cast-on that I want to tell you about is the *double-strand method of knitting on*. It is a very versatile way of beginning and is the method that I teach my beginning knitters first. The double-strand method of knitting on makes the first row of actual knitting easier to do. It is firm, yet elastic, and leaves a nice smooth finished edge.

The slip loop needs to be placed at a distance of three times the width of the finished piece, *plus at least six inches in order to leave a tail end long enough to finish in neatly later on.*

Look at the diagram that is included with your printed instructions to find out what the finished width should be. If, for instance, the back of a sweater is going to be twenty inches wide, you will need $20 \times 3 = 60 + 6 = 66$ inches.

If a diagram and the width in inches is not given, you may need to do a little detective work. Divide the total number of stitches to be cast on by the stitch gauge. For example, if your directions say "cast on 88 stitches" and your gauge is 4 stitches = 1 inch, divide the 4 into 88. The answer is 22, and your piece is intended to be twenty-two inches wide. Now multiply the twenty-two by the three-times rule and add six inches for the tail end. $22 \times 3 = 66 + 6 = 72$. You will need to place your slip loop approximately two yards from the end of the yarn.

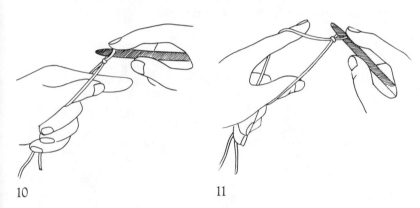
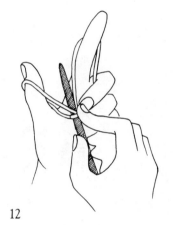

10   11   12

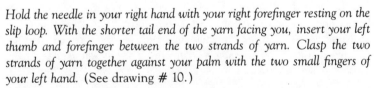

Hold the needle in your right hand with your right forefinger resting on the slip loop. With the shorter tail end of the yarn facing you, insert your left thumb and forefinger between the two strands of yarn. Clasp the two strands of yarn together against your palm with the two small fingers of your left hand. (See drawing # 10.)

Pull the needle in your right hand up and out to the right. Expand the distance between your left thumb and forefinger. (See drawing # 11.)

From the front to the back, insert the needle under the thumb yarn. (See drawing # 12.)

From the right to the left, go under the forefinger yarn and scoop that strand up and through the loop of the thumb yarn. (See drawing # 13.)

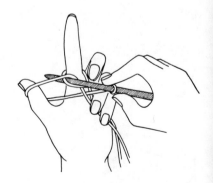

13

Drop the thumb. Reinsert the thumb between the two strands of yarn, expand the distance between the thumb and forefinger to adjust the tension, and move the right forefinger to rest on the new stitch. You may need to reclasp the strands against your palm.

This little maneuver with your two hands working together will soon become even, smooth, and fast with a little practice.

The loops on the right-hand needle need to be all the same size, loose enough to allow the first row to be worked, but not so loose that they slide off the needle or look sloppy.

When you cast on stitches by knitting them on with two strands of yarn and are going to be working next in stockinette stitch, *your next row will be purled.*

There is another way of making this exact same double-strand knitting on. It is done by holding the working yarn in the right hand. Sometimes it is called the American way of casting on. Again the slip loop is placed at a spot three times the finished width plus 6 inches from the end of the yarn.

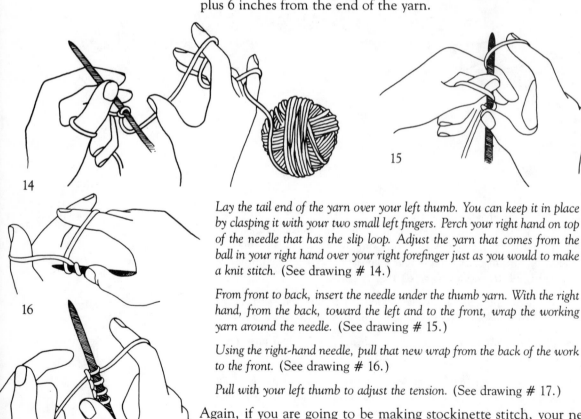

14

15

16

17

Lay the tail end of the yarn over your left thumb. You can keep it in place by clasping it with your two small left fingers. Perch your right hand on top of the needle that has the slip loop. Adjust the yarn that comes from the ball in your right hand over your right forefinger just as you would to make a knit stitch. (See drawing # 14.)

From front to back, insert the needle under the thumb yarn. With the right hand, from the back, toward the left and to the front, wrap the working yarn around the needle. (See drawing # 15.)

Using the right-hand needle, pull that new wrap from the back of the work to the front. (See drawing # 16.)

Pull with your left thumb to adjust the tension. (See drawing # 17.)

Again, if you are going to be making stockinette stitch, your next row will be purled.

CASTING ON A FEW STITCHES

When you have to cast on just a few stitches in the middle of a piece and you don't have two strands of yarn to work with, it is perfectly acceptable to use the simple *thread-over-the-left-thumb method* to cast on with a single strand. This is *not* a good method to use when beginning a piece, for the edge tends to look ragged. Neither is it a good method for casting on a great number of stitches because if you lose or drop one loop in making the next row, there is nothing you can do to save the situation because that loop is gone forever. However, it is ideal for casting on just a few stitches when you have no extra strand to work with.

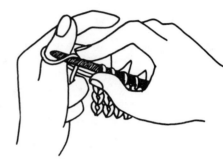

18   19

From-the-back-to-the-front, insert your left thumb under the working strand of yarn. (See drawing # 18.)

With the right-hand needle scoop up the strand from left to right and let it rest on the right-hand needle. (See drawing # 19.)

Slip out your thumb and adjust tension. (See drawing # 20.)

20

TWO-NEEDLE KNITTING OR PURLING ON

There is yet another way to cast on that first row of loops, and of course I am going to explain how to do it. But before I do, I need to tell you that I don't very often use it.

Knitting or purling on with two needles is a very effective way of beginning with a tight and inflexible cast-on row. I am not the only knitting instructor who has had to rip out such beginnings from customers' completed garments because they were so tight that they acted like a tourniquet and shut off the body's blood flow. Knitting or purling on with two needles is not advised for the bottom hipline casting on for sweaters. It may make a wrist cuff too tight for human hands. You may want to learn to do it, however, because it is ideal for the cast-on row of a buttonhole. It will not stretch, give, or bulge out of shape! It is a rigid cast-on, and has a sort of "beaded" appearance.

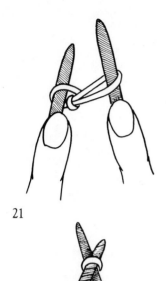

21

Place a slip knot on the left-hand needle. With the right-hand needle knit or purl a stitch into the front forward loop of the slip knot in the ordinary way, but do not remove the old loop from the left-hand needle. Pull forward on the right-hand needle. (See drawing # 21.)

Twist the tip of the left-hand needle so you can slide it from front to back into the front loop of the stitch on the right-hand needle. (See drawing # 22.)

Adjust tension.

Continue in this manner, working into the front forward loop of the first stitch on the left-hand needle. *(See drawing # 23.)*

If you cast on in this manner knitwise, and are going to be working in stockinette stitch, your first row should be purled. If you cast on purlwise, your first row should be knitted.

For the beginning of a ribbed piece, if you wish, you may alternate knit and purl stitches. Just be sure that the working yarn is on the appropriate side of the work so that you will not get an accidental yarn-over.

22

By and large, however, the best all-round method of casting on is the two-strand method. It is the way I almost always begin my knitting.

TECHNIQUES FOR CASTING ON

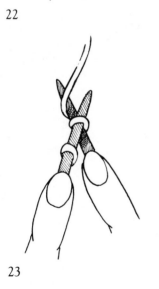

23

Regardless of what method of casting on you choose to use for your next article, I have some wonderful little helpers for you that I devised when I was a knitting instructor at a large department store in Southern California. During that time I found many simple ways to increase the joy of knitting with just a little forethought and some handy devices. Four of these unique techniques concern casting on.

1. It is important that your cast-on stitches be neither too loose nor too tight; that they slide easily enough along the needle to comfortably work the first row of stitches. If you find that you are casting on too tightly and seem not to be able to work more loosely without becoming sloppy, you have my permission to use a larger-size needle to make that original cast-on row *if* you promise to remember to change to the regular size after completing the cast-on.

2. When your instructions call for you to cast on more than twenty stitches at one time, there is an easy way to count and double check on the amount of stitches as well as to set up for a pattern stitch on the first row. Before you begin to cast the stitches on, reach into your supply pouch and take out some appropriately sized ring markers. Cast on the first twenty stitches. Slip a ring marker on the needle. Cast on another twenty stitches. Slip on another ring marker, and so on. That way, if you are interrupted in the process, you will never have to recount those groups of twenty stitches behind the marker again. It is easier to count by twenties—twenty, forty, sixty, etc.—than it is to go back to the beginning if the phone rings while you are casting on.

The twenty-stitch groups will also help you set up the first row of a pattern stitch. If your instructions call for ribbing, for instance, the markers will help you to stay on pattern. If the directions say, "Cast on 66. Row 1: Knit 1, purl 1 across," you should have a purl stitch just before you come to each 20-stitch marker. If you don't, there is something wrong and you can fix it before you get to the end of the row. I'd rather know at the end of 20 stitches whether or not I am on pattern than to find it out after 120 stitches.

Count the individual stitches themselves by "walking" your thumb and forefinger across them by twos. Using the "walking your fingers" technique, you eliminate the possibility of counting the same stitch twice or of skipping a stitch.

4. When you have completed casting on the required number of stitches, wrap the remaining tail end of yarn around your finger and secure the tiny hank with a small safety pin. Do this before you start the first row. Most knitters, at one time or another, have started to work the first row with the short end of the yarn instead of the yarn from the ball. Unfortunately the only cure for this is ripping out the whole thing. By forming a tiny hank of the tail-end yarn and securing it with a safety pin before you begin the first row, you cannot possibly use the wrong end and you won't have to pull apart what you've just knitted.

Please do not cut off the tail-end piece of yarn. It should be at least six inches long to be effectively, neatly, and discretely hidden when you are finishing up the article.

If in the finishing, you are going to have to attach two pieces together or weave a seam, plan ahead and make sure that the tail end is about eighteen inches long. Secured with a safety pin, it will not be in your way and will be handy to make the seam without adding new yarn. Any added new yarn would have its own tail end to hide. I'm lazy. Why hide two tail ends when, with a little planning, you can weave the seam or make the joining with the surplus casting-on yarn?

After you have worked a few rows of your piece, you will want to redo the little hank of yarn and move the safety pin up to attach it to the work itself.

Casting on is not the easiest part of knitting, but by understanding what you are doing and why, and using all of the helpers you can, it doesn't need to be a pain or detract from the joy of knitting.

11

THERE IS ONLY ONE STITCH, BUT YOU CAN DO IT A LOT OF WAYS

All this time we've been talking about knitting without really saying what it is. Now that we're down to the actual details of the craft, we need to take time out and say what it is we are doing.

Very simply stated, knitting is a way of making fabric by pulling loops of yarn through already formed loops of yarn. That's all there is to it!

Pick up something knitted and look at it. It doesn't need to be a handknit; anything knitted will do—a sweater, a sock, an afghan, or the ubiquitous T-shirt. It is all the same. Take a look at it, a really good and careful look. Hold a single thickness of the fabric up to the light. The fabric is just a series of rows of loops made into loops below them. Now turn the piece upside down.

Do you notice something that perhaps no one has pointed out to you before? Do you notice that with casual observation it is difficult to tell, especially in ordinary flat knitting, which way is up and which way is down; which row was made on top of the first row? Stretch your piece, wiggle it, turn it round and round to make sure for yourself that what I'm telling you is true.

On flat knitting, which is sometimes called *stockinette stitch* or *jersey* or *tricot*, there is a front side and a back side. The front side is smooth and flat. The back, or reverse side, of stockinette stitch is bumpy and has row upon row of pearllike beads.

I remember, as a beginner, thinking, "Oh, will I ever be able to learn and remember those stitches?" If you are a beginner now, you may be thinking the same thing. If you are more experienced, you may be smiling and saying, "I know better. There are only two stitches, the *knit* stitch and the *purl* stitch."

And I used to think that, too, until I really looked at a piece of knitting that I had just completed and thought about it. "That's funny, when I made that stitch, I made it a *knit* stitch. But when I turn the work around going back, it changes itself into a *purl* stitch. I wonder why? I wonder what is going on?"

Then one night I woke out of a sound sleep at three A.M. and I knew the answer.

There is only one stitch in knitting.

If that stitch faces you smooth and flat, it is *called* a knit stitch. If that very same stitch faces you bumpy, with pearllike beads at the base of it, it is *called* a purl stitch. Knitters must learn early to identify which is which *as the stitches face you.* Let your left thumbnail tell you the difference.

Run your left thumb down a piece of knitting—either finished or in progress. On the purl side of knitted fabric, you can feel with your thumbnail a series of bumps that are the pearllike beads of the purl stitch. At the base of the loops that rest on knitting needles, you will feel that same bead on the purl stitch. *(See drawing # 24.)*

Not so with the knitted stitch. Its base is smooth and flat. Your thumbnail will feel no bump or bead. It is important that you know how to identify the difference.

> All knitting, *regardless of how fancy or how simple it looks, is made by pulling loops through previously formed loops, and there is only* ONE STITCH. *Head on and straight forward it is termed* KNIT. *Backwards and opposite it is termed* PURL.

There are probably as many ways to form that one stitch, either straight on or backwards, as there are countries in the United Nations. Regardless of how it is made, the finished stitch looks exactly the same. All the various ways of knitting can be divided into three basic "schools." The English and North American "school," in which the working yarn is carried in the right hand; the European "school," wherein the working yarn is carried in the left hand, which has two variations; and the Arabic "school," in which the working yarn flows over the left shoulder.

Knitters from the various schools can get very uptight and opinionated about their special method of knitting. Obviously "their" way is the best way, just because that's how they do it. They may tell knitters from the other schools that they are doing it wrong. I have heard long tirades about how someone else's method of knitting cannot possibly be any good. Books have been written saying, "This is the *only* way to knit." Instructors have said, "It is impossible to

24

control tension *that* way." Teachers have insisted that their students learn only in a certain way.

Piffle and nonsense! There is more than one way to heat water. You can boil water in a tea kettle, a soup pot, or a frying pan.

There is more than one way to knit and all are correct.

Knit according to whichever "school" gives you the greatest joy. Form your stitches in whichever manner you find the most rewarding. Do your knitting in the way in which you are most comfortable.

It is true that the Arabic way is probably the fastest way to knit. (I can't read Arabic, and I've never gotten an Arabic knitter to slow down enough for me to see just exactly how the stitches are formed.) In the Arabic and European methods, the yarn flows from the direction in which it will be used, and it is much quicker to change the yarn to the opposite side of the fabric when going from a knit to a purl stitch or vice versa. It is true that in the American method, with the yarn in the right hand, the individual stitches are probably more perfectly formed. But it doesn't matter. The only difference in all the "schools" and methods of knitting is the way in which the working yarn is held. Knit in whatever way you choose!

In all methods, the knit stitch is formed with the yarn at the back of the work by inserting the right-hand needle into the first loop on the left-hand needle, wrapping the yarn around the right-hand needle beginning at the back, pulling that new loop up and through the old loop, then allowing the old stitch to drop off the left-hand needle.

Three different methods will be discussed on the following pages. Some of the material will be repetitive, because there is no better way to present it.

THE KNIT STITCH IN THE EUROPEAN METHOD

The *European Pic* and *Continental methods* carry the yarn in the left hand, over the index finger, under the second, over the ring finger, and the little finger crooks around the yarn to help adjust the tension. The right hand is perched on *top* of the right-hand needle. (*See drawing # 25.*)

Some people wrap the yarn completely around the index finger. Others wrap the yarn completely around the little finger. I do neither. I clasp the yarn against the palm of my left hand with my left little finger.

25

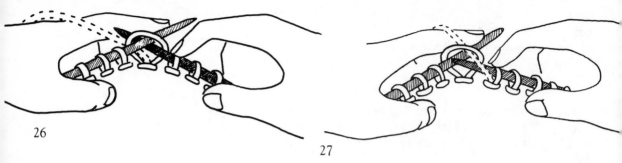

26

27

To form the stitch, with the yarn at the back of the work, the right-hand needle is inserted from the front to the back into the front forward loop of the left-hand needle. (See drawing # 26.)

The loop is stretched open to the right, and the yarn that comes over the left index finger is simply scooped up from right to left. (See drawing # 27.)

The old loop is then slid off the left-hand needle.

The right index finger now moves to the new stitch to keep it from getting too tight or too loose. It is done in one sweeping, swooping, flowing operation of *stretch*, *scoop*, and *slide*. The right-hand needle is held more horizontally than vertically, and the left-hand needle is held more vertically than horizontally. The wrists are closer together when you insert the needle and are more splayed back as you bring the new loop up and to the front. The left hand relaxes and tightens up in unison with the stitch being formed to control the flow of yarn. The right index finger rests on the stitch just completed to keep it from becoming too tight or too loose.

If you are a beginner, practice this knit stitch before going on. It is important that the bones, muscles, and nerves of your fingers develop a smooth and easy rhythm with the knit stitch before you go on to the purl stitch. Just knowing about it in theory is not enough. When you have a perfect four-inch square of knitting without any errors, you are ready for the next step. (The European purl stitches are found following the American knit stitch.)

THE KNIT STITCH IN THE AMERICAN AND BRITISH METHOD

In the *American way*, the yarn is carried in the right hand, over the index finger, under the second finger, over the ring finger, and under the little finger.

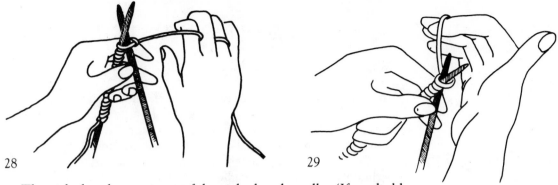

28

29

The right hand rests on *top* of the right-hand needle. (If you hold the right-hand needle like a pencil, you limit yourself in the number of stitches you can work on.) The left hand holds the left-hand needle in place and steadies the work while the right hand is momentarily lifted off its needle to wrap the stitch. (*See drawing #28.*)

With the yarn at the back of the work, the right-hand needle is inserted from the front to the back into the front forward loop of the first stitch on the left-hand needle. The right hand wraps the yarn around the right-hand needle beginning at the back from the right to the left. (See drawing #29.)

The new loop on the right-hand needle is brought through the old loop on the left-hand needle and to the front of the work. (See drawing # 30.)

Then the right-hand needle pulls the old loop off of the left-hand needle. (See drawing # 31.)

Insert, wrap, and *pull.* The whole operation is done very rhythmically and smoothly. It is a relaxing and easy procedure. If you are just learning, practice and get your flow and rhythm down perfect before going on. Simply knowing the words won't do it. Your hands have to know it as well.

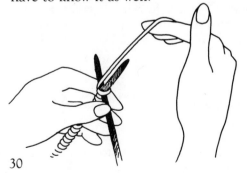

30

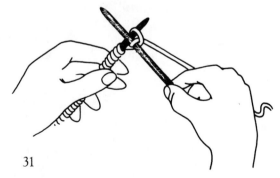

31

THE SLOPE OF THE LOOP

We need to stop here and discuss something very important. The direction of the slope of the stitch.

In giving you the instructions above, I said, "Insert the right-hand needle into the *front forward loop* of the stitch. . . ." This will become a very critical thing later on. Stop and inspect some knitting in progress on needles. Look at the stitches from a bird's-eye view as they rest on the left-hand needle. The stitches do not lie exactly crosswise on the needle; they slant. The stitches don't sit there perpendicular to the needle; they lie diagonally on it with the front forward loop sloping to the right. (*See drawing # 32.*)

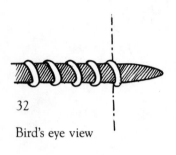

32

Bird's eye view

Pick up something very thin, like a tapestry needle or a tooth-pick. Insert it from the front to the back into a stitch as it sits on the left-hand needle. The front loop of the stitch will rest on the right side of the pick and the back loop on the left side of it.

33

Now hold that same piece up in front of you at eye level. Pull down firmly at the base of a stitch. You will see a bit of air space between the two loops of that stitch. (*See drawing # 33.*)

In the European Pic and the American methods of knitting, the front forward loop of all the stitches on the left-hand needle slope to the right. If they don't slope to the right, they are wrong! All methods of knitting will form the knit stitch in this way. It is in the formation of the purl stitch and the slant that it takes that the European Continental method differs from the European Pic and American-English methods.

In the *Continental method* of knitting, the purl stitch is formed in a way that throws the forward loop to the *back* side of the needle. Continental knitters can compensate for this on knit rows that follow purl rows by working into the back forward loop instead of into the front loop. If this compensation is not made, the stitches will be twisted. However, many knitters find this confusing, particularly if they are doing a pattern stitch that requires some manipulation of the individual stitches. It is so confusing, in fact, that I simply do not teach the Continental purl stitch to my students.

PURL STITCH BASICS IN GENERAL

Remember, earlier in this chapter I told you that the purl stitch was made backwards and opposite from the knit stitch. Since our definitions of the knit stitch began "With the yarn at the back of the work . . ." the purl stitch will have to begin "With the yarn at the front of the work. . . ." Likewise, since we said, ". . . from the front to the back . . ." to make the knit stitch, for the purl stitch we will have to say, ". . . from the back to the front, . . ." Finally, as we finished the knit stitch we said to pull the new loop to the front of the piece before sliding the old loop off. Now, for the purl stitch, we will say just the opposite. "Push the new loop to the back and slide the old loop off."

If you keep in mind that everything about the purl stitch is backwards and opposite, you'll have a much easier time and never get confused about what you are doing.

THE PURL STITCH IN THE EUROPEAN PIC METHOD

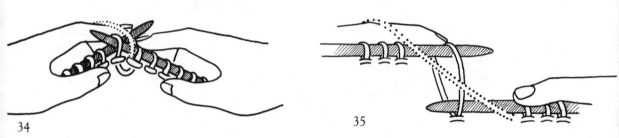

34

35

Holding the yarn in your left hand, with the yarn at the front of the work (toward you), from the back to the front, insert the right-hand needle from behind the new yarn into the front forward loop of the next stitch on the left-hand needle. (See drawing # 34.)

With the right hand, PULL the right-hand needle toward you to form a sort of hole or wide space. (See drawing # 35.)

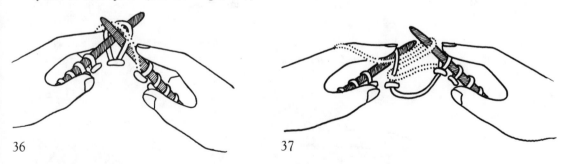

36

37

With the new yarn on the right-hand side of the right-hand needle, with the tip of the needle PUSH BACK that new yarn through the hole-space you made. (See drawing # 36.)

Slide the old stitch off the left-hand needle. (See drawing # 37.)

THERE IS ONLY ONE STITCH / 69

As the stitch slides off, the right forefinger moves on top of the new stitch to protect it from getting too tight or too loose. The right-hand needle is held more horizontally than vertically; the left-hand needle is held more vertically than horizontally. Splay your wrists back when you insert the needle from back to front and then bring your hands together as you push the new yarn through the hole. The motion is *pull, push,* and *slide*. Check to make sure that the front forward loop slopes to the right. If it doesn't, the stitch was made wrong.

Yes, it is harder to get the hang of the purl stitch than it is the knit stitch. And yes, it seems terribly awkward and difficult at first, but it is well worth putting your effort into learning it, because this method is *three times faster* than the American method. Pattern stitches that alternate knit and purl stitches will be just as fast to work as plain rows.

I often allow beginners to use a crochet hook as the right-hand needle for the first row when they are learning this Continental Pic purl stitch if they are having difficulties. With the open throat of the hook facing away from them to make the stitch, they can easily see what is supposed to happen. Just as soon as they understand and can form the stitch with the crochet hook, they transfer back to using a knitting needle in the right hand.

Hang in there and don't quit. If you give up, you cannot learn; and the rewards for learning are great.

THE PURL STITCH IN THE AMERICAN AND ENGLISH METHOD

With the yarn in the right hand at the front of the work (toward you), from behind the yarn insert the right-hand needle from the back to the front into the front forward loop on the left-hand needle. (See drawing # 38.)

Wrap the yarn around the back of the right-hand needle from the right to the left and to the front. (See drawing # 39.)

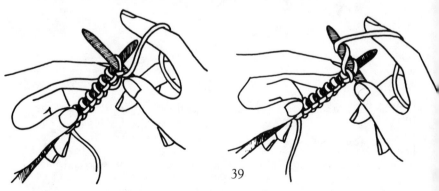

38

39

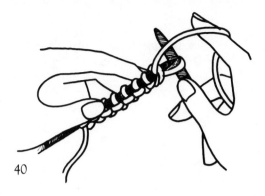

40

With the tip of the right-hand needle, push the new loop to the back of the work and slide the old stitch off the needle. (See drawing # 40.)

Insert, wrap, and *push.* Check to see that the front forward loop slopes to the right. If it doesn't, you've made the stitch wrong. Though it may seem a bit cumbersome at first, it will soon be just as relaxing and easy as the knit stitch. If you wish to see all of these stitches demonstated in motion, I recommend that you see my video tape called "Basic Knitting," which is produced and marketed by Jeanette Crews Designs, Lilburn, Georgia.

MORE ABOUT PURL STITCHES IN GENERAL

Many, many knitters make their purl stitches looser than they make their knit stitches. Often a conscious effort has to be made to firm up sloppy purl stitches. Think tight! Regardless of whether you are holding the yarn in your right or your left hand, hold it a little snugger and firmer when you make your purl stitches. Practice making rows and rows of the purl stitch before you try to intersperse them to make ribbing.

If your flat, back-and-forth stockinette-stitch fabric, which is one row of knit stitches and then one row of purl stitches, has ridges and open spaces on the reverse side, your purl stitch is too loose. Try to work tighter. If you *absolutely* cannot get a more-or-less even piece of fabric, seriously consider making your knitted articles in the round, where all stitches will be knit stitches. As a last resort, if you must work flat, you have my permission to use a smaller size needle in the right hand when working purl rows, but remember, this is a last resort—and it is a real bother reaching and grabbing for the correct size needle when you are changing rows.

When you have learned this one basic stitch of knitting and have learned to make it "forward and straight on" and "backwards and opposite," you are well on your way to a creative, relaxing, and rewarding future of handknitting, making fabric of rows upon rows of looped yarn.

12
SPECIAL THINGS TO DO WITH THAT ONE STITCH

Just because that stitch is sitting on your needle staring expectantly at you, it doesn't mean you have to work it in the same way every time. You don't have to just knit or purl. You can get very creative if you like.

THE SLIP STITCH

The easiest thing to do with a stitch is to move it from one needle to the other without doing anything to it. In knitting jargon it is called making a *slip stitch.* You just slip it from the left-hand needle to the right-hand needle *as if to purl.* Unless your instructions tell you otherwise, you keep the working yarn on the side of the work that it was on to start with and simply slip the stitch from one needle to the other. *(See drawing # 41.)*

You can move any stitch anywhere as many times as you wish to so long as you slip as if to purl it.

It really comes in handy when you want to stop and try on the piece or to spread it out to more accurately measure it.

41

Ordinarily stitches are slipped only every other row or round. They are worked on the alternate rounds to even up the fabric. Occasionally some pattern stitches will call for a certain stitch and its neighbors to be slipped for several rows to achieve a special effect. Bow and tucked stitches are examples of this. Occasionally some pattern stitches will call for you to take the yarn to the opposite side of the work when you slip the stitch, again to create a special effect. The directions will say "wool forward," or "y b," meaning take the yarn to the back of the work.

When working in stockinette stitch, if the same stitch on the knit side of the fabric is slipped every other row, it will give you a lovely fold line, which is a nice thing to have if you are making a cardigan with a fold-under front band. The band will turn under at the slipped stitch and lay flat.

The slip stitch also comes in handy if you want to make a pleated skirt. A single slipped stitch will make an elegant knife edge that will pull the pleat forward, while a single purl stitch will cause the pleat to fold in the opposite direction.

THE TWISTED STITCH

Usually when knitting in the American or European Pic methods, we work into the front forward loop, but we don't have to. We can deliberately *work into the back of the loop*. (*See drawing # 42.*) This will of course cause a *twisted stitch*. Twisted stitches are tighter than ordinary stitches, but perhaps we sometimes want a tighter stitch. Nordic sweaters traditionally use a knit 1, purl 1 ribbing with the knit stitches worked in the back loop in order to get just that effect, a tighter ribbing.

42

WORKING THE SECOND STITCH FIRST

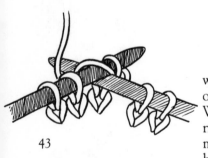

Okay, we can move the stitch without working it, we can twist it, what else can we do with it? Do we have to work the stitches in the order in which they appear on the left-hand needle? No, we don't. We can *work the second stitch* before we work the first stitch. If you never thought about it, try it and see what happens. You can simply move your right-hand needle over to the second stitch on the left-hand needle and knit it in the ordinary way from the front to the back. (*See drawing # 43.*)

43

Or, you can use the tip of the right-hand needle to stretch the second stitch on the left-hand needle over and across the first stitch and then knit it in the ordinary way. (*See drawing # 44.*)

The effect will be different, but both are nice. In either event, you then knit the first stitch and take both of the stitches off the left-hand needle at the same time.

On the following row or round, the crossed stitches are usually worked even in order to smooth up the fabric. Knitting the second

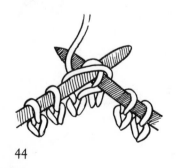

44

stitch before you knit the first stitch is a way of making a mini-cable, and it is often used as just that. It will have a nice raised effect and can make a good defining line to separate other pattern stitches. It is often used in Irish fisherman sweaters.

THE ELONGATED STITCH

There are still more creative things that you can do with that one basic knitting stitch. You can *elongate* it. If you wrap the yarn around the right-hand needle one or more times before you insert it into the next stitch, and then allow those wraps to fall off on the next row before you work the stitch, you will have a super-long stitch. (*See drawing # 45.*)

A whole row of elongated stitches will give you a lacy effect with very little labor and thought. (Something of the same effect can be achieved by using two very different-size needles for the right and left hand.)

45

KNITTING THE NEXT STITCH IN THE ROW BELOW

Just as you don't have to work stitches in the order in which they appear, neither do you have to work the rows in the usual sequence. You can *knit the next stitch in the row below.* Instead of inserting the right-hand needle at the base of the next stitch on the left-hand needle, you can move down one row and insert it there. (*See drawing # 46.*)

Don't worry, you won't lose the stitch. It will not drop. Knitting every other stitch in the row below is the basis of the very attractive "fisherman's rib" or "brioche stitch," of which the classic raglan sweaters of western Europe are made.

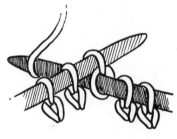

46

These are some of the different things you can do with the basic stitch of knitting. (I haven't mentioned it because it isn't often done, but you could do any of these variations with purl stitches as well.) These are the most common variations, but they're not all of them. (Knitting or purling more than once in the same stitch is called *increasing.* That is explained in chapter 14.) It is in varying the basic stitch that the thousands of pattern stitches are created. Some day, when I have nothing else to do, I am going to sit down with a pencil, paper, and a computer and try to figure out how many possible combinations of variations there could be. But don't hold your breath waiting for the results.

13

BINDING OFF AND BRINGING IT TO AN END

There are some things in life that we don't really want to come to an end—like the exchange of ideas and information, friendly support, and good times. But we always wanted knitted fabric to come to an end.

If there were not some way to stop the whole process of making loops on top of loops and to remove it from the needles, our precious knitting would be of no use to us. Thank goodness there is a way to stop, and it's called *binding off.* Some instructions and directions will call it *casting off.* I like that term. It reminds me of a little tiny boat pulling away from a big one to do its own thing. Either way you want to call it, it means sealing off in a safe and neat way a number of stitches that you don't intend to work any more.

If you're a beginner, learn it right to start with. Even if you are an experienced knitter, I'd like to walk you through it again. I want to make sure that you know how to bind-off knitwise, purlwise, in ribbing, forming a seam, and without working yarn.

Make yourself a stockinette-stitch swatch of thirty six stitches to do some experimenting on. It does not need to be more than an inch and a half or so long. Any needles and any yarn will do.

Pick up some plastic ring markers. The slip-on kind are great for this little project if you happen to have them. If you don't have slip-on markers around, it is very easy to make them by snipping an opening in the standard thin plastic ones. Place a ring marker after every 6 stitches on your swatch. I often have my students use slip-on ring markers when they are binding off. It is an easy way of keeping yourself on target because you do the counting ahead of time.

BINDING OFF KNITWISE

*Very loosely and sloppily knit the first stitch. * Very loosely and sloppily knit the next stitch (there are 2 loops on the right-hand needle). From the front, with the left-hand needle, lift the first stitch up and over the second stitch, and off the tip of the needle. * (You have worked 2 stitches, but you have only bound off 1 stitch knitwise.) (See drawing # 47.)*

47

You didn't read it wrong. That's the way I said it: "Very loosely and sloppily." Tight bind-offs cause students and their knitting instructors more trouble than any other mismade stitch! I used to say, "Make sure that your bind-off is not too tight." That didn't work. It was not emphatic enough. My student's bind-offs were still too firm and unwielding. Now I say, "Make it messy!"

Continue on across your swatch, loosely and sloppily, to the first marker, repeating the instructions between the asterisks (* *) in the paragraph above. When you get to the marker, you will have one loop remaining on the right-hand needle and you will have bound off five stitches knitwise. Run your fingers over those five stitches. Are they as elastic and as pliable as the fabric below them? They should be. If they're not, rip them out and try again. It is easy, oh so very easy, to make those bound-off stitches too tight—so tight, in fact, that the whole garment can be distorted and pulled out of shape.

If you can't get the bound-off stitches to be stretchy with the usual working needle, you have my permission to pick up a larger-size needle to use in the right hand to make sure that they are not too tight.

You do *not* have my permission to ruin the look of your precious handmade fabric with an ugly tight bind-off.

Look carefully at the stitches that you have just bound off knitwise. Notice that they roll to the front. Stitches bound off knitwise will always roll to the front. Nothing right or wrong about it, that's just the way it is.

BINDING OFF PURLWISE

Since you can form new stitches as purl stitches, do you suppose that you can bind off in purl? Of course you can! Nothing to it, but to do it. *To bind off purl-wise.*

*Purl 1. * Very loosely and sloppily purl the next stitch (there are 2 loops on the right-hand needle). Holding the yarn down to the front, and from the front, with the left-hand needle, lift the first stitch up and over the second* *stitch and off the tip of the needle. * (You will have bound off 1 stitch purlwise.)*

Continue in this same way to the next marker. You will have bound-off *six* more stitches and have one loop remaining on the right-hand needle. Stop and admire your work. You have learned a new technique.

But look one more time at those stitches that you just bound off purlwise. They behave differently than the stitches you bound off knitwise. They roll to the back of the work, don't they? You've just discovered that:

Stitches bound off knitwise roll to the front of the work. Stitches bound off purlwise roll to the back.

BINDING OFF IN ALTERNATING KNIT AND PURL

Ready for another experiment? What is going to happen if you alternate knit and purl stitches as you bind off? Try for yourself. First, bind off as if to knit, next bind off as if to purl, then as if to knit, and so on until you come to the marker.

Inspect your work and see what happened. Is the appearance of the edge different? Stop and examine it. Does it roll to the front, or to the back, or does it lie right on the top? Is it more elastic than either the knitwise or purlwise bind-offs?

Bind-offs made by alternating knit and purl stitches lie straight on the top of the piece. They roll neither to the front nor to the back, and they make a neatly elastic edge.

You should have three more groups of six stitches remaining on your swatch. Slip the first group of six stitches onto an extra double-pointed needle (any size or shape will do). Slip the next group of six onto another double-pointed needle. (For convenience, you might wish to put a rubber-tip stopper on the needle with the last remaining six stitches to keep them safe for later.) Fold the work back on itself between these two groups of stitches. It doesn't matter which group is at the front. You are going to learn to *make a seam while binding off two pieces together at the same time.*

BINDING OFF AND SEAMING

Hold the two double-pointed needles side by side, parallel, together. Insert the right-hand needle through the loop of the first stitch on the needle that is in front AND through the loop of the first stitch on the needle that is in the back. *Wrap the yarn around the right-hand needle to make a knit stitch. (See drawing # 48.)*

Pull it through both loops to the front of the piece. (See drawing # 49.)

Make another double stitch in the same way. With the tip of the left-hand needle, lift the outside stitch up and over the second stitch on the right-hand needle and off to bind it off.

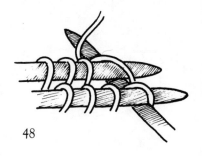

48

Continue across the row in the same manner.

Neat, isn't it? Two edges have been bound off and a seam formed all at the same time. I've said it before, and I'll say it again. Sometimes the lazy person's way of doing things is the neatest way. Inspect it from all angles and see if you approve.

Any time you have to do straight bind-offs of two separate pieces and then sew them together, you can accomplish all three steps in one! It comes in handy for sweaters that have flat shoulders.

Many of my advanced students enjoy making short rows instead of binding off shoulders in stair steps. After they have made the final evening-up row following the short rows, they form the seam by binding off the back and front together. They feel that that is easier and neater than binding off separately and weaving a seam. It is all a matter of preference.

49

To complete the final stitch that is resting on the right-hand needle when you have completed a bind-off sequence, and do not intend to continue knitting, clip off the yarn, leaving at least 6-inch-long tail end. Pull straight up with the right-hand needle and let that tail end come through the final loop.

BINDING OFF WITHOUT YARN

Now those last six stitches. They are stuck out there with no yarn to bind them off, but you can get rid of them securely anyway. To bind off without yarn:

Slip 2 stitches on to the right-hand needle. Then just lift one stitch over the other to dispose of it as in regular binding off. Slip another stitch and do the same thing.

If you choose, you may try alternating slipping as if to knit with slipping as if to purl. You can get rid of all but the last loop in this manner. (If you are not going to continue on, the last loop can be secured with an extra piece of yarn.)

Binding off stitches without yarn will come up again in the directions for the "neatest buttonhole" in chapter 16.

TROUBLESHOOTING THE DIRECTIONS

Some instructions will call for you to slip the first stitch when beginning a bind-off sequence. I do not feel that this is advisable. That one stitch will fall one row below the others. It makes that edge harder to finish off in whatever manner you intend to complete it.

Sometimes you will be required to continue working on after binding off a few stitches at the beginning of a row. The underarm bind-offs are such an example. Counting the required number of bound-off stitches can be confusing, because you must work two stitches in order to bind off the first one. Avoid all problems by placing a slip-on ring marker on the left-hand needle in the spot after however many stitches are specified to be bound off before you begin. When you find yourself at the slip-on ring marker, pull the marker off. *To avoid the ugly crossbar over the edge stitch when continuing after a bind off series:*

> *Bind off 1 stitch less than directed by the instructions. Place the loop that is remaining on the right-hand needle back onto the left-hand needle through the front loop. Decrease 1 stitch by working the 2 loops together, through the front loops, as if they were one.*

Please do yourself a favor and make it a habit on any knitting you may be doing to:

> *Bind off in the pattern stitch you are using even if the directions don't tell you to!*

A lot of designers really aren't very experienced in actual knitting and don't know about some of the nicer details. Even if they do, editors must always fight the battle of too many words. The instructions about how to bind off may have been edited out. Every knitting instructor in the country has seen lovely, perfectly knitted garments that have been bound off to less than perfection. The final ribbing of garments needs to be bound off in pattern stitch. If it is a knit one, purl one ribbing, bind it off knit one, purl one. If it is a knit two, purl two ribbing, bind it off knit two, purl two.

Another problem arises with bind-offs. I learned about it on my own, the hard way, and accounted for it in my own knitting. Unfortunately, as a knitting instructor, it is not always possible to pass on all you have learned to each and every patron. Customers may encounter problems on their own without a way to solve them.

One morning a woman appeared at my work table in tears. In her hand she carried a gift box. She brought her problem, still wrapped in its tissue paper. "I made this sweater as a birthday gift for my son. I worked so hard on it! I followed the instructions exactly. And he couldn't even get it over his head. I bought the yarn from you and it's all your fault."

True she had bought the yarn from me. True she had worked hard and had done a beautiful job on it. It was sad that it would not go over her son's head. She had followed the instructions in the purchased pattern booklet exactly. Unfortunately, the directions said, "Bind off 5 stitches at the beginning of the next 8 rows. Bind off remaining stitches for back neck," and "Bind off the center 24 stitches for the front neck." Not even a newborn could have gotten its head through the firmly bound off opening!

On a pullover where the opening will be completed with ribbing, place the neck stitches ON HOLDERS *rather than binding them off. Work the stitches from the holders rather than picking up stitches over bound-off stitches.*

Like virginity, once elasticity is lost it can never be regained. Better to have a head opening that is too large than too small. Large openings can be tightened up with a row of single crochet on the underside of the ribbing at the change line, or with a couple of strands of elastic thread run through the purl beads on the underside.

Small openings must have the ribbing removed, the bound-off stitches ripped back and reknitted, and the ribbing redone. Either that, or they are consigned to the bottom of the cedar chest as unusable family heirlooms.

Besides not binding off neck stitches that are to be later worked in ribbing, I finish off my pullover neck openings with a rolled-to-the-inside knit one, purl one crew-type rib. I bind off very loosely (knit one, purl one, of course) at the end of the ribbing, and use a sewing whip stitch to fasten the ribbing in place. I leave about half an inch unsewn so that a lingerie-type elastic can be slipped in if somehow the neck opening should prove to be too large.

Some knitters do not bind off that final row of ribbing at all for rolled necklines. Their neckbands roll to the front. They work a sewing backstitch directly from the stitches as they rest on the needle to fasten the band to the picked-up edge line.

Recently I was talking to the needlework editor of a national handcraft publication. Only a beginning knitter herself, she asked me why so many design models for sweaters came to her that had neck openings that were much too small. I had to tell her that many people didn't know any better. But now *you* know better and will slip those stitches to a holder rather than bind them off.

Regardless of where it occurs, don't let binding off get you into a tight spot. Don't ruin the grace and elasticity of your lovely handmade fabric with a firm and unforgiving edge. Whenever possible, all kinds of endings in life should be easy and graceful. Being firm and unforgiving hurts only ourselves.

14
MORE AND LESS OF A GOOD THING

AN INTRODUCTION TO INCREASING AND DECREASING

I remember somewhere, sometime in some art class, being told that the human body could be represented by a series of tapered cylinders. And I remember standing at an easel, with my chalk held long edge against the paper, drawing human bodies that looked like this. (*See drawing # 50.*)

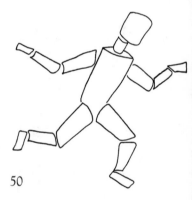

50

I recall it now because I want to introduce you to one of the pains—and joys—of knitting: making increases and decreases. If you can think of the human body in terms of cylinders, it will help you to understand what needs to happen to our straight pieces of loop-formed fabric as we try to utilize them to decorate and protect our bodies.

In *weaving* cloth, once the warp strands, the long vertical ones, are set up on the loom, it is difficult to change the width of the piece being woven. When the cloth is completed, it must be cut up and somehow fastened together to form the necessary tube for legs and sleeves and such.

Not so with knitting. Knitting can be *made* in the round—the tube being closed or fastened as you work. And that tube can be changed in width to allow for the difference in the girth of a calf and thigh or upper and lower arm *in the very process of making it* by increasing or decreasing stitches.

If you are working from the bottom up on a sleeve, you can increase the width from wrist to upper arm. If you are working down from the top, you can decrease that width from upper arm to wrist.

Likewise, you can decrease or increase from chest to shoulder, depending on whether you are going from bottom up or from top down. It is all the same difference.

There are umpteen different styles in which you can make those increases and decreases for different effects. In ordinary even, flat knitting, one loop rests directly on top of the one below and the fabric runs straight up and down. The "grain" of the fabric is vertical. Some decreases slope to the right or to the left, which will cause the grain of the fabric to change from vertical to slanted. Some increases will do the same. That is why the style of increase or decrease you choose to use is a matter of preference for a desired effect.

Both increases and decreases are customarily made *only* on knit rows. Purl rows are usually worked "even" and plain to even up and smooth out the fabric. Therefore, instructions usually say, "Decrease 1 stitch at each end of every *knit* row," or "Increase 1 stitch each side *every other* row."

If you repeat a certain style of increase or decrease over and over at regular intervals, a curious thing will happen. The increases or decreases will form a pattern against the background of the knitted fabric. A design element will appear, enhancing the piece and changing it from a utilitarian, protective article to an elaborate and wonderful decorative covering. Many pattern stitches, especially laces, are created by making a corresponding number of increases and decreases over a certain number of stitches.

As you read about and practice the increases and decreases described in the next two parts of this chapter, keep in mind that they serve *two* functions: to shape the knitted tube *and* to create changes in texture that will enliven the fabric. When you understand their function and their effect, they will never confuse you.

I've said it before, and I want to repeat it now. I am a lazy person. But I'm not *lackadaisically* lazy; I'm *methodically* lazy. I also have the kind of mind that keeps mumbling, "There has got to be a better way!"

KEEPING TRACK

There had to be a better way found to keep track of increases and decreases. I always had trouble trying to *keep* a sharpened pencil in my work basket and then *remembering* to find it to make little hash marks on the margin of my directions when I added or subtracted stitches. I would have to stop and count the remaining number of stitches and do a little arithmetic to find out how many more increases or decreases had to be made. Lazy people don't like to have to stop and count and do arithmetic!

And I found the easy way. I suggested to my customers that they purchase packets of very tiny safety pins, coilless ones when possible. These little safety pins are made into a chain at the beginning of a sequence of increases or decreases and fastened into the work. If the directions say, "Increase 1 stitch on each side every 6th row 18 times," we make a chain of eighteen safety pins. If the instructions say, "Decrease 1 stitch at each marker every 4th row 12 times," we make a chain of twelve safety pins.

My patrons are told to remove one safety pin from the chain each time they make the first increase or decrease on a row and to insert it into the increased or decreased stitch. They can then very easily see where they made the last increase or decrease, when they made it, and how many more they have to make. A methodically lazy way of saving time, effort, and energy!

Sometimes people, especially other knitters, will look at my garments in progress and say, "What in the world are all those safety pins for?" My answer is always, "To keep track of increases and decreases." Their response will be, "That makes sense." And it does. When your chain of safety pins is used up, your group of increases or decreases is completed. (Of course, you will stop and double-check your directions to see that you have the proper number of stitches remaining.)

Whenever you see a packet of tiny *coilless* safety pins, buy it. Sometimes they are rather hard to find, so stockpile them. The lack of a coil at the bottom end allows the pin to hang straight down in your work, and the yarn can never become entangled in a coil that isn't there.

WHERE TO INCREASE OR DECREASE

In the sections that follow I will frequently refer to increases or decreases "at the beginning" or "at the end" of a row. I do not really mean in the first and last stitch; I'll tell you why.

You can't weave a neat and inconspicuous seam over edge-increased or -decreased stitches.

Increases and decreases can often create an eye-catching pattern. Seams, however, should never be eye-catching; rather, they should be as close to invisible as possible.

I like to make what are termed full-fashioned increases and decreases. That is, I like to make increases and decreases that are placed two, three, or four stitches in from the edges. It allows an invisible seam to be woven and lets the increases or decreases add to the detail of the fabric. How many stitches in from the edge you choose to make these increases and decreases will depend upon the stitch gauge you are working with and upon your preference. So long as you are consistent on all the parts of a garment, exactly how far in you place the "full-fashioned" increases or decreases is strictly a matter of choice.

Therefore in the next two sections when I speak of the "beginning" or "end" of a row, or "right-hand edge" or "left-hand edge," please understand that I don't really mean it.

Most of the following increases and decreases are visually demonstrated in my video tape "Intermediate Knitting," which is produced and marketed by Jeanette Crews Designs, Lilburn, Georgia.

INCREASING TO MAKE MORE OUT OF WHAT YOU ALREADY HAVE

Most quantities of the stuff of life are not limited and finite. Joy and happiness can always be added to and spread around. And so it is with knitting. However many stitches you start with, you can always add to them and make more.

YARN-OVERS

The easiest and quickest way to make a new loop is to just throw an extra wrap of yarn across the needle between stitches. It is called making a *yarn-over*, because you lay the yarn over the right-hand needle before you work the next stitch. (See, knitting isn't complicated. It really makes sense when you stop to think about it.) This will cause an extra loop to sit on the needle. Of course it will also cause a hole in your fabric; that's part of the definition of a yarn-over increase. Most of us, when we were beginners, made lots of accidental yarn-overs when we were learning to do ribbing. We forgot to take the yarn between the tips of the needles to the opposite side of the work when we changed stitches. We didn't want yarn-overs then, but sooner or later we will want to make them on purpose, and we need to learn how.

Depending on whether you hold the working yarn in your right or your left hand, there may be a slight difference in the way you lay the yarn across the right-hand needle in the various situations. There is also a difference in exactly how you should lay the yarn over the right-hand needle before working the next stitch; it depends upon what kind of a stitch you just made and upon what kind of a stitch you intend to make next. The difference will show up in the length of the yarn-over loop and in the hole below it.

There are four possible combinations of circumstances in which you may be required to make a yarn-over. They are yarn-overs

1. between knit stitches

2. between purl stitches

3. between a knit and a purl stitch

4. between a purl and a knit stitch.

Some knitting instructional books will give very detailed instructions for each of these. I think that you can very simply describe all four by saying:

51
Yarn over between knit stitches

> Take the yarn to the side of the work from which the next regular stitch will be worked, to the back for a knit or to the front for a purl. Without inserting the needle into the next stitch, wrap the yarn around the right-hand needle as if you were making that stitch. Work the next stitch in the regular way. (See drawings # 51 and 52.)

> On the row following the one in which the yarn-over increase was made, the strand of yarn formed by it is worked as a regular stitch.

"Yarn-over" increases are abbreviated Y O or YO or y o or yo in standard knitting directions.

52
Yarn over between purl stitches

THE ENGLISH MAKE-ONE

The English make an increase that is very similar to the American yarn-over. They call it *make one English style. They*

> simply knit an extra stitch under the stand that lies before the next stitch. (See drawing # 53.)

The English make-one will fall one row below the American yarn-over and will leave a slightly smaller hole. Both of these increases *leave a hole in the fabric and neither of them change the grain and slope of the fabric.* The increased stitch will lie directly above its hole.

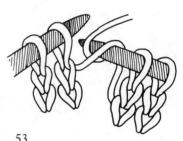

53

THE MULTIPLE INCREASE IN ONE STITCH

The next easiest way to make an increase is to knit into a stitch more than once. To *knit into the front and the back of the next stitch (KFB).*

With the yarn at the back of the work, knit the next stitch in the ordinary way, but do not remove the old stitch from the needle. Swing the right-hand needle wide around and to the back . . . (See drawing # 54.)

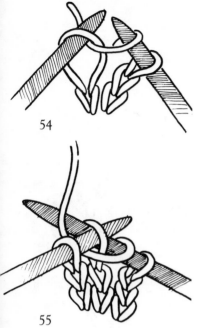

54

. . . and knit into the back loop of the old stitch. (See drawing # 55.)

Remove the old stitch from the needle.

You will have made two stitches out of one without a hole, and you will have caused the grain of the fabric to move one stitch to the left. You will also have a purllike bead at the base of the stitch that was knitted in the back loop.

I very frequently use this KFB increase in the knit-in-one-piece-from-the-top-down raglan sweaters that I love to make. The repetitious use of this increase and the resulting bead caused by it add an interesting detail to the garment.

55

While I have seen this type of increase abbreviated *KFB* in some instructions, more commonly the directions will simply say *inc.*

Occasionally you will be called on to *purl into the back and the front of the next stitch.* It is done in a similar manner.

With the yarn at the front of the work, insert as if to purl the right-hand needle into the back loop of the next stitch and purl, but do not remove the old stitch from the left-hand needle. (See drawing # 56.)

Swing wide and around, and purl into the front loop of the same stitch. (See drawing # 57.)

Remove the old stitch from the needle.

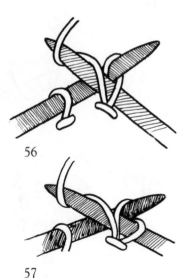

56

This increase will move the grain of the fabric one stitch to the right as it faces you.

You can knit into a stitch more than just two times. In making "popcorn" and "bauble" stitches, it is very common to knit into the front and the back of the next stitch five or six times. It is done in the same way, swinging the right-hand needle wide and around to the opposite side of the work before you take the old stitch off the left-hand needle.

57

It quite naturally follows that you can make more than one extra stitch into purl stitches in the same manner that you can with knit stitches.

Sometimes your instructions will direct you to knit, *purl, and knit* or *purl, knit, and purl* into the next stitch. The only thing to remember about this type increase is to know that you have to move the yarn between the tips of the needles to the opposite side of the work before each step. If you don't, you will get extra unwanted yarn-over increases between each one and you will have more loops on your needle than you intended.

THE BLIND STOCKINETTE-STITCH INCREASE

The disadvantage of yarn-over increases is that they leave a hole. The disadvantage of knit-in-front-and-back increases is that they leave a bead on the flat surface of the fabric. Each has its place and each is useful. However, there are times when working, especially in stockinette stitch, when we want an inconspicuous increase without a hole and without a bead. Thank goodness someone invented one. I call it the *blind-stockinette-stitch increase.* Some European directions call it *make-one.* Either name you choose to call it, it is a wonderful technique to know. No bead, no hole—in fact, it is so nearly invisible that you, the knitter, really have to look hard to find it after it is made.

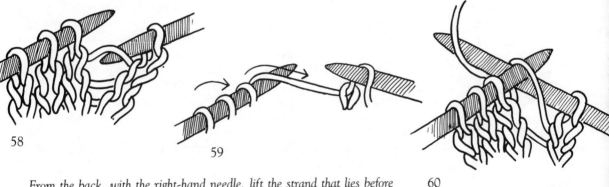

58

59

60

From the back, with the right-hand needle, lift the strand that lies before the next stitch . . . (See drawing # 58.)

. . . and place it on the left-hand needle sloping in the same direction as all of the other knit stitches. (See drawing # 59.)

Knit into the BACK LOOP *of this strand. (See drawing # 60.)*

The first time my students try it, they swear it can't be done. After the loop is placed on the left-hand needle, the trick is to slide the right-hand needle along the underside of the left-hand needle, then turn it into the picked-up loop. The second time my students try it they smile with approval. After that they sneak these invisible increases into their garments in lots of places—when they are short a stitch to make a pattern work, the center back of coats and jackets to make them hang better, near the underarm to make room for a large bust, in a collar to make the flare smoother. I hope that you get the idea that this one is well worth learning and remembering.

These increases are the most commonly used in ordinary knitting. They may be the only ones most knitters are ever required to make, but they are by no means all of the kinds of increases that can be made.

OTHER WAYS TO INCREASE

Stop for a moment and take a look at a knit stitch as it lies on the left-hand needle in the middle of a row. How many possible ways are there of making more stitches out of it? Could you *knit into the right-hand loop of the stitch in the row below?* Sure. And which direction would it move the grain of the fabric? To the right, of course.

What about the *left-hand loop of the stitch in the row below?* There is no difficulty with that. Knit the stitch, remove it from the left-hand needle to the right, then, with the tip of the left-hand needle, pull out and up on that loop and knit into it. The grain of the fabric will move to the left. Whether you inserted the left-hand needle from the front to the back or from the back to the front would make a difference in the appearance of the stitch.

Now look again at a knit stitch as it sits on your needle. There are probably a dozen more different ways that you could multiply it. We could go on for a dozen more pages describing ways to increase it, and as many pages more describing how you could multiply purl stitches. You may never be called upon to make these other increases, and I hate to waste space on them when there are so many other facets of this delightul way of making fabric that I want to tell you about. Just know that they can be done.

DON'T GET DIZZY OVER DECREASES

From time to time in our knitting we want to get rid of some of the stitches but still keep on knitting. We may want to dispose of just one, or several of the stitches along a row. We may want to narrow the width of a piece from chest to shoulders, or we may want to create a design in the fabric.

For whatever reason, the easiest thing to do would be to just take them off the needle and stop working them—simply remove them from the left-hand needle as we come to them and let them dangle in the air.

Unfortunately, they might not just hang there flapping in the breeze for very long; they might start to pull out and "run" off like a puppy after a stick, leaving a trail of destruction in their wake. If we weren't planning on a run, we would be disconcerted to see gaps and loose loops careening down our pretty fabric.

Getting rid of stitches, or *decreasing,* needs to be done in special ways so that the stitches we quit working on will be secure and stay in the spot where we took them off. Since decreases can change the vertical grain of the fabric and cause it to slope in different directions, we also have to plan which kind of decrease to use in a specific location.

KNITTING STITCHES TOGETHER

The easiest way to get rid of unwanted stitches in a safe and secure way is to work stitches together as if they were one. Just pretend several loops are one and work them all together. It is the simplest of all decreases and is easy to do.

To knit two together:

61

On a knit row, with the outside—the public side—of the work facing you, knit the next 2 stitches together, through the front loops, as if they were one. (See drawing # 61.)

You will have gotten rid of one loop, and the grain of the fabric will have moved over one stitch from the left to the right as it faces you. *(See drawing # 62.)*

This kind of a decrease is usually made at the end of a row. It is abbreviated *K 2 tog.*

Now that is hardly the only way to work two stitches together. Remember, I said *through the front loops.* Could you knit those same two stitches together *through the back loops?* Of course you could. Try it and see. It still gets rid of one loop, but it causes the grain of the fabric to move over one stitch from the right to the left, and not very tidily at that.

62

Sometimes some pattern stitch instructions will call for more than two stitches to be knitted together at one time, and there's nothing to it. Either through the front or the back loops, it is possible to knit as many as five stitches together at once for a special effect. More than five at once, though, and it becomes a real hassle and isn't worth the effort.

You can also *purl two stitches together* through the front or the back loops. The effects will be different, and it is not usually done on stockinette stitch, but it is still an option. Just as you can knit many stitches together, you can purl as many stitches together as you want to.

THE SLIP KNIT PASSOVER

Remember, the easy and common decrease of knitting two stitches together through the front loops causes the fabric to shift one stitch to the right. However, it is usually desirable to have the grain of the fabric go straight up as it is narrowed, rather than going off on a slant. Therefore, a decrease had to be devised that would move the fabric correspondingly one stitch to the left and allow the remaining stitches to lie perpendicular.

The simplest decrease that achieves this is a *slip knit passover*. To make it:

63

64

As if to knit, slip the next stitch from the left-hand to the right-hand needle. Knit the next stitch. Then, with the tip of the left-hand needle, lift the slipped stitch up and over the knitted stitch and safely off the end of the right-hand needle. (See drawings # 63 and 64.)

This decrease is abbreviated *SKP* or sometimes *S1, K, Psso*. It is usually made at the beginning of a row, for it slopes from the right to the left as the article faces you. *(See drawing # 65.)*

Alas, because the decreased stitch is slipped and not worked before it is dropped into oblivion, this decrease appears to have been made on the row below. Sometimes it matters greatly; sometimes it doesn't, as you'll see as you read on. Also, the decreased stitch will appear slightly elongated when closely inspected. And some people do inspect closely!

65

I had never really noticed that SKPs and K-2-togs did not really match until I was making a raglan sweater from directions that proudly called for "full-fashioned accentuated decreases." Once I was able to translate that phrase, I found it meant that the decreases were made four stitches in from each edge and that K 2 tog was made at the beginning of the row and the SKP was made at the end of the row, rather than in the usual opposite order. The two sides of my sweater did not match at all. It looked awful. I was sure that I was doing something wrong. I ripped and ripped. I thought that I was stupid.

I dug into an old knitting book to look up what was the matter. Nothing was the matter. It said right there in the book, "Of course, every good knitter knows that SKP and K 2 tog do not really match." At that time I was not a good knitter and I didn't know it. Neither did the designer of the sweater!

The next time it was brought home to me that these two decreases do not look alike or fall on the same row was when I was making one of my beloved multistriped sweaters. (I like to use up leftover yarn in wild and glorious stripes making emphatic and dramatic designs.) Making a SKP and a K 2 tog on a color change row looks terrible. And if you've only got a two-row stripe pattern, you have to look for another way in which to make the decreases.

OTHER WAYS TO DECREASE

To make *a decrease that more perfectly matches a knit-two-together decrease*, a little sleight of hand is required. It works like this:

66
67

With the tip of the right-hand needle, slip the first stitch on the left-hand needle as if to knit. Slip the next stitch on the left-hand needle in the same way. From left to right insert the tip of the left-hand needle through the front loops of these two stitches. Now knit those two strands together as-if-they-were-one. (See drawings # 66 and 67.)

This decrease which slopes from the left to the right as it faces you is commonly made at the beginning of a row and is abbreviated SSK or sometimes *S1, s1, K.*

Some creative knitter liked the way a SKP slope-to-the-left decrease looked and invented *a slope-to-the-right decrease to match SKP.* This one really takes some manipulation. I suggest that you find someone to read the instructions to you while you try it for the first time. It goes like this:

Knit 1. With the left-hand needle lift this stitch off the right-hand needle and put it back onto the left-hand needle. Lift the second stitch on the left-hand needle as if to purl, then pull it up and over the manipulated stitch and off the left-hand needle. The first stitch on the left-hand needle has already been worked once, so, as if to knit, move the stitch to the right-hand needle.

I don't know how to abbreviate that procedure; I guess you could call it *"K move psso move."* I do know that once done, it is easy to do again.

In practice, most of the time, I use SSK at the beginning of a row and K 2 tog at the end of a row. But don't let my bias influence you. If you are happier with SKP and K-Move-Psso-Move as your usual decreases, use them. At least you are now aware that SKP and K 2 tog do not match each other, and won't expect them to.

A couple of more things need to be said about decreases. You can combine them into one operation and get a *multiple decrease.* Often in making lace pattern stitches your instructions will tell you:

Slip as if to knit the next stitch. Knit 2 together. With the tip of the left-hand needle pass the slipped stitch up and over the K 2 tog and off the needle.

You will have decreased two stitches in this one maneuver and the fabric will continue on straight up. The abbreviation for this one is *S1, K 2 tog, Psso.*

There are other kinds of decreases and combinations of decreases possible. However, there just isn't space in this book to include all of them.

The last thing I need to say is *watch out.* When a pattern calls for you to make a lot of decreases, don't make them all in the same manner—you could get a corkscrew effect. For instance, you may be making a Nordic sweater on circular needles and, after joining in the sleeve portions, start to form the yoke, decreasing every few stitches when you change color patterns. Make every other decrease in a different manner. Make one decrease K 2 tog and the next one SSK, so that the yoke will go straight up and not drift off to one side. The same rule will hold true on knitted skirts and wherever the effect is gradual and circular with lots of decreases. Alternating right and left slope decreases is just a good habit to get into. I use the combination even if I'm making just one row of decreases.

Don't let yourself get dizzy over decreases. They are just a way of safely sealing off a loop that you don't intend to use anymore.

15

SOME FIRM REMARKS ABOUT SLOPPY EDGES AND JOINING JUDICIOUSLY

Beginnings and endings need special ceremonies. The first day of school and graduation from it, joining an organization and leaving it as an honorary member—these are events that deserve recognition and attention. By our attention to them, we give them definition.

So also we need to give special attention to the beginning and ending of our rows of knitting and balls of yarn. Without special care the first and last stitches of back and forth knitting tend to become loose and sloppy. Without forethought, ends of yarn become a problem. It would be a shame to have beautiful and even stitches in the middle of our work and uneven and untidy ones at the ends. What a sorry sight it would be to have short ends of yarn erupting helter-skelter from our piece.

NEAT EDGES

There is a very simple method of avoiding sloppy edges. Learn it and make it a habit. It is a simple little ceremony that goes like this:

Work the first stitch of a row. Insert the right-hand needle into the second stitch. Stop! Give the yarn a firm tug to extra-tighten that first stitch. Complete the second stitch.

This is just about the *only* time I will ever direct you to *tug* on the yarn. Yarn is to be treated kindly, with love and respect. In this instance, a firm tug to avoid a loose and sloppy edge is respect; respect for the fact that the yarn *will* stretch.

Establish the habit, now, of stopping after inserting the needle into the second stitch and giving the yarn a firm pull before completing that second stitch. Soon your fingers will automatically do it for you without your having to think about it, and you will always have neat and tidy edges.

This is the best method that I know of to handle edge or selvedge stitches. Years of work at the knitting table observing my students' work has led me to it.

Some schools of knitting advocate that you always slip the first stitch of every row. If you do that, you cannot weave a neat and flat seam. (And I happen to like neat and flat seams.) Or try crocheting evenly along an edge where the first stitch has been slipped. It takes a lot of juggling to make it come out even!

Other schools of knitting, especially European ones, maintain that you should always work the first three stitches of a row in garter stitch before changing to the regular pattern stitch. I disagree. Garter stitch gives a gauge of considerable less rows per inch than does stockinette stitch and most laces. It will render a vertical edge that is shorter by far than the rest of the piece. Short pulled-up seams are not my idea of fine workmanship.

Most admittedly, there are times and places when and where it is necessary to add an extra selvedge stitch. Especially in making laces, it is often necessary to have an edge or selvedge stitch to allow for yarn-overs at the beginning of a multiple. When this is necessary, that selvedge stitch can be worked in stockinette stitch. Simply tighten it before continuing on across the row.

JOINING YARN

There is another occasion in knitting that also requires its own little ceremony—joining yarn. Balls of yarn do come to an end before we are ready to make an end of our knitting. New yarn often needs to be added to our work.

Let me digress a moment and tie several loose ends together. In all yarns, cheap or dear, crummy or fine, there are knots, splices, and flaws. The flaw may be a twig or branch that somehow remained in the wool through the manufacturing process. It may be a discolored or oily spot. It could be a blob or a length that isn't properly spun. Maybe it's a knot where strands had to be joined together. These flaws should not be worked into your precious fabric.

No manufacturer wants these knots, splices, and flaws to occur. The spinner wants to produce good yarn. Yet, no matter how careful the process is, flaws do occur.

If you should happen to receive a "bad" lot of yarn, a skein or ball or a group of them that are full of knots, splices, and flaws, *you don't have to use it!* Both the manufacturer and the local yarn supplier want to know when "bad" yarn is slipping past production inspectors and into the marketplace. Return the yarn with your receipt and the labels indicating color and dye lot number to the supplier to be shipped back to the factory.

In any event, we do not want knots, ours or others, and flaws, to be worked into and show up on our precious piece over which we have so diligently labored. When you come to a bad spot in the yarn, *cut it out,* and treat the place where the good yarn continues as if it were a new ball.

You must always leave a 6-inch tag end of yarn whenever changing yarns in order to have enough to finish in and hide with a tapestry needle.

Most assuredly, thrift is to be admired, and we don't want to wantonly waste yarn. Neither do we desire to cheat ourselves and endanger the life of a knitted article by leaving short tag ends that cannot be successfully secured and hidden.

When you find that you must add new yarn, *stop and check out the situation.* The procedure may be different according to whether you are working on a flat piece or in the round, changing colors or just adding fresh stuff.

1. *If you are working flat,* that is back and forth, do you have enough yarn to get across the row plus a six-inch tail? The rule of thumb of three will tell you. It is discussed in the chapter about casting on. If you can, it is preferable to join yarn at the beginning of a new row. If you haven't enough yarn to complete the row you are on, and do not wish to rip back to its beginning, you may choose to join in the middle of a row.

2. *If you are changing colors,* you will probably want to add the new color at the beginning of a row, unless you are working in the round.

3. *If you are working in the round,* there is no end of a row, and you must join in the middle of the piece.

4. *If the rows are very long,* you may want to join in the middle in order to economize on yarn.

5. *If you must economize on yarn,* you may want to join in the middle.

To add new yarn at the beginning of a row:

Leave 6 inches of both the old and the new yarn free. Hold the 6-inch ends firmly with the little fingers of your hand that does not carry the working yarn. Start working with the new yarn and complete about four stitches. STOP. *With the tag ends, tie the first half of a square knot—just as you would begin to tie a shoelace—right over left, around and through. Place the work on a flat surface with the public side of the work facing up. Inspect the edge stitch. Does it look the same as all of the other stitches? If it's okay, turn the work to the private side, the inside, and complete the square knot—left over right, around and through. If it does not look okay, go back and adjust the stitch until it does. Later on you will work in those two 6-inch tag ends of yarn.*

To add new yarn in the middle of a piece by overlapping:

Give yourself at least 6 inches plus 6 stitches' worth of the old yarn to work with. Leave 6 inches of the new yarn free. Overlap the old and the new yarn. Work about 6 stitches with the doubled strand, that is the old and the new yarns together as if they were one. (You do not have to twist them together or fuse them.) (See drawing # 68.) After you have worked about 6 stitches with the doubled strand, just drop the old yarn. Making sure that you have left 6 inches free, simply cease to use the old yarn and continue with the new. Later on you will work in those two 6-inch tag ends.

68

An exception to using the overlap method may occur when using extremely bulky yarns or in making very airy lace.

When you cannot join at the beginning of a new row *or* use the overlap method, you have my permission to "very neatly and carefully" tie a knot in the middle of a row, but be sure that you leave those six-inch-long tail ends.

Before we leave the subject of joining yarn, I need to stop and talk about "bad advice" and "gardens of misinformation." We have all encountered them. You know by now that I learned to knit from books. Books that were in all probability written by persons who did not know how to knit. And that's understandable. Knitting is a skill and an art. Writing is a craft and an art. That all these aptitudes and abilities should reside in one person is a rarity.

Very often, craft books are written by people who know very little about their subject. They may know how to manipulate words, but not yarn. When writers do not themselves know how to do a thing, they go to the library and look up what other writers have written about it.

And someone, somewhere in the dim distant past, said that the best way to join yarn was at the end of a row with a *slip knot*. You may have encountered the admonition, "Always join yarn only at the end of a row as follows: tie a slip knot in the yarn and push it up to the edge." Rubbish and horse feathers! There are three errors in this advice:

1. Only one strand of the yarn in a slip knot moves. It is impossible to push it up to the edge. I know; I have sailed little boats on big oceans, and I have put the slip knot on the wrong piece of line, and I have lost the halyard to the winds.

2. Most knitters have been neither boy scouts nor seamen and don't know how to tie a slip knot at all.

3. You don't *always* have an end of a row handy.

Whoever it was that first wrote it was wrong. Yet ever since then, other writers have been quoting the first writer as an "authority."

Another bit of poor advice concerns joining yarn in the middle of a row. Some gardens of misinformation will tell you to cut half the strands on the ends of both the old and the new yarn, then overlap and twist together these cut strands to resemble the original yarn, or, with a tapestry needle, to thread the new yarn through the last two inches of the old yarn to make a perfect joining.

Lots of luck! I wonder if the writers ever tried to do it. It doesn't work. I have knitted myself since I was fourteen years old. I have seen piles and piles of other people's knitting, and I have *never* seen either of these two methods succeed. Oh, I have had people tell me that I just wasn't trying hard enough and that they knew someone who knew someone who could do it. But when I asked the know-it-all to bring that someone in to show me how to do it, the perfect-joiner disappeared. I have even offered to pay and pay handsomely for someone to do it successfully before my very eyes. No one has ever taken me up on my offer.

The point of this little lecture is that the written word is not always *the best* or *the last*. (Not even mine!) Trust yourself. Trust your own good common sense. Try the "book" way, but if it simply doesn't work, try something else. If "necessity is the mother of invention," then "variety is the handmaiden of success." Do what succeeds!

Give ceremony and success to your work. Firm up your edges and join your ends judiciously. You deserve the best.

16

BUTTONHOLES ARE BASTARDS

I had been putting off writing this chapter, stammering and stalling and hanging back like a salesman caught with an inferior product. I didn't want to write this chapter because I didn't know the ultimate answer about making fine and beautiful buttonholes in handknits. Though I had tried all of the various kinds suggested in other books about knitting, I was not really happy with any of them, and I had no honest solution of my own.

In my quandary I called Evie Rosen, one of the finest knitting teachers in the country, and asked her, "Evie, what is your answer to buttonholes in handknits?"

"The sewing machine," she said. "I don't know of a worked-in buttonhole that I really like. And I'm not a purist. I don't mind treating handknits like any other fabric, and I see nothing wrong with knitting the thing without them and then making buttonholes on the sewing machine after it is finished. Of course," she said, "I take a tapestry needle and yarn, and work over the machine stitching with a buttonhole stitch so it won't be obnoxious."

We both burst out laughing over the phone, each knowing that the other had tried everything possible to make worked-in buttonholes work and had given up in frustration.

After I hung up, I recalled that my Aunt Ruth had come to somewhat the same conclusion. When I had asked her years ago how she made knitted buttonholes, she said, "I don't! They always look terrible. I prefer to make pullovers. If I have to make a cardigan, I crochet the front bands and make the buttonholes in them, or I put a zipper down the front."

The solution of one other knitter came to mind. She was a patron of mine in California where I worked as the "Knitting Lady." A fine seamstress as well as a fine knitter, she, too, avoided making worked-in buttonholes. After completing the cardigan plain, without any buttonholes, she attached the buttons to the opposite side of the garment and then sewed large fabric-covered snaps directly under the buttons to both sides of the sweater. Unless you happened to catch her in the act of fastening the sweater, you would never have realized that they weren't any buttonholes at all.

If in the past you have been baffled by buttonholes and have felt that they were bastards, rest assured that you are not alone in your thinking. In this chapter, I'll tell you how to make several different kinds of knitted-in buttonholes. I don't really like any of them, but be my guest—try them out and see what you think. If you prefer to use any of the above solutions and never work in a buttonhole for the rest of your life, you'll never get any criticism from me.

THE EYELET BUTTONHOLE

The simplest hole for a button is just that, a hole—an *eyelet buttonhole*. It is also the easiest. *(See drawing # 69.)*

An eyelet is produced by a yarn-over followed by a knit-two-together through the front loops. (On the following row the yarn-over is worked as a stitch.

69

This makes a small and innocuous opening. If you are planning to use tiny wee buttons, give it a try.

Unfortunately, the only place that I have ever used very tiny buttons is on a baby's or very small child's garment. Bigger buttonholes for ordinary buttons aren't so easy or so invisible.

THE THREE-ROW BUTTONHOLE

There is a *three-row buttonhole* that Virginia Newell recently showed to me at a knitting seminar that is as good as I have ever seen. In any pattern stitch it goes:

Row 1: On an outside row, work to the desired location of the buttonhole. Yarn over twice, then through the back loops knit the next two stitches together. Continue across row.

Row 2: Work across to the YOs of the previous row. P one YO and drop the other one off the needle. Continue across row. (It looks terrible, but hang in there and have faith.)

Row 3: Work across row to buttonhole. K one stitch THROUGH THE HOLE and allow the old stitch to fall off the needle. Continue across the row.

It's neat and tidy! It requires no final finishing work! And it's large enough for an ordinary sized button. Give it a try.

THE VERTICAL BUTTONHOLE

The next best looking knitted-in buttonholes that Evie and I know of are *vertical buttonholes. (See drawing # 70.)*

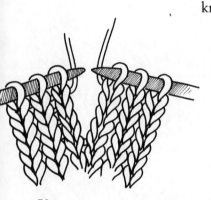

At the place where you want the hole to begin, add a new ball of yarn. Drop the other yarn and continue across the row with the new stuff. On the next row, when you come to the place where the yarn was added, drop it and go back to working with the old yarn. In effect you are making two separate pieces with two balls of yarn. A split will occur where you change the yarns and that is the buttonhole. When the split is as long as you want it to be, go back to working the whole row with one ball of yarn. After the garment is finished and you are tidying up your sweater with a tapestry needle and yarn, work a row of buttonhole stitch around the opening.

70

THE HORIZONTAL BUTTONHOLE

There are endless formulas for *horizontal buttonholes.* Standard instructions call for binding off the required number of stitches on one row and then casting on the same number of stitches in the same spot on the next row. Unfortunately, it is ugly and leaves a weak and stretched spot at its beginning. Inventive knitters have tried in many ways to remedy the situation.

Whichever formula you choose to try, horizontal buttonholes should *not* be worked in the very middle of the front band. Those of you who are fine dressmakers will know what I am talking about. As a garment is worn, the button will rest against the leading edge of the buttonhole. It will not ride in the middle of the hole. If the buttonhole has been exactly centered in a front band and the button sewed in the center of the corresponding band on the opposite side, the garment may pull apart and show part of the front band of the under side. It is just a minor detail. But if you are a perfectionist, it is something that has to be taken into account.

The answer is easy. Rather than centering the buttonhole in the front band, begin to make it nearer the center stitch of the front band and work it toward the underarm. When you sew the button in place, fasten it corresponding to the leading edge of the hole.

THE NEATEST BUTTONHOLE

The instructions for the best knitted-in buttonhole that I know about were given to me by a thoughtful student years ago. I still have her handwritten directions, encased in a plastic sheet, which I drag out every time I have to make a buttonhole. Where she got these instructions, I have no idea.

Before you try it on a swatch, I suggest that you do three things. First, reread the section in the chapter on casting on and review the instructions for purling on with two needles beginning with a loop on the left-hand needle. Next find some kindly and patient soul to read the instructions to you while you follow them. Last thing, just before you start, unplug the phone. You don't need any interruptions when learning to make *neatest buttonholes*. *(See drawing # 71.)*

71

Work the required number of stitches before starting the buttonhole.

As if to knit, slip one stitch. Between the tips of the needles, bring the yarn to the front of the work and drop it. As if to knit, slip the next stitch from the left-hand needle to the right-hand needle and pass the first slipped stitch over the second slipped stitch and off the needle. Not using the dropped yarn, bind off the required number of stitches in this manner.

Slip the last stitch on the right-hand needle back to the left needle. Turn the work around. Bring yarn to the front. At the edge where the buttonhole was started, using the twisted method of casting on purlwise, cast on one more stitch than the number that you bound off.

Turn the work around. Slip the first stitch from the left-hand needle to the right needle. Slip the extra cast-on stitch over the next stitch and then slip this stitch back onto the left-hand needle. Work to the end of the row.

It is the best-looking buttonhole that I know about, but it is not perfect and it is not easy to remember. I think that Evie Rosen's sewing machine solution is easier than getting out these directions every time.

WORKING WITH STANDARD
BUTTONHOLE INSTRUCTIONS

If you choose to use "standard buttonhole instructions" of binding off the required number of stitches on one row and then casting them back on on the next row, there are a few things that you can try to make them look a little better.

To get ride of the horizontal bar that will appear across the next stitch where the last stitch was bound off, try this maneuver. Bind off one less stitch than required. Place the loop that remains on the right-hand needle onto the left-hand needle. Through the back loops, knit it together with the next stitch.

To make the leading edge of the buttonhole look a little neater, cut an extra twenty-four-inch-long strand and use it to form the cast-on with a two-strand method. When you are finished, use the tag ends of the extra strand to make a duplicate stitch over any stretched or elongated stitches.

Or you could cast on one more stitch than specified. On the return row just before you get to the buttonhole, knit that last original stitch together with the extra cast-on stitch to decrease back to the correct number of stitches.

Some knitters try a different tactic. They increase one stitch in the left-side-loop of the last stitch on the right-hand needle before they cast on for the top of the buttonhole.

Still others will swear by the *pull-out method*. They knit the required number of stitches for the buttonhole with a bit of cotton crochet thread. Next they slip those cotton stitches back onto the left-hand needle and work over them with the regular yarn as if nothing had happened. When the garment is finished they use a yarn needle and a doubled strand of the working yarn to run through the loops all around the cotton thread and secure the stitches in that way. After the loops are safely caught, they pull out the cotton thread.

A variation of the pull-out method is the *contrasting yarn method.* In it the required stitches are worked in a different yarn. The working yarn is just carried across at the back of the piece while they are worked. When the article is completed the contrasting yarn is pulled out, and the exposed loops are fastened over each other with a crochet hook in a slip stitch all around the opening. The final loop has to be caught with another fresh strand of yarn.

Then there is the *lost buttonhole method.* Just knit the thing without any. When the piece is finished, mark the locations of where you want buttonholes to be. Reach in with a pair of scissors and clip one strand of yarn. Undo enough stitches to make the hole and finish off the hole with slip-stitch crochet.

How do you make a buttonhole in handknits? Just like you get a hippopotamus out of water—any way you can!

Southerners have a marvelous and fitting expression that can be used to describe worked-in buttonholes in handknits. When describing a messy situation, they say, "It was as uncomfortable as a bastard at a family reunion." And buttonholes are bastards.

17

HEMS AREN'T
HOPELESS

I learned to be a fine seamstress long before I learned to be a fine knitter. And I learned in my dressmaking that hems should be invisible and undetectable to the casual observer; that their purpose was to give enough weight or flair to the garment so that it would hang to its best advantage. In my ignorance I supposed that the same would hold true for knitted garments.

My first experience with knitted hems was on a gray wool car-coat type of sweater. In those days I was still following instructions like a puppy follows a little boy—eager, expectant, and undemanding. The instructions called for the jacket to be made in pieces starting at the bottom of the back, with the hem, of course. It wasn't until the garment was completed that I realized how bad the hem looked, and I didn't know what to do about it. It bulged and stretched out the bottom of the otherwise attractive article. I was not pleased with the way it looked.

In those early days I also thought that blocking was a cure-all, so I blocked it. The hem only looked worse; it bulged even more. I didn't know what to do. I had never heard of ripping out from the cast-on end of a piece, and I wasn't about to rip out the whole thing, so I wore it as it was. (See chapter 27, on altering.) Every time I wore it I was uncomfortable because I thought it looked downright tacky.

The sweater was only a few months old when a very dear friend admired it and asked to try it on. She loved it, and being smaller in the hips than I was, the bulge was not so objectionable on her. I gave it to her on the spot and stayed away from hems in knits for years.

Several years later, when I was working part time at the local knit shop, Ruth, the owner, taught me the secret of making fine hems in knitted garments.

The underside of a hem should be worked in knit 1, purl 1 ribbing on a smaller needle with a lighter-weight yarn, if possible. A purl ridge row on the public side should separate the hem from the garment.

It is as simple as that!

Hems do have their place in handknits and hand-machine-made knits. We do not always want ribbing or a border stitch on the bottom of jackets, coats, capes, and such. Sometimes we want a garment to flare out and away from the body, and sometimes the only way to achieve this is to make a hem. There is no reason why it cannot be an almost invisible hem as in fine dressmaking. There is no reason for ugly, bulky, bulging globs.

Often heavier garments such as jackets, coats, and capes are worked with multiple strands of yarn. If your next hemmed project is, simply eliminate one strand of yarn for the underside of the hem. If the garment is made with only one heavy strand of yarn, check around at your neighborhood yarn dealer and see if you cannot purchase a small amount of the same color in a lighter weight of yarn.

It makes no difference whether you are working from the top or from the bottom of the garment, the same rule holds true. Use a *smaller* needle for the knit 1, purl 1 ribbing. Drop for instance, from a size 8 to a 4, or from a size 10½ to an 8. And use that same smaller needle for the purl ridge row that will form a neat and even turning-under line. If you are binding off at the end of the hem, be sure to bind off in pattern—that is in knit 1, purl 1 ribbing.

As far as securing that carefully made hem in place, I like to use a sewing whipstitch on it. I catch together *only* the single outer loop of the cast-on or bind-off row and *only* a single purl-bead of every other stitch of the garment fabric. I work that whipstitch firmly but not tightly.

I've read in knitting books and in knitting-machine manuals that hems can be easily and beautifully made by casting on with waste yarn and then secured in place by knitting together the first row of the real yarn with the appropriate row of the fabric. I don't think that's either easy or beautiful! I always get an unsightly tight row at the joining. I have tried it over and over, and I have ripped back and ripped back. I have come to the conclusion that the knitting together of the first row of the underside of the hem and the appropriate row of the garment fabric pulls the stitches of the fabric no matter how carefully I try to do it. As I said, I prefer to whipstitch the hem in place with yarn and a tapestry needle.

Please notice that in all of this discussion I have not mentioned hems in skirts. I am not fond of them! Knitted pleated skirts should never be hemmed. Hems interfere with their lovely flare and undulating ripple. It is usually sufficient to use a knit one, purl one bind-off on them.

Neither am I fond of plain stockinette-stitch, straight-knitted skirts, hemmed or not, for anyone weighing over ninety-eight pounds. I don't mind a properly made hem in a softly flared stockinette-stitch skirt, but I prefer three rows of single crochet. Notice I said *rows,* not rounds. Rounds of crochet have a tendency to roll inward and can give a balloon effect. If you choose to not make a hem in a flared skirt, be sure to crochet the first row from the outside, the public side, of the garment, join with a slip stitch, turn, and work the second row from the inside, the private side. Again join with a slip stitch, turn and make the final third row from the outside.

I no longer avoid hems in knitted garments. I just follow Ruth's rules and make them properly.

18
PICKING UP NEW STITCHES AND OLD ONES

Picking up and starting over again. How often we have to do it in life. Sometimes it's counting our losses, putting them behind us and going on. Sometimes it's starting off in a new direction, building on the foundation of what has gone before. In either event, the way in which we start off afresh can determine the success or failure of the project. Maybe that's why I like knitting so much—it's so much like life itself.

RESCUING STITCHES

Let's talk first about picking up and *rescuing stitches.* The subjects of picking up dropped stitches and ripping back will be discussed in chapter 24, but here I want to talk a little about the way in which you replace stitches that you are currently working that have accidentally fallen off your needles.

If in football the best offense is a good defense, in knitting the easiest solution is the best possible protection. Rubber needle-tip protectors are so cheap and so easy to put in place and such a defense against the needle slipping out that it is silly not to use them. But even with protection, needles can and do slip out of your work. I find the problem worse with straight needles than with circular ones, but nonetheless it happens with all needles, and usually at the most inconvenient time. When I pick up my knitting to relieve the boredom of a dull committee meeting, or when there is a good program on TV and my hands want some easy repetitive activity while I watch the show, that's usually the time I find my needles have slipped out of my work.

When this happens, you must replace them before you can go on. You already know from chapter 11 that stitches do not lie across the needles at right angles. Rather, in both the American right-hand method and the Continental left-hand Pic method, the front forward loop of the stitch slopes to the right. You also know from chapter 12 that so long as you slip any stitch as if to purl, the front forward slope to the right will be maintained. Knowing these two things will enable you to understand that, if possible, you merely slide the needle into the stitches as if to purl. (If you try to rescue those stitches as if to knit, you will have a row of twisted stitches that will stand out like Christmas decorations on the Fourth of July.)

But it is not always possible to fit those stitches back onto the working needle easily. Sometimes it seems as if the working needle is too large, and putting one stitch on it makes the next stitch drop down. The answer is easy. Put a rubber tip protector on one end of that small-size circular needle that you now carry in your goodie pouch and slide the stitches onto it. Since it is double-pointed, you can't possibly end up on the wrong end of the needle. When the stitches are safely "saved," you can then slide them onto the working needle as if to purl, and you are in business once more.

If your needle has slipped out of a pattern stitch where you are using ring markers to keep you on pattern—and I hope that you are using ring markers—one little extra step is desired. Before you begin to "save" the stitches, take a handful of little tiny safety pins and place them in appropriate spots at the multiple repeats. As you come to the pins you can easily replace them with ring markers.

PICKING UP NEW STITCHES

Building new stitches on an old foundation is also called *picking up stitches*. It's a bad term, because the stitches are not "picked up" at all, but rather new ones are manufactured on an old platform of finished fabric. Neckline stitches for ribbing are a good example. When the back and front of a sweater are completed and put together, or in the case of knit-from-the-top-down sweaters any time after the neckline shaping is completed, a separate bit of knitting will be done. Usually it is ribbing worked directly from the existing fabric.

Loops have to be made on that existing fabric in order to work the ribbing. It is the making of this first row of new loops that is called "picking up stitches." Many instructions will tell you to "pick up and knit 134 stitches around neck opening," and then leave you on your own to figure out how and where. Some instructions will helpfully tell you to "slip 44 stitches from holder at back neck, pick up 12 along right front neck edge, 28 from holder and same number from left neck edge." You still have to do some figuring on your own.

Stitches are always picked up from the outside, the public side, of the work.

No matter how careful you are or how close you work to the edge of the fabric, there will always be an unsightly and uneven area on the underside, the private side, of the work where stitches are picked up. The exception to the outside rule is the rolled crew neck that some European designers are fond of, which is fastened to the outside of the garment with a sewing back stitch. I don't like it because I've had to help many knitters redo it when there wasn't enough elasticity for the head to go through.

The exact location at which you pick up these new loops is critical, and yet of no importance at all! What you are after is a fine-looking finished garment. I've seen lots of knitting books and read their hard and fast rules about *exactly* where along the edge you should pick up. Concerning cast-on and bound-off edges, some say, ". . . ¼ inch in from the edge." Some say, ". . . behind the two loops of the cast-on or bind-off row." Others say, ". . . from under only the front forward single loop of the cast-on or bind-off row." Concerning vertical edges, some say, ". . . go into the knot of a vertical row." Others say to ". . . avoid the knot of the vertical rows." Almost no one gives you credit for having good common sense.

Exactly where the picked-up stitches come from is not nearly so important as how they look!

If you are not pleased after an inspection of your first attempt, try again in a different spot.

As the place where they come from is not terribly important, neither is the exact amount of stitches picked up. True, if you are going to make a patterned rib, the multiple will be important. Likewise it usually looks better to have the same number of stitches on each side of a garment. But if your instructions tell you to pick up 156 stitches for a knit 1, purl 1 ribbing and you can only get 144 comfortably, don't sweat it. Go with the 144 rather than end up with a bungled looking article.

The rule of thumb that designers use for figuring out how many stitches should be picked up is threefold:

1. Pick up stitch for stitch along horizontal edges.

2. Pick up the number of stitches per inch called for in the fabric gauge on vertical edges, and

3. Pick up three stitches for every four rows on diagonal edges.

If your picked-up stitches seem crowded, the designer could have made a mistake, or it could be a typographical error.

Wherever *you* decide to pick up the stitches on a particular garment, and however many stitches *you* decide to pick up, I have some handy-dandy devices and techniques to help you do a good and easy job of it.

Before you begin to pick up stitches the next time, get yourself prepared by having ready a circular needle smaller than the size on which you plan to do the edging. (It is ever so much easier to work your way into tight places with a smaller needle.) Have rubber point protectors handy for this small needle, and for the working needle, so that the carefully picked-up stitches won't slide off the other end. Get out some small safety pins and some ring markers. You also may want a pencil and paper or some "idiot tags." (See chapter 8—I prefer the idiot tags.) In knitting, as in life, being prepared makes any undertaking easier.

Begin by dividing up the areas into manageable-sized chunks. For instance, divide the edge of a V neck opening in half, mark it with a safety pin, and then divide it in half again, marking these divisions with safety pins. It is easier to pick up fifteen stitches evenly over a three-inch area than it is to pick up sixty stitches over a twelve-inch space. You may not be doing a V neck, but the same idea holds true that smaller is easier.

To pick up and knit stitches:

Holding the garment in your left hand with the outside (the public side of the fabric) facing you, pick up the smaller needle in your right hand. Beginning at the place where your instructions have told you, or at a safety pin, insert the needle into the fabric near the edge of the piece. Making sure that you leave a 6-inch tail end of yarn free, with the yarn at the back of the work, form a knit stitch around the needle and bring it up and to the front. (See drawing # 72.)

72

One stitch has been picked up. Continue in this way until you have the number of stitches you want before you get to the first safety pin. PLACE A RING MARKER ON THE NEEDLE. *You'll never have to count those stitches again!*

Remove that safety pin and continue to pick up stitches till the next one. Count the new stitches to be sure you have what you want and place another marker on the needle.

See, it's not hard at all! It does take a little concentration, and that is why I use the "idiot tags." I write on them the total number of stitches to be picked up. Half and then half again. And I write down how many stitches I actually picked up and where. Outside problems have a penchant for arising when I'm picking up stitches, and I take no chances with my memory. Neither do I like counting stitches over and over again. I am not an idiot, but I like idiot tags.

Continue to pick up and knit until the area is covered. As you work the next row, you can get rid of the ring markers; they will have served their purpose. That next row is of some concern. You will, of course, change to whatever size needle you have been directed to work the ribbing on. And I like to add a designer detail regardless of whether the pattern calls for it or not. I form a purl ridge on the outside of the sweater. If working flat, back and forth, I knit a row. If working in the round, I purl a round. I think that gives it a finer, more jewel-like appearance to the garment. But it is a matter of taste and your own preference.

Another matter of taste and appearance concerns changes of color. Even if the edging will be of a different color, I like to use the main garment color to pick up and knit that first row, changing to the contrasting color with the row on which I change to the other needle. That way any rough spots where I either pulled the fabric together or eased it out will be invisible to the eye.

I only wish that picking myself up from sticky situations in life were as easy as picking up stitches!

19

SHAPE IT UP WITH
SHORT ROWS

I have talked before in this book about how, very basically, the human body can be described as a bunch of cylinders or tubes and how we wrap up these shapes with fabric to form clothing. I have talked before about how knitted fabric is forgiving and easy to work with. And I have told you the truth, but not the whole lumpy truth.

Some of these cylinders that are arms and legs and torsos have very big bumps on them that must be allowed for. The place where a leg becomes a foot is a protuberance called a *heel*. At that point our tube of clothing, called a *sock*, will need a little help to fit the human form. The female of the species has other lumps as well, and they are called *breasts*. Sometimes straight tubes of knitting don't fit over them very well without assistance.

Our early foremothers in the art of knitting devised very clever ways of accounting for these projections unobtrusively, neatly, and without seams. They formed their fabric into special shapes with *short rows*, or *partial knitting* or leaving *stitches in waiting*. All three terms mean the same thing. They mean turning around in the middle of a row and going back from whence we came in a very special way that will not leave a hole in the work.

I don't know of very many knitters who have not at one time or another made accidental short rows in their knitting when they have had to set their work down in the middle of a row and then started working in the wrong direction when they picked it back up. The result was a hole, and one side of their work was longer than the other side. That kind of a short row is a mistake.

But short rows carefully made on purpose can do wonderful things. They can form the heel of a sock. They can make bust darts. They can supply the necessary fullness to cover a diaper-padded baby's bottom. They can form elegant shawl collars. Short rows can create extra length for the crown of the head or a "dowager's hump." Some instructions for yoked sweaters that are knitted from the bottom up require you to make short rows just before you begin the yoke.

Some instructions will call the technique *short-rowing* because the rows are not worked all the way to the end. Other directions will call it *partial knitting* because only part of the row is knitted. It is also called *keeping stitches in waiting* because some stitches are waiting for subsequent rows to be worked.

Just as one may never in all their life be called upon to swim across a rushing river, you may never in all your knitting adventures be called upon to work short rows. Still, I would be a poor instructor if I did not tell you about them. If you don't want to bother with them here and now, that's okay. Just know that they do exist, that they can be done, and that they really aren't very hard.

Regardless of what it is called, and the exact procedure by which it is done, short-rowing is simply turning around in the middle of the row, wrapping the base of that turning stitch with a strand of the working yarn, and then going on back across the row in the regular way. When all of the short rows are completed, that strand is worked together with its stitch to "heal the hole."

You could manufacture a short row by holding the turning stitch in your left hand and just winding a strand of yarn around it with your right hand. I often have my students do just that on the first short row so that they will understand exactly what the compli-cated-sounding instructions are all about.

Before you tackle the instructions that follow for short rows, make sure that you are feeling good, are alert and confident. It is a help to have a "reader" who will call out the written words while you follow the directions, which are for short-rowing four stitches three times from both the right and the left side of a piece the dimensions of which are given below. You are going to work each row four stitches shorter each time for six turnarounds. A "dart" will be made at each side of the piece. The center of the swatch will be six rows longer than the outside edges of the swatch. Abbreviated instructions might say, "Short-row 4 sts 6 times."

Remember: *As if to purl* means to insert the right-hand needle from the back to the front of the work.

These instructions are "all purpose," that is to say that you can begin on either the knit or the purl side. Once you master the technique, you can even use them on pattern stitches and change the numbers and the times to suit your own purposes.

Start with a swatch of stockinette stitch about 30 stitches wide and 2 inches long, and 6 ring markers.

1. *Work to within 4 stitches of the end of the row or the last marker near the end of the row.*

2. *As if to purl, slip the next stitch to the right-hand needle.*

3. *Take the yarn between the tips of the needles to the opposite side of the work.*

73

4. *Transfer, as if to knit, that same slipped stitch back to the left-hand needle by putting the left-hand needle in the back loop of the stitch, and then take it off the right-hand needle. (See drawing # 73.)*

5. *Again take the yarn between the tips of the needles to the opposite side of the work.*

6. *Place a ring marker on the right-hand needle.*

7. *Turn the piece around, and going in the direction from which you came, work the next 2 stitches, leaving the 4 stitches on the other side of the marker unworked.*

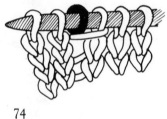

74

8. *Stop. Check your work. There should be a strand of yarn wrapped around the base of the unworked stitch next to the marker. (See drawing # 74.)*

You have made one short row.

9. *Continue on across the row following the instructions in step 1.*

Repeat these 9 steps all over again five times more. Four stitches short-rowed six times looks like this: *(See drawing # 75.)*

When the four stitches have been short rowed six times,

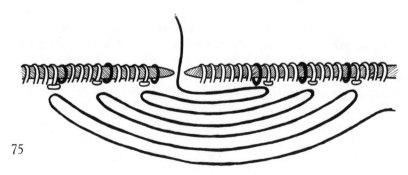

75

To avoid holes in the work, it is imperative that on the next row you pick up the strand that you so carefully wrapped around the base of the stitch at the turning point and work it, together as one, with the turning stitch. You will pick up that strand differently depending on whether you are on the knit or the purl side of the swatch.

We don't care what the back side, or purl side, of the piece looks like. We do care how the front side, or knit side, looks. That wrap must be picked up so that it will not be seen by the public. (Double-check to determine which side of the fabric will be the outside, the public side.)

Work whichever you are supposed to be doing, knitting or purling, to the first turning point.

76   77

If it is the purl side, tilt the work toward you. With the tip of the right-hand needle, pick up the strand and place it on the left-hand needle. (See drawing # 76.)

Work the strand together with its stitch. If it is the knit side, from below with the tip of the right hand needle scoop it up . . . (See drawing # 77.)

. . . and work it together with its stitch.

Discarding the markers as you go, work one row more so that you can see the full effect of what you have just accomplished. You have learned to do something that many knitters have never heard of.

I force all of my advanced students to learn to make short rows. What they choose to do after the class is over is their business. Many students truly enjoy the technique. They would rather make short rows on the shoulders of a sweater than form stair-step bind-offs. (These knitters will then use the double bind-off technique described in chapter 13 to make the shoulder seams.) Some students will put short-row bust darts in every woman's sweater they make. Others, after they have done the compulsory bit in class, never ever want to do it again.

At least now you know the whole lumpy, bumpy truth about cylinders and tubes and turning heels and shaping them up with short rows.

20

DUPLICATING AND GRAFTING ARE NOT CHEATING

When used in knitting, the terms *duplicating* and *grafting* are perfectly respectable words. They refer to some things you can do to and with your lovely handmade fabric after the last stitch is knitted. Duplicating and grafting are not cheating!

THE DUPLICATE STITCH

The *duplicate stitch* is simply the tracing over of a completed knitted stitch using a tapestry needle and yarn, following it up, under, around, and down again. It is a handy thing to know and very easy to do.

On the last project I completed, a colorful "sampler" afghan, I used a duplicate stitch on plain stockinette stitch to make a signature square. I put in my initials and the year so that my great-great-grandchildren, who may never know me, will know that I made the lovely blanket.

On the project before that, I used duplicate stitch to reinforce a couple of stretched stitches at the underarms of a gray battle-jacket-style sweater that was knit in one piece from the top down for my favorite electrician who installed the wiring for the computer on which this manuscript was written. I also used a duplicate stitch to cover over a bad piece of yarn that a student had knitted into the center front of a striped pullover. See how versatile and useful the duplicate stitch can be!

Please find or make yourself a swatch of stockinette stitch knitting and grab a bit of contrasting color yarn of the same weight. Thread that yarn into a tapestry or blunt-tipped metal yarn needle. (I can write words all day long, and you can read them, but actually doing it as you read is the best way of learning.) Check to be sure that the cast-on row is at the bottom of your piece and the bind-off row is at the top.

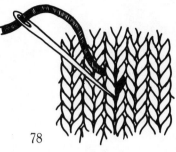

From the back of the work, insert your needle into the base of a stitch in the middle of the swatch. Be sure to leave a 6-inch-long tail end hanging free. Bring up the needle at the front of the work and let the yarn lay up and toward your right side.

Slide your tapestry needle under the 2 loops at the top of that same stitch. Making sure that the tail end stays put, pull the yarn through and adjust the tension.

Now take the needle down to the back of the work and insert it in the base of the stitch again. (See drawing # 78.)

78

A duplicate stitch is merely the tracing over of the path of an existing stitch, adjusting the tension carefully to match the original stitch. Make half a dozen duplicate stitches horizontally across your swatch and then make half a dozen in a vertical line.

You can make your next duplicate stitch either into the row above or to the right or to the left. I have read instructions that insist you must move in a certain direction, but I don't think that it makes any difference so long as you carefully adjust the tension of the contrasting color yarn.

Mending and strengthening your knitted fabric with duplicate stitch in the same color yarn can be a real joy. Stretched, weak, or discolored stitches will fairly disappear before your eyes.

With a duplicate stitch, patterns of contrasting color can be embroidered over a base of stockinette stitch. You can add not only initials and years as I did, but rosebuds and leaves, animals and houses. Do keep in mind that the duplicated stitches are now of double thickness. Duplicated stitches will never be as elastic and pliable as the surrounding fabric, so please be careful about trying to use huge areas of it. You may end up with a garbled and blobby effect.

GRAFTING

Grafting is manufacturing a row of knitting with a needle and yarn in order to join together two pieces of knitted fabric. Very simply put, it is making a row of duplicate stitch out of thin air between pieces that need to be joined seamlessly and invisibly together. It is sometimes called *making a kitchner stitch*.

The toes of socks are grafted together. Sometimes the center back of a collar will need to be joined with a Kitchner stitch. Often neckbands are joined to each other in this manner. I have seen instructions that called for a bottom-up skirt and a bottom-up top to be grafted together to form a dress. It might be called for on every other project you make, or you might go for years and never hear of it.

I have read all sorts of difficult-to-follow instructions about how to graft. At one time they frightened me terribly. Then I learned the duplicate stitch and began to understand the journey that a single strand of yarn takes across a row of knitting. After that it was easy.

I've had the best luck in teaching grafting by having my students make a four-inch-wide swatch of two inches of stockinette, two inches of garter stitch, and two inches of ribbing. I have them make a horizontal row of duplicate stitch with crochet cotton across the middle of each of the three sections, from right to left. Then we clip out the original yarn on the stockinette stitch section and leave the crochet cotton in place. Next we thread yarn on our tapestry needle and follow the path of the crochet cotton.

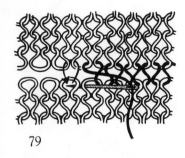

*Up in the base of a stitch, across the gap, down in the first loop and up in the next one, * across the gap. Down in the spot we came out of before, up in the base of the next stitch, across the gap and down in the stitch we were in before, up in the next one. * Repeat between the asterisks. (See drawing # 79.)*

79

Even beginners can zoom across stockinette stitch grafting. After they have learned by following the path of the cotton crochet thread across a swatch, they can hold two needles parallel horizontally with stitches on them and graft across thin air.

Garter stitch grafting can be a little more difficult; it is important that the knitting be stopped on the same row on both pieces. Learning to do it by first making an accurate duplicate stitch with cotton crochet thread is the easiest way I know of explaining it. *(See drawing # 80.)*

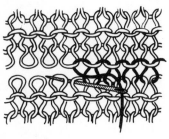

80

Grafting ribbing can drive even an experienced knitting instructor up the wall. Sometimes I have gotten so frustrated with it that I have used the double bind-off method instead (see chapter 13). If you need or want to learn to do it, try making duplicate stitch across a swatch first, making sure that you have plenty of patience, peace, and quiet on hand.

The graft that politicians are accused of taking, the duplicating that video pirates do daily are not at all in the same league with the Kitchner and duplicate stitches. Ours is an honest effort and adds to the fine handmadeness of your project.

21

MAKE SURE YOUR WORK MEASURES UP

I was blessed with a wonderful father-in-law. I really looked forward to Pop's visits. Besides being a wonderful person, he was a superb cabinetmaker. He lived up the coast about 250 miles, so when he came to visit he'd stay a week or two. After he had been in the house for a few days and had gotten reacquainted with the grand-children, he would shyly say, "Maggie, don't you think those kids need a special shelf for their record player?" or "Maggie, would you like to have a cupboard to keep the card table and chairs in?" Of course I'd say yes.

Pop was a quiet and careful craftsman. Sometimes his meticu-lousness got on my nerves. One time I said, "Pop, you've already measured that board twice."

"Yes," he said, "yes, I did. But I want to be sure it fits right. Once you cut a board, you can't uncut it. Maggie, there are two kinds of carpenters in this world. The kind of carpenter that measures three times and cuts once and the kind that measures once and cuts three times. And I don't like sawdust."

Thank goodness that knitting is much more forgiving than wooden boards! I'm glad that we can alter and adjust our precious handmade fabric. Still, the concept of measuring three times and cutting once makes sense.

Stop frequently to admire and measure your work. If you can't admire it and if it doesn't measure up, stop what you're doing. There are many parts to the joy of knitting: the pleasure of making knitted stitches and the pleasure of a fine finished article, the pleasure of pride in accomplishment and the pleasure of acknowledging compliments of others. Measuring frequently and accurately assures you of all of these pleasures.

A good measuring tape is a necessity. Guessing and eyeballing just won't do the job.

How you use the tape is important. How you measure the body that will wear the garment and how you measure the garment in progress are of equal importance.

Garments made of handknit fabrics do not fit the body in the same way that woven cloth garments do. Knits are much more pliable, expansive, and forgiving than regular cloth. They do not "drape" and "hang" in the way that cloth does. The same rules of thumb that apply to dressmaking measurements do not always apply to designing and fitting knits. (In planning woven-cloth fabric garments, extra inches of "ease" in excess of the actual body measurement must be added to allow the body to move.) The length "ease" allowance for knitted long sweater sleeves can be less than for cloth sleeves because the hand-knitted fabric will give more at the elbow than woven cloth will. The chest allowance for a cotton sweater-blouse knitted at a large gauge of four stitches per inch can be two inches *less* than the actual body measurement and still not look tight or stretched. That is what I mean by "forgiving." On the flip side of the coin, a simple straight knit skirt needs to be twenty to thirty inches wider at the bottom than at the hip to flatter and fall gracefully.

If your knitting instructor designs for you, trust her judgment as to sizing and amount of ease. She knows the yarns she sells. She has worked with knits and knows how they behave on human bodies.

If you are following commercially designed patterns, be sure to check out the actual intended width. If it is not given in the instructions or on the drawing of the piece, you can find out what it will be by dividing the number of stitches per inch, as given in the gauge, into the total number of stitches at the widest point. A back that has eighty-eight stitches at the underarm on a gauge of four stitches to the inch will be twenty-two inches wide (88 divided by 4 = 22). The whole sweater will finish out to be forty-four inches wide.

"STANDARD" VS "NON-STANDARD" MEASUREMENTS

In the United States most contemporary designers work from a single standard body measurement chart called the National Knit and Crochet Standards Simplified Guidelines. The amount of "ease" and extra width that they choose to add is a matter of style, shaping, and fashion according to the particular yarn that they are designing for.

A copy of this chart of "standard" body measurements can be found in the appendix section of Maggie Righetti's *Universal Yarn Finder* for sale at your local yarn supplier.

Check the measurements of the intended wearer against this standard size chart. Always try to follow the instructions for the size nearest the person's actual *chest* measurement. In knitting it's easier to alter instructions for lengths than it is to change them for widths.

Be sure the person is wearing the undergarments that they will wear under the finished article. Use a good nonstretchy tape measure and pull it firmly, but not so tightly as to strangle around the body. If the tape measure starts to fall down, you have held it much too loosely.

Not all human bodies are "standard," however, and changes may be necessary.

For instance, I have very heavy upper arms. My arms are also long in proportion to the rest of my body. Before I learned to chart patterns for myself, I found that things worked out much better if I made a medium-size body and a large-size sleeve for myself. My teenage sons had smaller hips than were allowed for in standard men's sizes. On the backs and fronts of their sweaters I'd cast on the number of stitches for a smaller size and then gradually increase stitches at the edges until I reached the number of stitches necessary for their chest size. After that I'd follow the printed directions from there on.

Some people are happiest following directions exactly as they are written. If you are that kind of person, then by all means follow the instructions exactly. If you like to follow directions more or less and still make changes, do so. If you want to totally design your own garments, you'll have to learn to chart. I can't teach you that in this book. Charting is another whole book in itself.

KEEP ON MEASURING!

Continually *measure the length of the piece.*

To measure the length of your work in progress you need a clean flat surface to lay it on and that good tape measure I told you about. Set the tape measure at the base of the stitches as they rest on the needle in a middle part of the article and measure down to the beginning of the piece.

We do not usually include the row of stitches that is on the needles themselves in our measuring. Occasionally, if we are measuring for a very narrow border or a buttonhole, we may want to take into account the row that is on the needles. Also, if we are using a bulky yarn on very large needles, the row on the needles will have to be accounted for, but not at the full diameter of the needles. The vertical edges may be a bit distorted, so it is not usually wise to measure along them.

Sleeve caps and armhole lengths should be measured in the middle of the piece from a horizontal marker. Chapter 8 tells you how to place horizontal markers for measuring points.

Also, continually *measure the width of a piece in progress.*

To measure the width of your article in progress you may need to use extra circular needles or a piece of cotton crochet thread or ⅛ inch knitting ribbon to hold the stitches as you spread the work out public side down on a clean flat surface. Without stretching or scooching together, measure across the total width from edge to edge or marker to marker.

Remember that in chapter 12, "Special Things to Do with That One Stitch," we said that you may slip stitches whenever and wherever you wish so long as you slip them as-if-to-purl.

It is important that you measure the width of your piece when you have made about two inches. Why in the world would anyone want to go any farther than two inches on something that was too wide or too narrow, unless they simply loved the making of the stitches and cared nothing about the finished article. Checking the whole width is the best way to prove to yourself that you are indeed working at gauge. And remember, gauge determines size!

Recently I came across the statistic that more than 55 percent of all the yarn sold in this country was used to make afghans. Sometimes I wonder if afghan making is so very popular because people love the knitting of the stitches, but don't understand gauge and don't know how to make sure that their work is measuring up. Differences in coverlet sizes don't matter much, so afghan makers aren't often concerned about gauge.

Make afghans and handknitted coverlets if you choose. They are lovely examples of the fine and ancient art of knitting, but never let me hear you say that *you* don't understand gauge or that you couldn't measure your work in progress.

Measure and admire your work in progress frequently, carefully, and accurately. Never guess. And be glad that your knitting is more forgiving and adaptable than Pop's boards.

22

A TREASURY OF TEXTURES

Variation, change, the interplay of light and shadow, undulating ridges and hollows, spaces and globs dancing together—all these things are possible with the way in which we alternate and intersperse the knit and purl stitches, increases and decreases. The possibilities are almost endless! Just as a computer uses only two functions—on and off—to accomplish all its wizardry, we have at our fingertips the knit and purl stitch, which we can jumble in almost as many ways.

And the results are textured treasures, some serving very useful and practical purposes, some simply delightful because they're fun to look at, all of them interesting. There's not enough space in a book such as this to include more than just a small handful of them. And those that are included here are, by necessity, restricted to the most common.* Get acquainted and make friends with them, but don't limit yourself to them.

COMING TO TERMS

Before you begin to investigate the pattern stitches described below, some simple terms need to be explained:

- An *odd* number of stitches means a number that cannot be divided by two. Three, five, and seven are odd numbers.

---

*Many of the pattern stitches included here are demonstrated in my video tape, "Knitting Pattern Stitches."

- An *even* number of stitches means a number that can be divided by two. Four, twelve, and twenty are even numbers.

- A *multiple* means the number of stitches required to perform the pattern stitch. For instance, one by one ribbing will be a multiple of two because it takes two stitches to make it work—one knit stitch and one purl stitch.

- A *repeat* means how many times you do *either* the multiple *or* the sequence of rows over and over again.

- The term *plus* (+) means that it takes extra stitches at the end of the repeat of multiples to make the pattern stitch work correctly.

- *Charts*, sometimes called *graphs*, can be made for all pattern stitches and color work. They are a symbolized picture of the way the knitted fabric looks from the outside, the public side, of the piece. All charts read from the bottom up to the top. The first row starts at the bottom of the chart and reads from the right-hand side of the page to the left-hand side of the page. For knitters in the round, the charts mean "do what you see" on all the following rows.

- For knitters working flat—that is, back and forth—the second row reads from left to right *backwards and opposite* so that what appears on the chart as a "knit" must be made as a "purl" and vice versa. The third row again reads from right to left, and so on.

- On charts:
    The symbol I means to make a knit stitch.
    The symbol — means to make a purl stitch.
    An O means a "yarn over."
    Slanted lines (/ \) or an X means that the stitches are crossed or
        twisted.
    K 2 tog = ⟋|
    SKP = |⟍
    S1, K2 tog, psso = ⟋|⟍

THE STITCHES

Beginners are advised to work through the pattern stitches that follow in the order in which they are presented. I have set them up to follow a logical procession from easy to more intricate. What you learn from one pattern stitch, you will carry with you to help you on the next.

If you want to play with making a swatch of each of these stitches, you will want to be careful to cast on in full multiples with the addition of any "plus" stitches.

GARTER STITCH

This is the simplest of all knitted fabric stitches. It has a multiple of one and can therefore be made over any number of stitches. *(See photo # 1.)*

In flat, back-and-forth work, knit every stitch of every row. The instructions would read:

Row 1) Knit.
Repeat row 1.

In the round, knit every stitch of the first round and purl every stitch of the second round; repeat these two rounds. The directions would say:

Round 1) Knit.
Rnd 2) Purl.
Repeat rnds 1 & 2.

The chart for garter stitch is:

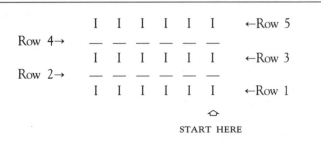

```
                 I   I   I   I   I   I      ←Row 5
      Row 4→     —   —   —   —   —   —
                 I   I   I   I   I   I      ←Row 3
      Row 2→     —   —   —   —   —   —
                 I   I   I   I   I   I      ←Row 1
                            ⬠
                       START HERE
```

Garter stitch fabric lies flat and is reversible. Both sides look the same. It takes two rows to make one "ridge." Garter stitch expands crosswise and when used as the bottom edge of a garment will cause the sweater to flare. It is elastic lengthwise.

You are aware, of course, that there is really only one stitch in knitting; that the purl stitch is simply the knit stitch made backwards and opposite. It naturally follows that garter stitch can be made by purling every stitch of every row instead of knitting them.

STOCKINETTE STITCH

Stockinette stitch is the most common knitted fabric. It is also called *Jersey, flat knitting,* and *tricot.* It has a multiple of one and can therefore be made over any number of stitches. *(See photo # 2.)*

In flat, back-and-forth work, rows of knitting are alternated with rows of purling. You knit across on one row and purl back on the next. Most standard instructions call for you to begin with a knit row; this is incorrect if you have used a double strand method of casting on. If you use one of the preferred two-strand methods, start with a purl row and realize that the designer or pattern writer didn't know any better. The standard instructions would read:

Row 1) Knit across.
Row 2) Purl across.
Repeat these 2 rows for pattern stitch.

Knitters in the round have it easy. They knit every stitch of every round. Their directions will say:

Round 1) Knit around.
Repeat round 1.

The chart for stockinette stitch is just a series of straight lines:

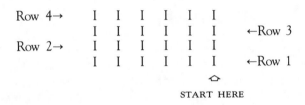

Row 4→   I   I   I   I   I   I
            I   I   I   I   I   I   ←Row 3
Row 2→   I   I   I   I   I   I
            I   I   I   I   I   I   ←Row 1
                            ⇧
                     START HERE

Stockinette stitch rolls to the back, the purl side along vertical edges, and also curls up to the front at the top and bottom. The edges of it must be finished in some way to make it lie flat. The fabric looks different on each side. When worn knit side out, it has a tendency to stretch lengthwise.

REVERSE STOCKINETTE STITCH

This is just a fancy name for stockinette stitch used with the purl side outside. Its multiple is, of course, one also. *(See photo # 3.)*

For flat knitters, it is sometimes begun with a purl row instead of a knit row, but it is the same fabric. If you use the preferred two-strand method of casting on, begin with a knit row. Standard directions will say:

Row 1) Purl across.
Row 2) Knit across.
Repeat these 2 rows for pattern stitch.

3

Knitters in the round may make it by purling every stitch of every round:

Round 1) Purl around.
Repeat rnd 1.

The chart for reverse stockinette stitch is:

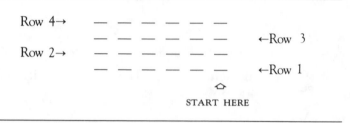

Reverse stockinette stitch has all of the good and bad characteristics of regular stockinette stitch (see above). In addition, when used purl side outside it will expand widthwise.

QUAKER RIB

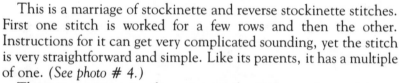

This is a marriage of stockinette and reverse stockinette stitches. First one stitch is worked for a few rows and then the other. Instructions for it can get very complicated sounding, yet the stitch is very straightforward and simple. Like its parents, it has a multiple of one. *(See photo # 4.)*

These instructions are for a six-row alternation and a twelve-row repeat, but generically speaking Quaker rib can be made in any combination of row alternations.

In flat, back-and-forth work, you would make six rows of stockinette stitch and then six rows of reverse stockinette stitch as follows:

Row 1) Knit across.
Row 2) Purl across.
Repeat rows 1 & 2 twice more.
Row 7) Purl across.
Row 8) Knit across.
Repeat rows 7 & 8 twice more.
Repeat these 12 rows for pattern stitch.

In the round, knit every stitch of every round for six rounds and then purl every stitch of every round for six rounds. Directions might say:

Rnds 1 thru 6) Knit.
Rnds 7 thru 12) Purl.
Repeat these 12 rounds for pattern stitch.

A chart for this combination would be:

```
Row 12→      —   —   —   —   —
             —   —   —   —   —      ←Row 11
Row 10→      —   —   —   —   —
             —   —   —   —   —      ←Row 9
Row 8→       —   —   —   —   —
             —   —   —   —   —      ←Row 7
Row 6→       I   I   I   I   I
             I   I   I   I   I      ←Row 5
Row 4→       I   I   I   I   I
             I   I   I   I   I      ←Row 3
Row 2→       I   I   I   I   I
             I   I   I   I   I      ←Row 1
                         ⟁
                    START HERE
```

Quaker rib lies flat; it does not curl at the edges. Both sides of the fabric look alike. It will stretch a bit lengthwise if it hangs with weight on the bottom.

ONE-BY-ONE RIBBING

The definition of all ribbing is: the regular alternation of sets of knit and purl stitches along a row, wherein on the second and all subsequent rows the stitches are worked as they face the knitter. Boiled down, it means you're making a fabric of ridges (knit stitches) and valleys (purl stitches). I teach my students that once the first row of any ribbing is set up, on all the following rows to work the stitches as they face you, knitting the knits, and purling the purls.

Beginners should be reminded that it is necessary to take the yarn between the tips of the needles to the opposite side of the work when changing from one kind of stitch to the other.

One-by-one ribbing has a multiple of two stitches. However, when worked flat, back and forth, as the final edging of a garment, it should be done over an odd number of stitches so that when a

5

seam is woven the edging will appear continuous to the eye. On the outside of the piece you would begin and end with a knit stitch. *(See photo # 5.)*

For flat knitters, instructions will vary according to whether there are an odd or even number of stitches to be worked over. Instructions for an even number of stitches will be:

*Row 1) * K 1, P 1 *, repeat between the *s.*
Row 2 and all following rows) Repeat row 1. (As the sts face you K the K sts and P the P sts.)

Instructions for an odd number of stitches will be:

*Row 1) * K 1, P 1 *, repeat between *s ending K 1.*
*Row 2) * P 1, K 1 *, repeat between *s ending P 1. (As the sts face you, K the K sts and P the P sts.)*
Repeat these 2 rows for pattern stitch.

Instructions for round knitters will always be for an even number of stitches. They will say:

*Round 1) * K 1, P 1 *, repeat between *s around.*
Repeat rnd 1 for pattern.

A chart for one-by-one ribbing over an odd number of stitches is:

	I	—	I	—	I	—	I	←Row 3
Row 2→	I	—	I	—	I	—	I	
	I	—	I	—	I	—	I	←Row 1

⬦

START HERE

All ribbing is reversible; when folded over on itself, it looks the same. However, the underside of the fabric is one stitch off the pattern of the upper side. It is elastic crosswise and because it will stretch lengthwise, it is *not* a good choice for cardigan front bands.

TWO-BY-TWO RIBBING

Please read the definition for, and characteristics of, ribbing given under one-by-one ribbing above.

Two-by-two ribbing is a multiple of four stitches. (When used as the outer edge finishing of a garment where seams will be woven, it should be used over a multiple plus one so that a seam can be neatly woven.) *(See photo # 6.)*

Instructions for flat knitting would read:

*Row 1) * K 2, P 2 *, repeat between *s across.*
Repeat row 1 for pattern stitch.

For round knitters, over a number of stitches divisible by four, the directions would read:

*Round 1 and all following rounds) * K 2, P 2 *, repeat between *s around.*

A chart for two-by-two ribbing is:

6

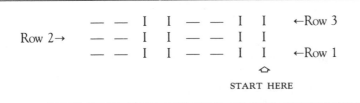

This ribbing is not as elastic as one-by-one ribbing.

MINI-CABLE RIBBING

Remember, in chapter 12 we talked about how you didn't have to knit the stitches in order as they sat there on the left-hand needle. This ribbing is going to put that idea into practice. If you need to, go back and review just how to work that second stitch.

Sometimes a mini-cable ribbing is just the touch to set off the elegance of a garment. I use it quite a bit. It looks particularly handsome in heather tone yarns. It is a multiple of three stitches plus one (for the final edge). *(See photo # 7.)*

For back and forth knitters the instructions will read:

*Row 1) * P 1, K the second st, K the first st *, repeat between *s, ending P 1.*
*Row 2) * K 1, P 2 *, repeat between *s, ending K 1.*
Repeat these 2 rows for pattern stitch.

For knitters in the round, instructions would differ for the second round. They would say:

*Round 1) * P 1, K the second st, K the first st *, repeat between *s.*
*Round 2) * P 1, K 2 *, ending P 1.*

7

A chart for this stitch is:

```
                —  X  —  X  —      ←Row 3
Row 2→          —  I  I  —  I  I  —
                —  X  —  X  —      ←Row 1

                         ⌂
                    START HERE
```

This is not a reversible ribbing. It is just as elastic as one-by-one ribbing and much more decorative.

SEED STITCH

Such an uninviting name for such a wonderful and easy pattern stitch. European books may call it *moss* or *rice stitch*, but I don't think that is much better. Four stitches or rows of it make an ideal edging for stockinette-stitch articles. (*See photo # 8.*)

Seed stitch has a multiple of two and a repeat of two rows. The first row is set up just as one-by-one ribbing is, and on all the following rows the stitches are worked the opposite of the way they face you. If you will remember this, you will never get lost. Formal instructions will vary according to whether you are working over an odd or an even number of stitches.

For flat knitters over an even number of stitches, directions will read:

Row 1) * K 1, P 1 *, *repeat between* *s across.*
Row 2) * P 1, K 1 *, *repeat between* *s across. (As the stitches face you, P the K sts and K the P sts.)*
Repeat rows 1 & 2 for pattern stitch.

8

When working in the round, the instructions will say:

Round 1) * K 1, P 1 *, *repeat between* *s around.*
Round 2) * P 1, K 1 *, *repeat between* *s around. (As the sts face you, P the K sts and K the P sts.)*
Repeat these 2 rounds for pattern stitch.

The chart for seed stitch over an even number of stitches is:

```
Row 4→    I  —  I  —
             —  I  —  I    ←Row 3
Row 2→    I  —  I  —
             —  I  —  I    ←Row 1
                   ⇧
              START HERE
```

Seed stitch is marvelous. It lies flat and does not roll or curl. It is reversible and is ideal for front bands of cardigans. For some knitters it will have a tendency to expand widthwise, as it is wider than the same number of stockinette-stitch stitches.

IRISH MOSS STITCH

This stitch has a wonderful diagonal texture. It is a marriage of one-by-one ribbing and seed stitch. Like its parents, it has a multiple of two stitches, but unlike them it has a repeat of four rows. The first two rows are worked as one-by-one ribbing. Then, on the third row, you move over one stitch and purl the knits and knit the purls. The fourth row is like ribbing again, you knit the knits and purl the purls. (*See photo # 9.*)

9

If you understand what is going on you can work Irish moss stitch over an odd or an even number of stitches.

Standard directions for flat knitters for Irish moss stitch over an even number of stitches would read:

Row 1) * K 1, P 1 *, *repeat between* *s across.*
Row 2) Same as Row 1. (As the stitches face you, knit the K sts and P the P sts.)
Row 3) * P 1, K 1 *, *repeat between* *s across. (As the sts face you, P the K sts and K the P sts.)*
Row 4) Same as Row 3. (As the stitches face you, P the P sts and K the K sts.)
Repeat these 4 rows for pattern stitch.

For circular knitting, Irish moss instructions say:

Rounds 1 & 2) * K 1, P 1 *, *repeat between* *s around.*
Rounds 3 & 4) * P 1, K 1 *, *repeat between* *s around.*
Repeat these 4 rounds for pattern stitch.

When working flat in Irish moss stitch, I find it helpful to place a safety pin at the edge of the fabric on the beginning of the first row as a marker so I recognize which row is a change of pattern row. A chart for Irish moss stitch on an even number of stitches is this:

```
Row 4→      I   —   I   —
            I   —   I   —        ←Row 3
Row 2→      —   I   —   I
            —   I   —   I        ←Row 1
                    ⌂
                START HERE
```

Irish moss knitted fabric is reversible. It lies flat and does not curl or roll. An article made of it will have a tendency to expand somewhat crosswise, and the stitches may "seat" themselves with the first washing. Therefore, garments made in this pattern stitch should be planned to finish at the actual chest measurement of the wearer *before the first washing.*

FOUR-STITCH, FOUR-ROW FRONT-TWIST CABLE

All cables are made over a base of ribbing. The "ridges" of the ribbing are at least four stitches wide. The "valleys" of the ribbing can be of any width and of any pattern stitch. On the public side of the piece, on certain rows half the knit stitches are worked out of sequence.

That's all there is to it. It is easy, rewarding, fun, and adds an interesting texture to the fabric. Because shadows cause the twisted stitches to stand out against the background of the other stitches, all cable patterns look best when made in light- to medium-colored yarns, especially heather tones. They are lost in dark colors.

Four-stitch, four-row front-twist cable is the simplest and most basic of all cable pattern stitches. In this instance, on every fourth row, two stitches are placed on an extra needle and held to the front of the work while the next two stitches are worked. Then the two stitches waiting on the extra needle are worked. (*See photo # 10.*)

Holding the waiting stitches to the front of the work will cause the cable to twist from the right to the left hand side of the fabric.

This pattern is a multiple of five plus one and requires a repeat of four rows.

For flat knitters the directions will read:

10

Row 1) * *P 1, K 4* *, *repeat between* **s across, ending P 1.*
Row 2) * *K 1, P 4* *, *repeat between* **s across, ending K 1.*
Row 3) * *P 1, as if to purl, slip the next 2 sts to a cable needle and hold*
    at the front of the work, K the next 2 sts, K the 2 sts from the cable
    needle *, *repeat between* **s across, ending P 1.*
Row 4) Same as row 2.
Repeat these 4 rows for pattern stitch.

Of course, cables may be made in circular knitting. The only difference is that the "plus one" is not required in setting up the pattern. Instructions for round knitters would read:

Round 1) * *P 1, K 4* *, *repeat between* **s around.*
Round 2) * *P 1, as if to purl, slip the next 2 sts to a cable needle and*
    hold at the front of the work, K the next 2 sts, K the 2 sts from the
    cable needle *, *repeat between* **s around.*
Rounds 3 & 4) Same as round 1.
Repeat these 4 rounds for pattern stitch.

A chart for this pattern is:

```
Row 4→      —   I   I   I   I   —
            —   \   \   /   /   —      ←Row 3 (front twist)
Row 2→      —   I   I   I   I   —
            —   I   I   I   I   —      ←Row 1
                        ⇧
                   START HERE
```

The interplay of light and shadow gives this particular cable pattern a heavy, rugged, and richly textured appearance.

In planning garments that contain cables, designers will add one stitch for every cable twist horizontally across a row to make up for the space that is lost in the twist. Don't be surprised if a garment that has a cabled front and a plain back has many more stitches on the front than on the back.

SIX-STITCH, SIX-ROW BACK-TWIST CABLE

Please read and try the four-stitch, four-row front-twist cable stitch before tackling this one.

In this cable, six stitches make up the knit "ridge" and the "valley" is two purl stitches. Half of the stitches of the "ridge" are twisted *to the back* on every sixth row. *(See photo # 11.)*

11

Holding the waiting stitches at the back of the work will cause the cable to move from left to right across the fabric as it faces you.

The multiple of this pattern is eight stitches plus two and the repeat is six rows.

Instructions for flat knitting will read:

Row 1) * P 2, K 6 *, repeat between *s across, ending P 2.
Row 2) * K 2, P 6 *, repeat between *s across, ending K 2.
Row 3) * P 2, as if to purl, slip the next 3 sts to a cable needle and hold to the back of the work, K next 3 sts, K the 3 sts from the cable needle *. Repeat between *s across, ending P 2.
Row 4) * K 2, P 6 *, repeat between *s, ending K 2. (Same as row 2.)
Row 5) * P 2, K 6 *, repeat between *s, ending P 2. (Same as row 1.)
Row 6) * K 2, P 6 *, repeat between *s, ending K 2. (Same as row 2.)
Repeat these 6 rows for pattern stitch.

Directions for round knitting will eliminate the "plus two." They will read:

Round 1) * P 2, K 6 *, repeat between *s around.
Round 2) * P 2, as if to purl, slip the next 3 sts to a cable needle and hold at the back of the work, K next 3 sts, K 3 sts from cable needle*, repeat between *s around.
Rounds 3, 4, 5, & 6) * P 2, K 6 *, repeat between *s. (Same as round 1.)

The chart will be:

```
Row 6→     — — I I I I I I — —
           — — I I I I I I — —        ←Row 5
Row 4→     — — I I I I I I — —
           — — \ \ \ / / / — —        ←Row 3 (back twist)
Row 2→     — — I I I I I I — —
           — — I I I I I I — —        ←Row 1
                      ⇧
                 START HERE
```

The appearance of this cable is very different from the four-stitch, four-row one. It appears lighter and more delicate, even though the general principle is the same in making any cable pattern.

ANTLER CABLE

Please read the remarks for four-stitch cable and six-stitch cable and make them before starting this one.

By combining the twisting of stitches to the *back* and to the *front*, very lovely patterns can be formed. This antler cable is just one very easy example. The first two stitches of the "ridge" are twisted to the back. The two center stitches of the ridge are worked plain. The final two stitches of the ridge are twisted to the front. The twists are made only every eighth row. The multiple of stitches is twelve plus two, and the repeat is eight rows. (*See photo # 12.*)

In flat knitting the directions might read:

Rows 1, 5, & 7) * *P 2, K 10* *, repeat between* *s, end P 2.*
Rows 2, 4, 6, & 8) * *K 2, P 10* *, repeat between* *s, end K 2.*
Row 3) * *P 2, as if to purl, slip next 2 sts to cable needle and hold at back of work, K 2, K 2 from cable needle, K 2, slip next 2 sts to cable needle and hold at front of work, K 2, K 2 from cable needle* *, repeat between* *s, end P 2.*
Repeat these 8 rows for pattern stitch.

For circular knitting, the "plus two" is not required. Directions will say:

Rounds 1 & 2) * *P 2, K 10* *, repeat between* *s.*
Round 3) * *P 2, as if to purl, slip the next 2 sts to a cable needle and hold at back of work, K 2, K 2 from holder, K 2, slip next 2 sts to cable needle and hold at front of work, K 2, K 2 from holder* *, repeat between* *s.*
Rounds 4, 5, 6, 7, & 8) Same as round 1.
Repeat these 8 rounds for pat st.

A chart looks like this:

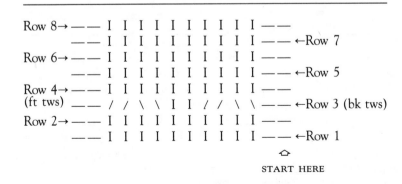

RAISED EYELET LACE

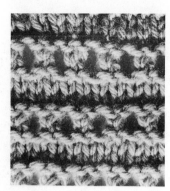

By combining equal numbers of increases and decreases across a set number of stitches, knitted lace is made. In eyelet lace, the same number of yarn-overs (an increase) as K-2-togs (a decrease) are made over a set of two stitches. It is made over a multiple of two stitches plus two, and a repeat of four rows. This is the simplest and most basic of all laces. It gives the knitted fabric eye-catching appeal and is fun to make. *(See photo # 13.)*

For flat knitters the instructions say:

Row 1) (outside the piece) P.
Row 2) K 1, * Yarn over, K 2 tog *, rpt bet *s, end K 1.
Row 3) P.
Row 4) (Inside of piece) P.
Repeat rows 1–4 for pattern stitch.

Circular knitting directions do not need the "plus two" and will say:

Round 1) (outside of work) P.
Round 2) * Yarn over, P 2 tog *, rpt bet *s around.
Round 3) P.
Round 4) K.
Repeat these 4 rounds for pat st.

The chart is simple and straightforward:

Row 4→	I	I	I	I	I	I	I	
	— — — — — — — —							←Row 3
Row 2→	I	O	X	O	X	I		
	— — — — — — — —							←Row 1

X = K 2 tog
O = Yarn-over

⌂
START HERE

If you are going to make rows upon rows of this lace pattern, it may be wise to change the type of decrease from a K 2 tog to a SKP on alternate times that you work the pattern to avoid getting a slant in the fabric. (See decreases in chapter 14.)

Raised eyelet lace may be made without the raised purl ridges, but I like the effect they give. At times I have made this pattern in a different color on a plain stockinette stitch background and was really pleased with the effect. (If you want to try it, be sure to read chapter 23 about changing color first.)

FEATHER AND FAN LACE

This is such an elegant and satisfactory pattern stitch you'll find lots of uses for it. It is an excellent beginner's lace pattern because you can keep ring markers in place at the end of each multiple to help you stay on pattern. Try it out on scarves or baby blankets in Class B sport-weight yarn with a four-stitch edging of garter stitch for starters. *(See photo # 14.)*

14

Feather and fan lace, sometimes called Old Shael in English books, is made over a multiple of eighteen stitches and requires a repeat of four rows.

In flat knitting the instructions will say:

Row 1) (outside of piece) K.
Row 2) P.
*Row 3) *[K 2 tog] 3 times, [Yarn over, K 1] 6 times, [K 2 tog] 3 times,*
   *place a ring marker in the work *, repeat between *s across.*
Row 4) (inside of piece) K.
Repeat these 4 rows for pat st.

For circular knitting the directions are:

Rounds 1 & 2) K.
*Round 3) * [K 2 tog] 3 times, [Yarn over, K 1] 6 times, [K 2 tog] 3*
   *times, place a ring marker in the work *, repeat between *s around.*
Round 4) P.
Repeat these 4 rounds for pat st.

Before you begin to make this pattern (or any other complicated lace pattern), please make yourself a *lace book*. A lace book is nothing more than a stack of 3 × 5- or 5 × 8-inch index cards— one for every row of the pattern plus a cover and a back—all punched with a hole and tied together with a scrap of yarn. On the cover is written the name of the pattern, the number of stitches in the multiple and the number of rows in the repeat, and the source where you found the pattern. The card for the first row will say in letters large enough for you to see easily, "Row 1: (outside) Knit." The card for row 2 will say, "Row 2: Purl." For row 3 the card will be written out, "Row 3," and the necessary steps will be listed one under the other in this fashion.

K 2 tog—3 times
Y O, K 1—6 times
K 2 tog—3 times
Marker

The card for row 4 will say, "Row 4: Purl." The back cover may say whether or not you liked doing the pattern and what you made out of it. Get yourself a large paper clip to secure the lace book on whichever page you are working on. When you start a new row, turn the page and clip it again. The lace book will keep you on the right row, just as the markers will keep you on the right stitch.

```
Row 4→  I  I  I  I  I  I  I  I  I  I  I  I  I  I  I  I  I  I  I  I  I  I  I  I
         I  I  I  I  I  I  I  I  I  I  I  I  I  I  I  I  I  I  I  I  I  I  I  I  I   ←Row 3
Row 2→  ─  ─  ─  ─  ─  ─  ─  ─  ─  ─  ─  ─  ─  ─  ─  ─  ─  ─  ─  ─  ─  ─  ─  ─  ─
           ⋏     ⋏      ⋏  I  O  I  O  I  O  I  O  I  O  I  O  I     ⋏     ⋏      ⋏   ←Row 1
                                                                        ◇
                                                                  START HERE
```

SNOWDROP OR TULIP LACE

Viewed from the top, it appears to be the snowdrop flower that blooms in the very early spring; viewed from the other direction, it is a vibrant tulip. I am very fond of this elegant pattern. *(See photo # 15.)* I have used several multiples of it as the front panel of a soft sweater/blouse, in an afghan, and on a dress that was all-over lace. The instructions for it sound much more intricate than they really are. Nonetheless, make yourself a lace book before you start. The structure of the lace pattern allows me to carry ring markers at the beginning of every multiple, which keeps me on pattern if I should be interrupted.

Instructions for knitting it flat are:

15

All alternate rows are purled.
*Rows 1 & 3) (middle of flower) * Yarn over, slip 1,*
*K 2 tog, psso, y o, K 5, place ring marker in the work *, rpt bet *s, end y o, sl 1, K 2 tog, psso, y o.*
*Row 5) (begin to taper flower) * K 3, y o, SKP, K 1, K 2 tog, y o *, rpt bet *s, end K 3.*
*Row 7) (make flower stem and start new petals) * Sl 1, K 2 tog, psso, y o, K 1, y o *, rpt bet *s (there are 2 of these "rpt bet *s" between the ring markers), end sl 1, K 2 tog, psso, y o.*
Repeat these 8 rows (including the 8th row as a purl row) for pattern stitch.

Instructions for working in the round are slightly different. If made circular, all alternate (even-numbered) rounds are knitted even, also no plus or end stitches are required. Otherwise the instructions read the same.

A chart for this pretty pattern is:

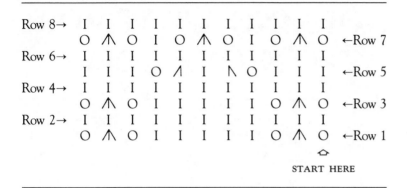

Row 8→	I	I	I	I	I	I	I	I	I	I	I	
	O	∧	O	I	O	∧	O	I	O	∧	O	←Row 7
Row 6→	I	I	I	I	I	I	I	I	I	I	I	
	I	I	I	O	⟋	I	⟍	O	I	I	I	←Row 5
Row 4→	I	I	I	I	I	I	I	I	I	I	I	
	O	∧	O	I	I	I	I	I	O	∧	O	←Row 3
Row 2→	I	I	I	I	I	I	I	I	I	I	I	
	O	∧	O	I	I	I	I	I	O	∧	O	←Row 1

⇧

START HERE

I hope that working progressively through this handful of pattern stitches will have given you the courage to tackle other distinctive pattern stitches. With the experience under your belt of reading formal standard directions and of understanding just what is supposed to be happening, you are prepared to go on to fancier and more intricate-textured treasures.

23

WORKING WITH MORE THAN ONE COLOR

As much fun and as rewarding as it is to work with textured stitches, sooner or later almost all knitters want to venture into color combinations within the same piece, and work with the interplay of stripes and two or more color patterns.

It's just plain fun to watch what happens as motifs pop out and colors dance together, as the richness of tone on tone emerges, as contrasting colors become more elegant by their juxtaposition.

The actual working of the stitches with different colored yarns is no different from any other knitting, but, as always, there are tricks of the trade that make the work easier and better looking.

Really, in working with more than one color there are only two basic types of interchange, though the two may be combined to produce a myriad of effects. One method is making whole rows of different colors, the other is interspersing different color stitches in the same row.

DIFFERENT-COLORED ROWS

Let's tackle the subject of different-colored rows first and talk about when, where, and how to change yarns.

To avoid unsightly purl-like beads on the public side of the piece when changing yarn, always make the first row of a new color so that it will appear as a knit row on the public side.

Make yourself a swatch and prove my rule for yourself.

Look in your supply stash and grab two different colors of the same weight yarn and the appropriate size needles to work with. Cast on about four inches of stitches and work a few rows in stockinette stitch. Beginning with a knit row on the flat, public side, change to the other color. (Refer to chapter 15 about joining yarn at the end of a row.) Smooth and good looking on the outside, isn't it? But look at the underside and you'll see the purl-like beads I'm talking about.

Work a row or two more and now change colors again, but this time make a purl ridge row on the public side to see what it looks like. Now the purl-like bead has been thrown up on the flat outside. I don't like the looks of it. Do you?

Try an experiment. After a few rows of stockinette, change colors again with a smooth transition by making a knit row of the new color on the flat public side, *then* on the next row throw up a purl ridge on the outside.

It's amazing. The knit row of the new color almost disappears and the purl ridge stands out bright, clear, and sparkling.

Let's try something else on the swatch. Make a pattern stitch— an easy one like seed stitch or Irish moss—for a few rows and change colors again without a plain row in between.

Looks like a mess, doesn't it! Purl beads destroy the rhythm of the pattern stitch. But don't stop. Continue a few rows more in the same pattern. Now change colors again, making sure to work the first row plain so as to appear as a knit row on the public side. On the next row, resume the pattern stitch and watch the plain row disappear!

Try another experiment on your swatch. Work simple ribbing for a while, maybe four or five rows, enough for the pattern really to show up. Then, on the same row, change color and begin working stockinette stitch. Do you like the effect? I don't! Though lots of instructions may tell you to change colors as you have just done, I'll tell you a tidier way to do it.

CHANGING COLOR AND PATTERN

Continue your stockinette stitch a bit and then in a different way change to another color and ribbing. With the new color, knit one row on the flat, public side. Now work another knit row that will appear as a purl ridge row on the flat public side. After that, begin ribbing for about four or five rows, long enough to notice the difference in the appearance of where you changed color and pattern before on the same row. The new rule you have just proved is this:

Never change color and pattern on the same row.

THE TAIL-END PROBLEM

Your swatch now has a veritable fringe of tail ends. If the swatch were to become a part of a garment or an afghan, all those tail ends would have to be worked in. It is just a necessary evil—sometimes.

When your repeated stripes are six rows or less in width, you don't have to cut off the old yarn. If you are careful, you can just carry up the yarn and use it again. That's one less tail-end fringe to bother with.

WORKING IN THE ROUND

Though all this experimenting has been worked back and forth on a flat piece, the results hold true for knitting in the round as well. Working in the round, I plan to make my joinings at an imaginary underarm side "seam." Sometimes I later work one half of a duplicate stitch over the joining stitch to help smooth over the spot. I am willing to trade off an almost imperceptible joining for the joy of working in the round.

Working in the round has another advantage as far as tail ends are concerned, too. I once made a multistriped jacket that I called "Joseph's Coat" and used Elizabeth Zimmermann's method of making two vertical double lines of sewing machine stitching a few knit stitches apart and then cutting between the lines of stitching with scissors to form an opening. When I cut the opening, I also cut off all of the tail ends, which were now secured by the sewing machine stitches!

DIFFERENT COLORS IN THE SAME ROW

Interspersing stitches of separate colors along the same row can be a real joy or an utter pain. I always loved and "lusted in my heart" after Nordic and Fair Isle patterns, but hated the drudgery of making them. That was back in my "olden days," when I only knew the conventional American way of knitting with the yarn in the right hand, working back and forth on flat pieces.

In Nordic and Fair Isle patterns, the different-colored stitches form an integral part of the fabric. The strands not currently in use are carried at the back, or purlside, of the work. These traditional designs are carefully planned so that there are only a small number of stitches between the use of each color to avoid long dangling loops of yarn on the underside.

To make Nordic and Fair Isle designs in the American yarn-in-the-right-hand method, it is necessary to first read the directional graph backwards and opposite on all purl rows *and*, each time a different colored stitch is called for, to drop the working yarn and to pick up *from underneath* the waiting yarn. Every time this is done, care must be taken to assure that the tension is even. (If you don't pick up the yarn from underneath, you will get a hole in the knitting.)

But making these designs in the traditional way—round and round—each row on the graph reads from right to left and one yarn is carried in each hand. Working round and round, the yarn most in use on a particular row is carried in the right hand, American method, and the yarn or yarns least in use are carried in the left hand, European Pic method. There is none of this business of having to drop one yarn and pick up another from underneath, because the yarns are carried along as you go. (*See drawings # 81 and 82.*)

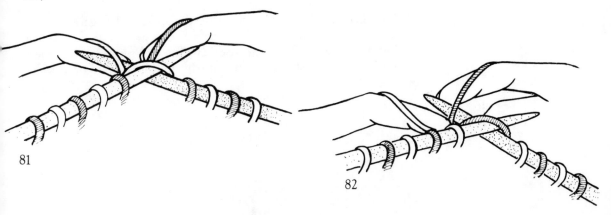

81

82

"CATCHING" THE YARN

The rule of thumb is that yarn can be successfully carried along at the back of the work for four or five stitches without any difficulties. More than that and you run into problems like catching it on fingers as you put on and take off the sweater. When there are more than four or five stitches between the use of a color, it is necessary to "catch" the yarn by laying it across the right-hand needle as a

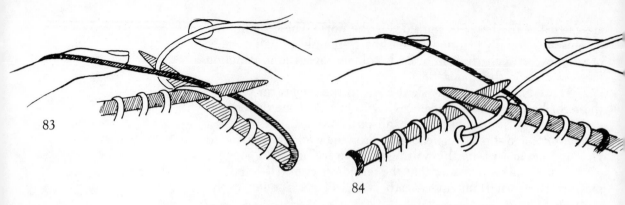

83

84

different color stitch is being made. That unused strand is *not* incorporated into the main color stitch. *(See drawings # 83 and 84.)*

Beware of gorgeous-looking but treacherous-to-make designs where there are gobs of stitches between different colors on a single row. There may be a faint color shadow where you have to "catch" the long strands. If the background is a light color, you'll have a messy-looking fabric.

NORDIC AND FAIR ISLE CARDIGANS

Don't get the idea that because Nordic and Fair Isle garments are knitted in a circle that they have to stay that way. You can use the sewing machine stitching and then cutting technique to turn them into cardigans. Finishing for the cut edge may be formed by knitting or crocheting.

24
DON'T LET MISTAKES RUIN YOUR FUN

There are no mistakes in life: there are only learning lessons.

I always tell the patrons around my work table that it is all right to make mistakes. The person who never made a mistake is the person who never made anything. Sometimes I think that if the old saying about necessity being the mother of invention is true, then mistakes may well be the mother of creativity. And creativity is okay by me! The only trouble that mistakes can cause comes from not being able to admit having made them and thus being unable to learn from them.

I'm human. Of course I make mistakes.

I'm lazy. I don't like to rip out hard-earned inches of my knitting.

I'm also proud. I don't like to finish a piece that doesn't fit, looks tacky, or is sloppy and messy.

Being all these things in one complicated person, I've accumulated a lot of ways to work around the inherent problems and the inevitable mistakes that arise in being a human knitter.

AN OUNCE OF PREVENTION . . .

To begin with, I try to avoid mistakes before they can happen. I have already talked about wise choice of design, good pattern instructions, appropriate needles and quality yarns. Now I'll delve into my personal bag of quick tricks.

THE TWO-PROJECT PLOY

I *always* try to keep two projects going at the same time. One project is a simple, easy, relaxing sort of thing. Then I can carry on an intelligent conversation while my fingers fly. I can utterly relax to the tune of its easy, repetitious rhythm.

At other times, I work on my other project. This project can be as complex and intricate a thing as possible, one that will never have an easy moment of work. Challenging and rewarding in its complexity, I keep this piece to work on during private times.

I work on whichever project matches my mood and the situation.

There are other special benefits of the two-projects-at-once idea. Don't consider it extravagant or willful. Do consider it wise and thoughtful. With two projects to choose from, you don't have to sit there with nothing to work on when you are temporarily stymied by what needs doing next on your knitting and you can't get help right away or are out of yarn or need a special tool you don't have and the stores are closed.

Furthermore, you don't have to be rude and say, "Shut up! I'm counting." Knitting is never an excuse for bad manners. Knitting should be fun, and hopefully you will radiate with the joy of it.

BE ACCURATE

Remember that on any project, a few simple, easily learned tricks will cut down on mistakes. The old adage "A stitch in time saves nine," is no joke.

Never guess. Measure frequently. Measure gauge. Measure length correctly. Measure width by slipping part of the stitches to another needle and spreading the work out. Double check. Half of a size 40 sweater should measure twenty inches across. And for heaven's sake, *stop* when the measurements aren't right. Do work on your other project until you can solve the problem.

USE THOSE MARKERS!

Use lots of markers—horizontal thread markers for lengths (as described in the chapter on measuring), ring markers for increase and/or decrease points (as described in chapter 14); ring markers for pattern stitch repeats.

Use safety pins for safety's sake. You can use safety pins to mark the rows of a pattern stitch if you do not choose to use a row counter; to mark the inside and the outside of a reversible pattern stitch; or, using a safety pin chain, to keep track of increases and/or decreases.

Have reference points. Know, for instance, that when you get to the ring marker with the thread tied to it you *must* have a purl stitch on the wrong side. That way, if you do not have a purl stitch, it is immediately obvious that something has gone wrong and something can be done about it *now*.

Write yourself notes and attach them where they cannot be missed. Like, "Remember to make a buttonhole at the start of row," placed where the next row will start. Or, "Count yarn in box at home. Maybe order more," wrapped around your door key so that you will remember the minute you get home. Note down, "Recheck Jim's sleeve length." Don't guess and be forced to rip back three inches of ribbing and add one inch of stockinette stitch and redo the ribbing.

ADMIRE!

Most important of all:

Please stop frequently and admire your work and yourself for having done it. Knitting is not like fine wine; it does not improve with age. If you cannot honestly admire it today, rip it out. It will not look better next week.

DEALING WITH DROPPED STITCHES

Everyone, especially those who do not know how to knit, knows all about *dropped stitches* and how "terrible" they are. Even little boys at the beach, after they have baptized you with sand accidentally(?) will say, "Didn't make you drop a stitch, did I, lady?"

Nonsense! Real knitters know that dropped stitches are not all that bad. The following statement may brand me as a heretic to some, but I am going to say it anyway, and years of experience will not allow me to recant.

One stitch more or less is not going to kill you or your work, unless you are working an intricate pattern stitch or getting a huge gauge, or losing or acquiring that stitch has caused a hole.

By using ring markers to define pattern repeats and stopping frequently to admire your work, it is highly unlikely that you will discover a dropped stitch three inches back in a lovely lace, an intricate Aran pattern, a Fair Isle, or even on flat, smooth stockinette. But it *can* happen—and there is almost no alternative to ripping back. Anything you do to manufacture an extra stitch in a pattern will look as obnoxious as cracked black pepper in a creamy white wine sauce.

GO ON—OR RIP BACK?

In a textured or knubby yarn, however, one dropped stitch three inches back is no great loss and certainly no cause for tears or ripping back. Put a small safety pin through the stitch itself and through its adjacent stitches the minute you discover it in order to keep it from running down, and go ahead and finish the piece. When you're finished, you can secure any dropped stitches to the fabric with either yarn or sewing thread.

In relatively thin, light colored yarn worked in stockinette stitch, a dropped stitch may be a different matter. The criteria here is, does it show? Can *you* still admire the piece? Some knitters will go back, some will go on. The decision is yours. After all, the knitting is yours and the knitting is for fun. So do what makes you happy.

To be truthful, I must say that I have never seen a long-since dropped stitch *successfully* picked up after more than three rows, certainly not after three inches. There just isn't enough available yarn between the two adjacent stitches to work with to pull the dropped stitch up onto the needle without a tight looking spot resulting. You will often find yourself faced with the decision to either fasten the dropped stitch to those adjoining it on the underside, or to rip the area out.

If you decide to go on and not to rip back, you will have one less stitch than the instructions specify when you reach the next stage. If it is the end of a flat piece, you will simply have one less stitch to bind off. If the next stage is the underarm bind-off, you're in luck again, as it's a great place to conceal a cheat. I'll never tell if you bind off five stitches on the right underarm and six on the left. I'll probably never notice.

Straight-across-the-neck bind-offs on center fronts or backs are a natural cheating spot, too. Or if you are making a single shoulder stairstep bind-off, just bind off one stitch less on the final stairstep. It will not show when the final shoulder seam is woven.

If you are short-rowing shoulders in order to bind off back and front together to form a seam and discover that you have one less stitch on one side or the other, do not despair. Quickly and quietly knit two together as you bind off, either at the neck or at the armhole edge. Some custom designed garments for either full-busted or round-shouldered women do not have the same number of stitches front and back on purpose, in order to solve the figure problem without resorting to shoulder darts.

PICKING THE DROPPED STITCH UP

I sometimes wonder what kind of cells the people lived in who started the idea stated in many knitting instruction books, "Never start a row you will not have time to finish." They didn't live in my house. They never tried to knit with four sons, their friends, three dogs and a perpetual kitten, a telephone, a doorbell, friends and relations. Sometimes it takes me hours to complete one row between interruptions. If I stuck to rules like that, I would never even have started to knit and I would've missed all the fun and joy of it.

So I throw my work down sometimes and sometimes I drop a stitch. When I'm able to safely return and pick up my work again, I always stop and admire it, inspect it for dropped or stretched stitches, check to see in which direction I'm working and what I'm supposed to be doing. Disaster has led me to observe this ritual. If there is a dropped or stretched stitch—or a whole row of them—I can easily and inexpensively correct them now. *Picking up a dropped knit stitch* is a breeze when you think of the area where the stitch has been dropped as a ladder. The good adjacent stitches are the uprights, and the strands where the stitch has dropped are the rungs. Help ease the dropped stitch up the ladder and back into place with a suitably sized crochet hook.

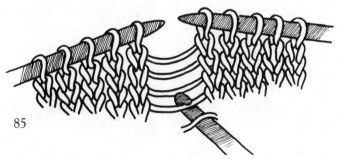

85

*Turn the work so that the knit side faces you. From under the bottom rung, with the open end of the hook facing you, insert it in the dropped stitch. *Slide the tip of the hook far enough up to catch the rung of the ladder. (See drawing # 85.)*

*Pull down on the hook to let the dropped stitch slip over the rung. * (See drawing # 86.)*

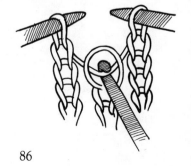

86

Repeat between •s. When you have eased the stitch onto the final rung of the ladder, BE SURE *the stitch is placed on the left-hand needle with the front forward loop sloping to the right.*

Anyone can pick up a dropped stitch, but many people forget to put it back on the needle sloping the correct direction after they have done it. If it slopes in the wrong direction, it will become a twisted stitch and stand out like a mink coat at a beach party!

There is also a way to *pick up a dropped purl stitch,* but it's more difficult, so I usually don't bother with it. Instead, I turn the work around so that the stitch faces me as a knit and pick it up the easy way.

If the lost stitch has only dropped down one row, it's not even necessary to reach for a crochet hook. The stitch can be picked up with the tip of the needle you are using.

First turn the work so that the stitch faces you as a knit stitch. Insert the right-hand needle in the stitch that has dropped. (See drawing # 87.)

Pull the strand through and place it, facing in the correct direction, on the left-hand needle.

87

THAT MYSTERIOUS EXTRA STITCH

Mysteriously acquired stitches happen to all knitters who forget to throw the yarn from back to front between the tips of the needles when changing from a knit to purl or vice versa. This results in an unwanted "yarn-over," a hole, and an extra stitch. If the error is discovered on the next row, stop and correct it. Simply drop off the unwanted loop and go on. Later, you can "even up" the stitches as I will describe shortly. Do not, I repeat, *do not* make a stitch in the yarn-over loop. Do not work it together with the next stitch; just drop it.

Sometimes extra stitches seem to appear from out of nowhere. Getting rid of the extra stitch is not the real problem. When you find an extra stitch, stop and try to discover where it came from. The problem is what the fabric looks like where the extra stitch occurred.

- If the extra stitch was formed long ago by an accidental yarn-over, which was then knitted as a stitch, there will definitely be a hole. That is why yarn-overs are made—to form an extra stitch with a hole under it. It can perhaps be darned in on the underside of the fabric with either yarn or matching sewing thread as described in chapter 25, on finishing.

Please, stop and try to mend it just as soon as you discover the hole. Do not finish the whole thing and then discover that the hole cannot be successfully concealed.

- If it was just a stitch you forgot to decrease at some earlier point, the extra stitch can be bound off or decreased at the next appropriate place.

- If the extra stitch was caused by splitting the yarn and making it into two stitches instead of one, your own eye and temperament will have to decide what to do. How does it look?

- Some people sometimes get an extra stitch when joining new yarn in the middle of a row. They fail to work the two strands of overlapped yarn as if they were one. If it doesn't look bad, there is no cause for distress. The extra stitch can be bound off or decreased at the next appropriate place.

CORRECTING MISMADE STITCHES

If you have gotten off sequence on a ribbing pattern, seed stitch or other simple pattern, don't get hysterical. You may not have to rip. You can *correct mismade stitches.* Knit stitches can be changed to purl stitches, just as purl stitches can be changed to knit stitches. If it's not more than a few stitches and a few rows, deliberately drop the incorrect stitch down (one ladder rung at a time) and then pick it up as it should be.

Once you understand the concept of deliberately dropping stitches to correct an error, a misplaced or mistwisted cable becomes not a problem, but rather a challenge. These can easily be corrected by dropping the stitches of the last half of the cable-rib down to the place where they were incorrectly twisted, correcting the twist, and picking up those stitches again.

EASING LOOSE STITCHES

Long ago I learned to stop frequently and check my progress and rip back *loose or stretched stitches.* That was before a marvelous mother of four daughters taught me better. I was a house guest in her home, and one evening, after her twelve-year-old had been sent off to bed, Beatrice picked up the piece of knitting her daughter had been learning on that day. Out of her own work basket she took a double-pointed sock needle. Quietly and patiently as we talked she "evened out" her daughter's first faltering stitches. Neatness, pride of self, and fine craftsmanship were part of Beatrice's personal makeup; so was loving understanding.

She explained as she worked that if her daughter saw her own work the next morning with its sometimes loose and irregular stitches and compared it to her mother's neat and nearly perfect piece, she would become discouraged and quit, defeated. This mother was not having a contest with her daughter, one in which the younger would surely lose. Beatrice knew that her daughter's work would improve as her fingers grew more agile and her pride of accomplishment increased. She gently eased the stitches into uniformity without ripping back and destroying the girl's work.

Remember how, in making the duplicate stitch (chapter 20), we traced the course of the yarn across the row? In the same way, Beatrice lifted a loose stitch and pulled it firm with the double-pointed needle. She moved to the adjacent stitch and also pulled it firm. All across the row she went, pulling up the slack to the end of the row. The extra long loops could be securely fastened into the seam when the piece was finished. (If a work is tubular or the loose stitches are quite far from the edges, the long loop of extra yarn can be fastened in the middle as if joining yarn.)

I learned two things that night: that it is a rare mother who can lovingly ease her daughter to equality and success at a new skill, and that loose stitches do not always have to be ripped; they, too, can be eased. Please do not cry or bemoan the fact if your mother was unable to help you. Mine didn't and most mothers can't. Learn to ease your own way.

ALMOST THE ULTIMATE: RIPPING BACK

When the time comes that the only way to salvage a situation is to rip, rip I do. It really isn't so hard to *rip back successfully*, it's just the idea that galls.

1. *Put a safety pin through the last good stitch that you can save and in the stitch in the row directly above it so that you won't accidently rip back too far.*

2. *If you are working an elaborate pattern stitch, you will have to keep track of the number of rows removed.*

3. *The final row ripped must always be done stitch by stitch, no matter if you are taking out a lot or a little.*

4. *Slide out the working needle.*

5. *If you have a long way to go, it is helpful to roll the piece vertically to contain the width in a small area, and hold it between your knees with the edge to be unraveled pointing up.*

6. *Winding the yarn as you go, proceed to rip back grossly until your safety pin stops you when you are one row away from where you need to be. (Whenever you reach a spot where the yarn has been joined previously, stop and start making a new ball.*

7. *Pick up a smaller size circular needle. The exact size is not important. Three or more sizes smaller will do. There will be much less chance of dropping or splitting stitches if the picking up is done on a smaller-size needle. To say the very least, it is difficult to try to force those poor homeless stitches back onto the same size needle they were originally worked on. Make it easy on yourself by using the smaller size.*

8. *Fasten a rubber band on one end of this extra needle. (Regular rubber point protectors do not usually fit tight enough for this operation. While it is not wise to leave rubber bands on needles for a long period of time because they can leave sulphur deposits, I do recommend it here.) Do not fall into the trap of picking up raveled stitches carefully and lovingly only to have them slip off the other end of the needle.*

9. *Turn the work so that the yarn is in your left hand, held as if you were going to crochet.*

10. *With the empty circular needle in your right hand, insert it from the back side in the row below the stitch where the yarn is. Gently pull the yarn with the left hand just enough to free it from the stitch so that the stitch is not dropped, not twisted, and not split. (See drawing # 88.) (Sometimes with knubby or fleecy yarns such as mohair, or with a very tightly knitted piece, it will be necessary to use your right thumb to push free the stitch as you gently tug on the yarn with your left hand.)*

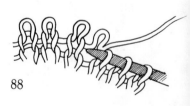

88

11. *Repeat the process over and over until all the stitches are on the smaller-size circular needle.*

12. *Put a rubber band or point protector on the open end of this same needle so that both ends are now stoppered.*

13. *Rest. Stop and inspect. Mark any stitches with safety pins that do not appear to be absolutely correct. You will perfect them as you transfer them.*

14. *Pick up the needle on which the piece is supposed to be worked. Remove the stopper from the far end of the needle used to pick up the stitches.*

15. *Knit, or slip as if to purl, one at a time the stitches from the pick-up needle to the regular needle, adjusting any stitches that need it.*

16. *You are off and knitting again.*

You might take time out to draw a deep breath, sip a cup of coffee, and admire your work. Not only is the piece back on the straight and narrow path to success, but again, you were the one who saved it.

As you continue to work, don't be dismayed if there is a soil line at the point to which the yarn was raveled. Remember that re-worked yarn has run through your fingers three times. Just write yourself a note and pin it to the piece to be sure to give the area extra attention as you block it. (See chapter 26.)

Next time you have to rip, take time out to go over these directions again carefully. A poor job with turned, dropped, or split stitches isn't necessary. You *can* do a good job.

Once you understand the process of easily and successfully rip-ping back, alterations of knitted garments can be looked at with a new perspective. There is an entire chapter in this book called "Altering Is an Alternative." Please read through it.

WHAT TO DO ABOUT BAD YARN

Avoid the mistake of knitting in a piece of *bad yarn.* All yarns, no matter how cheap or how dear, sometimes have bad spots—a piece too thick, a length too thin, an area discolored or with grease spots. Sometimes a foot or two simply isn't twisted or worsted.

Do not knit in yarn like this. Even a bit that may seem just a little off will stand out like a streak of lightning in a dark sky when the piece is finished! Cut out the "bad" area and join the yarn where it is again good as described in chapter 15 in the section about joining yarn.

But still, there are times that you may not realize the yarn is "bad" until it has been worked in. Like the day we were sailing off Santa Cruz Island. I had my dark glasses on with a sailor hat pulled down over my ears to keep my hair from blowing. The yarn was black knubby stuff, and the piece was a simple tubular skirt on circular needles. Cuddled in the shady corner of the open cockpit on a bright sparkling ocean, I looped on miles of yarn before we had to change the tack. When we did and the sun shown on my work, I was horrified to discover a brown streak of yarn about four inches long across the skirt "way back yonder."

I did not want to destroy the happy mood by taking out what I had just put on. The brown streak could not be left in, I had to *replace the bad yarn*, so I dug into my knitting bag for a fresh strand of yarn, a pair of scissors, a tapestry needle and two double-pointed sock needles. This is what I did—and what you should do:

1. *Cut the "bad spot" where it first appears.*

2. *Begin to remove the "bad" yarn, picking it out with the tapestry needle, and slipping both the upper and lower loops to double-pointed sock needles as if to purl. (See drawing # 89.)*

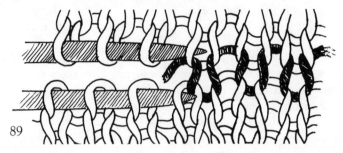

3. *Put point protectors on the ends of the sock needles and work the other direction in the same manner until all the "bad" yarn is removed, all the upper and lower loops rest on the sock needles, and there are ends of free yarn at least three inches long.*

4. *Thread a tapestry needle with fresh good yarn.*

5. *Work in the new yarn. (See grafting instructions, chapter 20.)*

6. *Even up the stitches.*

7. *Finish in all the ends of yarn into the piece. (In this particular knubby yarn, all I could do was tie knots and secure the ends. Many times in lighter weight or smoother yarn I have overlapped several stitches.)*

8. *Stop and admire your efforts.*

Some knitters might have preferred to rip back to the bad yarn in order to replace it. I didn't because I wanted to see if I could correct the error. To me, that was challenging and more fun. Besides, I'm lazy and I hate to rip. Whatever your solution to the discovery of a streak of bad yarn "way back yonder" may be, the streak must come out.

Since that sailing cruise, I have used the same technique many times. I have shown it to others as a simple, easy way to repair a broken strand of yarn, mend a moth hole, or make a spot for a forgotten buttonhole or pocket. It works; try it.

GETTING LOST

"Tell me what row I'm on." Have you ever gotten lost in a lovely lengthy labyrinth of lace? It happens to people frequently. (More often to "book" knitters, less often to those who are creative and use innovative aids.) Many a morning at my work table in the store has been spent in helping a lost lace knitter find her place again.

Laces are one of the more rewarding types of knitting. I personally shied away from them for too long, because my first attempt at lace thirty-plus years ago was a disaster. I didn't understand the multiples and repeats theory behind the idea, and certainly how not to get lost. It's a pity that I was so timid after that first misadventure.

I think many other knitters are timid, too, because they don't understand either. Actually, laces are logical. There is a section in the chapter on pattern stitches (chapter 22) that step by step leads you to understand them.

Still, even using all the precautions of markers, row counters, "lace books," and just plain understanding what you are doing, it is possible to get lost. Okay, so you're lost; so help find yourself. As my grandmother, who was a crocheter, not a knitter, used to remind me, "The Lord helps them who help themselves."

First, dig out your instructions. (You *did* make a second copy, didn't you?) From the instructions, if you have not already done so, make yourself a pattern book of file cards. (See chapter 22.)

Now, look again at your working piece. Really *look* at it. *See* if there are any "yarn-overs" or "K 2 togs" along the last row. Thank goodness most lace patterns read, "Row 2 and all even rows; purl." That statement cuts in half the number of possibilities. Were there any YOs or K 2 togs made on the last completed row?

If there were YOs and K 2 togs, you completed an odd-numbered row, which is fine. If there were none, you finished after completing an even-numbered row and must rip back one row. Sometimes it is possible to just look at the stupid thing and tell whether the last row was done on the inside or the outside of the fabric.

Now then, pick up spare needles and a spare ball of yarn, and using ring markers to define them, cast on three multiples of the pattern plus whatever extra stitches are called for in the instructions. For instance, "pattern stitch multiple of 6 + 2," means in this particular case, "cast on 6 sts times 3 patterns equals 18 sts plus 2 sts equals 20 sts."

Work the first row of the pattern according to your pattern book. Compare these stitches that you have just made with the actual piece. Look the same? No, then work rows 2 and 3 on the spare piece and compare it with the real thing. Still not the same? Then go on with your swatch until it is. It has to be there. You will find it. You can help yourself to find yourself and get on your way again.

MORE CREATIVE SOLUTIONS

There are other ways to correct mistakes. I began this chapter about correcting mistakes by saying, "I'm human. I'm lazy, and I'm proud." Now I will add two more "I ams." "I am ambitious and I am a quitter, too!"

Sure, I've gotten in over my head on complicated stitches and horrible yarns. When I have bitten off more than I could chew, I have spit it out.

Long ago, I "lost" the half-made back and instructions for a very complicated lace baby sweater in a bus station. I simply was not ready for that type of pattern. I was pregnant and tearful. I had just moved to a new town. I did not know a soul. I did not know how to find help. So I ripped and cried and ripped and lost ground. Finally I "lost" the thing in the old Los Angeles Pacific Electric Station.

If you should decide to "lose" something, take care in selecting the correct place in which to "lose" it. Make sure *you* cannot find it. Make even more sure that *it* cannot find you!

I started an afghan once in a miserable cheap yarn in an ugly dumb-dumb pattern (because I had not planned ahead and had rushed into a store to buy "something to knit" while on vacation). After the vacation was over, I found that the pattern was just too dumb and stupid to be interesting. The cheap yarn was not worth saving. But when a local rehabilitation hospital issued a plea for donations of easy handicraft projects, I was more than delighted to donate it, rather, to dump it into their outstretched arms.

I always smile remembering my beloved Aunt Ruth's solution to an overly ambitious, multicolored, every-stitch-according-to-the-graph project at the time her husband first retired—when he was always home all day every day. A visiting acquaintance admired the very thing that was driving Aunt Ruth up the wall. (She admired the knitting, not my uncle.) Aunt Ruth said, "If you like it so much you can just have it and finish it for yourself," and gave it to the appreciative and astonished lady.

There are more ways to correct mistakes than just to rip out and pick up dropped stitches. The admitting to the mistake is the hard part.

III

AFTER THE LAST STITCH IS WORKED

25

A GOOD FINISHING JOB COVERS A MULTITUDE OF ERRORS

After the last stitch of a project is knitted and the final row bound off, there comes a very important part of knitting—finishing.

And after you have spent countless hours making your stitches even and perfect it would be a shame to have the finishing touches botch the lovely appearance. Good finishing is critical to the difference between fine handmade and just homemade articles.

Gone are the days when average knitters could afford to put all of the parts of a garment into a paper sack, carry it to their local friendly knit shop and say, "Finish it off for me. I'll pick it up day after tomorrow." In this day and age, even if the proprietoress of your yarn shop had the time and energy to do it, she will not finish it for you for fifty cents an hour. Neither would you work for someone else for that price.

Finishing is an art that you must learn for yourself. I wish there were hard and fast rules to guide you in learning to finish a fine handmade piece. I wish I could say, "Always do thus and so." I wish I didn't have to say, "It depends."

But, I do and it does! You have loose stitches, seams, and tail ends of yarn to contend with. There may be crocheted edges to add and buttons or other fastenings to secure in place. And there are sometimes stretched stitches or points of stress that need to be reinforced. Though there are general rules that I will tell you about, each and every situation will vary.

WHAT TO USE FOR THE JOB

Some things that will not vary are the tools you will need to do a good finishing job. You will need a *metal tapestry or yarn needle with a blunt point*. You will need a blunt pointed needle because you want to go *beside* the strands of yarn rather than *through* them.

Let's stop now and take a moment to talk about threading the yarn into that needle. Please don't moisten or lick the yarn in order to taper it into a point so it will go through the eye of the needle. That is time consuming and unnecessary. There is an easier way to thread the needle.

Hold the eye of the needle in your right hand. Fold the yarn over the tip end of the needle. Pull very firmly down on the folded yarn with the thumb and forefinger of your left hand.

Slide the tip of the needle out of the fold, turn the needle around and place the eye of the needle over the fold. From the front to the back, roll the eye over the tightly held fold of yarn. The folded spot should just slide into the eye of the needle.

Practice it a few times and it will soon become quick and easy. You'll need to thread that needle often in your finishing job.

You will also need a good pair of *scissors* or *yarn clippers*, a pair that will cleanly cut the yarn rather than chew it up.

Usually you will use the yarn with which you knitted the article to weave any seams and do any reinforcing. Occasionally the working yarn may be so knubby, fleecy, or fragile that it will not be serviceable enough to work with. If that is the case, you may want to use a lightweight yarn that is the same color as the background color of the project.

THE ART OF SEAMING

Seams are usually the first part of a finishing job. I have told you in other parts of this book how I avoid making seams whenever I can, but totally avoiding them isn't always possible. How we join together these unavoidable seams is critical to the way our finished garment will look and wear.

Seams in knitted garments should have three characteristics: (1) They should be unnoticeable; (2) they should be flat and not bulky; (3) they should be resilient and "give" with the garment.

Please don't crochet your seams together. By its nature, crocheting is not elastic. By its nature, knitting *is* elastic. Attaching flexible, resilient pieces together with firm, unforgiving stitches is like spooning red hot Mexican chili sauce on a creamy smooth vanilla custard, absurdly destroying the whole concept you were striving for. Moreover, crocheted seams are also thick and bulky. The extra weight and girth are unnecessary.

Please don't use a sewing backstitch from the underside for your seams. While you are working from the private side of a garment, you absolutely cannot see what is happening on the public, the important side of the garment. When I have tried to sew backstitch seams from the wrong side of a piece I have had the tendency to wander between stitches and to split the yarn. It seems as silly as arranging cut flowers without water to work endless hours to produce a glorious and perfect fabric and then botch it with less than perfect seams.

Please do spend a little time and energy learning to *weave invisible seams from the outside of the piece.* Your efforts —and your project— will be rewarded with a fine and elegant finished appearance. Make yourself three four-inch squares of stockinette stitch to practice on. I'll teach you to weave together all the possible combinations of seams that you'll encounter in any finishing job.

Before you can begin to make a neat and elegant invisible woven seam you need to look at the edges that you will be working with. Pick up a piece of knitted fabric and look at the edge of it, where the rows turn around and go back. The edge will normally curl under to the purl side of stockinette-stitch knitting. Use your thumb and forefinger to uncurl it and see what it is that you have to deal with. (See drawing # 90.)

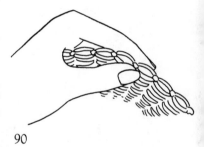

90

When you roll the vertical edge up and to the front, you are faced with a series of long loops and small knots. The knots may be too small to easily insert the blunt metal needle. The long loops may look a bit stretched and you may be doubtful about using them to make your seam. Don't be afraid. The process of weaving the seam will make them even up.

THE ROW-TO-ROW SEAM

The most common seam that you will be making in knitting will be *joining the vertical edge* of one row to the vertical edge of another. You will be joining the long loops of one piece to the long loops of the other piece in a very special way that will give you an imperceptible and elastic seam.

Pick up two of the stockinette-stitch squares that I asked you to make and lay them side by side, rows of stitches next to rows of stitches, *public side up.* Check to make sure that both of the cast-on edges are at the bottom of the pieces. Place a couple of safety pins to join the two swatches together at the top and in the middle. Thread a tapestry needle with a piece of yarn about twenty inches long. Yarn tends to fray, weaken, and "wear-out" as you use it, so work with short lengths of it.

Use the thumb and forefinger of your left hand to roll the knitted fabric out to the very edge. Bring your threaded needle up from underneath in the bottom-most, outer-most spot on the left-hand piece. Be sure to leave a tail end about six inches long. Now use your needle to take your yarn from above down into the bottom-most, outer-most spot on the right-hand piece. Stop and tie a square knot in the yarn to secure it and to join the two pieces together.

> *From underneath, bring the needle up in the first long loop on the right-hand piece. Go across the gap between the two pieces and take your needle down in the first long loop and up into the next long loop of the left-hand piece.*
>
> *Go across the gap and go down in the same loop you came out of before and up in the next long loop on the same side. (See drawing # 91.)*

Just keep repeating the last sentence over and over again. Get rid of the safety pins as they get in your way. They were put there simply to give you an indication of where you were going and to make sure that the correct pieces were woven together.

> *After you have made about 6 or 8 weaving stitches, stop and pull* QUITE *firmly on the weaving yarn to adjust the tension. The two squares will pull together and look as if they were one piece.*

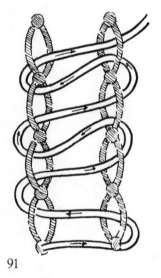

91

Continue to work on up the edges in exactly the same way. Be sure to use the thumb and forefinger of your left hand to roll the knitted fabric out to the edge. A gentle pull on the weaving yarn will show you where you came out of the long loop on the opposite piece before. Stop after every half dozen stitches to adjust the tension of the weaving yarn and to inspect your work. (If it doesn't pass your inspection, take it out now and do it over. It won't look any better the next time you look at it!)

As you approach the top bound-off edge, you may need to juggle one side or the other because of a difference in the number of rows. If the knitting is loose enough, you may use the knot between the long loops to lengthen a stitch. If the knots are quite firm, you may move up to the second long loop on the long side of the swatch to shorten one side.

At the upper end of the square, as you finish the seam, you may want to turn the piece over to the wrong side and whip the two edge knots together once.

As long as your needle is still threaded and you are on the private side of the work, *hide the tail end of the yarn* before you clip it off.

Whipstitch the remaining yarn to ONE *side edge along the long loops for a few stitches.*

Please don't add bulkiness by whipping the tail end of the yarn through both sides of the seam or through every loop. You went to the effort of making a fine woven invisible seam, don't make it any heavier than it has to be. Now clip off the excess yarn and congratulate yourself. You have learned to weave a "row-to-row" seam!

WHERE TO START THE SEAM

Great discourses have been written about from which direction a seam should be joined, whether from the direction the piece was knitted or in the opposite way. None of them give you any credit for common sense. Your own good intelligence will tell you from which direction to make the seam. If you need to weave an underarm seam that has ribbing at the hips or wrists, it is important that the bottom edge be smooth and even. Start there! If you are working on a raglan sweater that has been made in pieces, you will want the neck edge to be even and perfect. Start there! Any differences in the number of rows can be absorbed at the underarm. There is no "always" rule in finishing knitted articles.

WEAVING BOUND-OFF STITCHES

So now you know how to weave row-to-row seams, and from which direction to make them. But in knitting we are not always faced with a row-to-row joining. Sometimes we need to *weave together bound-off stitches to bound-off stitches* as in the case of shoulder or underarm stitches.

Pick up that third square of stockinette stitch that I asked you to make and let's tackle this situation. Lay the third swatch on top of the right-hand piece so that bound-off stitches abut bound-off stitches as they would on a shoulder. Place a couple of safety pins to hold the pieces together and in place.

Now stop and take a good look at the problem that faces you. The bound-off edges have a ridge of lengthwise stitches that were formed in the process of ending the pieces. They were necessary to the

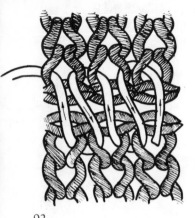

92

process, but you don't really want that ridge to show on the completed garment, and still you want to weave the seam from the outside, the public side, so that the stitches will match perfectly and evenly. The solution is easy. Thread a needle with a twenty-inch-long piece of yarn and I'll lead you through it.

From the back side, insert your needle between the first and second strand of yarn on the right-hand outer edge of the lower piece *just below* the bind-off ridge. Go across the gap and insert the needle down into the corresponding spot on the upper piece. Stop and tie a square knot on the underside. Bring your needle up in the upper piece two whole strands to the left above the bind-off ridge.

Go across the gap and into the opposite piece, going down in the same spot you came out of before, and up two strands to the left. (See drawing # 92.)

Just keep repeating the last sentence over and over again. Get rid of the safety pins as they get in your way. After you have made four or five stitches, stop and adjust the tension by pulling firmly on the working thread. Almost like magic, the bind-off ridge will disappear and the two swatches will merge together into a nearly continuous piece.

JOINING BOUND-OFF SHOULDERS

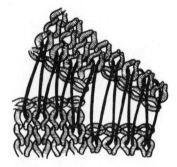

93

But I can hear you protesting that your shoulder seams have stair steps of bind-off ridges. Of course they do, but you had to learn to weave a straight seam first, before you could learn to weave a crooked one. The weaving of stairstep bound-off shoulders follows the same idea of inserting the needle back in the same spot beyond the bind-off and bringing it up on the same side two threads later. The only difference is that as you approach the row change you gradually slant between the two strands as you bring the needle up. The stitches are taken at an angle, that's all! *(See drawing # 93.)*

I know, I know. There is another solution, also. If you are so inclined, you can short-row the shoulder shaping instead of binding off in stair steps. After the short-rowing is finished, leave all the stitches just sitting on an extra-smaller-size circular needle or a stitch holder. When both the back and the front are completed, from the inside, the private side, you can bind off both pieces together at once to form the seam! That is described in chapter 13.

JOINING STITCHES TO ROWS

There is one other kind of weaving seam that you may be faced with. Sometimes, as on saddle shoulders, you must *join stitches to rows*. I'll bet that you can now figure that one out for yourself. Remember that there are usually more rows than there are stitches in an inch of knitting. You will have to juggle a bit to make it come out even. Remember that you want to go beyond the bound-off ridge on the stitches piece.

Pull the third swatch over across the top of the left-hand square and give it a try. The only thing to keep in mind is that you go across the gap and go back in the same spot you came out of before. (*See drawing # 94.*)

In chapter 24, on mistakes, you were taught how to even out loose stitches to the edge of the piece. If you have any loose stitches that need tightening up that have not already been taken care of, do it now. Once the seams are made, any loops of excess yarn can be whipped to the edge of the underside of the seams.

In chapter 20, on duplicating and grafting, you were taught how to trace over the path of a stitch or of a row of stitches. The duplicate stitch comes in handy to cover over a discolored or imperfect bit of yarn that escaped through your fingers unnoticed as you knitted. It also comes in handy to reinforce the inevitable stretched stitches at the division of the body from the sleeves at the underarms of knit-in-one-piece-from-the-top-down sweaters. This should be taken care of after the seams are woven.

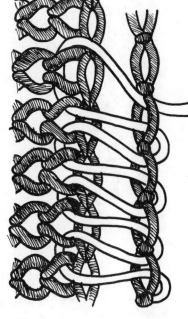

94

TIDYING UP

Don't be discouraged when you turn your garment inside out and see all the *tag ends of yarn that need tidying up.* You and your trusty blunt-pointed yarn needle will quickly make short work of them. Find a comfy place to work, a wastebasket, some sharp scissors, and someone or something to absorb your attention and work the ends in. A neighbor to chat with or a good show to watch on TV are what I look for when I am tackling yarn tails.

Your job of concealing those ends will have been made infinitely easier and quicker because you will have read the chapter on joining in new yarn and will have left at least six inches of tail-end yarn to work with. Less length than that and it becomes a messy and unhappy job with a crochet hook trying to catch the end and stretching stitches in the process.

95

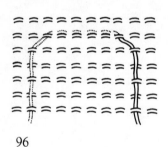

96

When yarn has been joined at the end of a row and the tail ends now rest next to a seam, dealing with the end is a quick and easy matter:

Thread the yarn onto your tapestry needle and whip it through the long loops of one side of the seam for about 5 or 6 whips. Stretch the seam gently to make sure that the whipping isn't too tight. With the sharp scissors, snip off the yarn, leaving a quarter-inch tail.

Since you won't want to add any more bulk than necessary, whip one strand up one side of the side of the seam and the other strand down that same side of the seam. *(See drawing # 95.)*

Yarn that has been joined by overlapping in the middle of a piece won't take much longer or much more effort to hide. First check the outside of the piece to make sure that the tension is correct and the joining invisible. It should be, but if it is not, smooth it out just as you would smooth out loose stitches, and carry any excess yarn to the underside of the piece.

Thread one of the tag ends on your needle and then work it down the fabric, catching it on EVERY OTHER purl bead for 1 or 1½ inches. Gently stretch the fabric a bit. Turn the piece right side out to make sure the hidden yarn is invisible and then clip off the yarn ¼ inch from the last catchpoint.

Repeat the procedure with the other tail end. (See drawing # 96.)

The yarn will never come loose and will probably never migrate to the outside of the garment. If it ever does, just push it back through to the inside.

When joinings occur in ribbing, laces, or other pattern stitches, the tail ends are hidden in the same general manner, but with an extra bit of care to make sure that they don't interfere with the detail of the outside. In ribbing I usually whip a tail end to one side of a knit stitch on the underside. In laces I weave up and down in every other purl bead until the end is worked in. Sometimes you just have to finagle it to make the ends secure and still not visible from the outside.

Yarn ends where stitches have been picked up can usually be whipped to the underside of the original edge in every other stitch.

Hiding the yarn left over from casting on at an edge that isn't joined to something else need not tax your imagination. If it is ribbing that you are dealing with, travel along the cast-on edge with a whipstitch or two until you come to a knit ridge on the purl side. Whip the tail end of yarn into one side of one stitch in every other row for an inch or so.

I have the best luck hiding casting-on leftovers in seed stitch and garter stitch by whipping it into the long loops of the first few rows. Sometimes I have run it diagonally away from the corner in the purl beads, and that works well, too.

Tag ends of yarn that are going to be hidden under facings really don't need to be given much attention, time, or effort. Just make sure that the joining knot is firm, then secure them under purl beads one or two times and clip them off an inch or so long.

FINISHING EDGES

Crocheting edges as finishing on knitted fabric can be a real joy. It is like wallpapering. The transformation is glorious and the result is instantaneous.

Because stockinette stitch left to itself will roll under to the reverse side along vertical edges, open areas of it must be finished off in some manner. Crocheting gives the firmness that is necessary; it is quick and easy, and solves the buttonhole dilemma. If you're unfamiliar with crochet terms, please see the glossary. The only hangup in making crocheted edges is that there are no hard and fast rules concerning hook size and number of stitches per knitted inch. All I can suggest is, *Try it out and see how it looks.* If one hook size doesn't make a nice edge, try another. If four single crochet stitches per inch is too tight, try four and a half or five. The object is to make the article look fine and finished. I usually have to try four or five times over a space of about six inches before I'm satisfied and have worked out a good formula to follow.

WHAT COLOR TO USE?

Some instructors insist that the first row of single crochet must be made with the main garment color even if the rest of the crocheting is to be done in contrasting color. The theory behind the idea is that if there is any "evening up" to be done, it won't show.

I don't agree that the same color row is always necessary. I did it for a while, but I don't any more. I'd rather use the finish color and yarn to begin the crocheting. I do it slowly and thoughtfully, stopping to inspect and admire after every few inches, and ripping back when I'm not proud of the way it looks.

THE WAY TO GO

Before you begin to crochet an edge, mark it in several places with small safety pins. A neck edge, for instance, needs to be marked at the center front, the shoulders and at the beginning of the slope from the horizontal center toward the shoulders. Center front openings in cardigans should be marked off into quarters. The pin markers on the two sides of the neck will aid you in measuring to be sure they are the same in finished form. On cardigans the markers will let you know when to tighten up or loosen your crochet stitches to achieve the overall length that you desire. (Before I started using the pin markers, I made one side of a jacket finish up 2 inches longer than the other side.)

Place a slip loop on the hook and work with the public side of the article facing you. Make a couple of inches of single crochet along the edge. Stop. Give the piece a very firm pull to "seat" the stitches. Take a look at it. Would it look better if the crocheting was made deeper into the fabric or closer to the edge? Are there enough stitches, or too many? Maybe you want to do the same number of stitches only with a smaller hook. (I usually find myself using a *much* smaller hook than the instructions call for.)

I have the best luck working into every long loop at the very edge of the piece. It is sometimes a little full and not quite tight enough, but I make a decrease stitch on the second row in about every fifth stitch to shorten it.

The object of the crocheting is to make a firm edge that will lie flat and will prevent the knitting from rolling under. In order to get the effect that I'm after, I have better luck making *rows* of crochet rather than rounds. (Rounds tend to curl.) When I have worked completely back around to the starting point, I turn the work around and work the second row in the opposite direction. It is done like this:

> At the completion of the first row, join to the beginning stitch with a slip stitch, chain 1, turn, and work a second row with the inside of the article facing you.

When working single crochet as finishing on knitted pieces, watch out for corners and curves. Try and see what works. Usually outside corners need three single crochet stitches in one spot to lie flat. Inside corners usually need crochet decreases to keep them from rippling. Just how many decreases it will take will depend upon your tension and the kind of curve or corner you are working with. Keep in mind that the object is to make a nice-looking finished piece. If it doesn't look right the first time, rip it out and try again.

Frequently, I find that two rows of single crochet and one row of crab stitch (or backwards single crochet, as it is sometimes called), are just the touch that I need to finish an edge. The crab stitch gives a braided-like look that is a nice detail.

Crab stitch is made by working single crochet backwards instead of forwards—from left to right instead of from right to left. The only trick to it is to draw up a good healthy loop after the first yarn-over-the-hook before you get rid of the two loops on the hook.

PUTTING IN ZIPPERS

When zippers are going to be added to knitted garments, it is usually wise to make a row of single crochet around the opening before you put the zipper in. If it is a placket that you are putting the zipper in, be sure to make a crochet triple decrease at the bottom of the placket. After the crocheting is completed, sew the zipper in place from the outside of the garment, using the bottom of the base of the crochet stitches as a guideline for stitching. Either hand back-stitching or sewing machine stitching will practically disappear from sight if you follow that base line.

RIBBING PROBLEMS

Sometimes ribbing worked on garments made of nonresilient yarns such as cottons, silks, or linens just won't behave as you want them to. It is very difficult to get ribbing on these yarns to be elastic and to snap back into place. Even if you use smaller needles than are called for, and work into the back loop of the knit stitch to make a twisted ribbing, you may find yourself with sloppy edge bands. Reinforcing these ribbings with elastic thread is the best answer that I know of.

If you have not chosen to knit in elastic thread, you can still salvage the situation by adding elastic cord after the garment is finished and woven together. Lay out lengths of the elastic cord about eighteen inches longer than the total length of the area you want to reinforce. Cut enough of these lengths to insert at the top, bottom, and about every half inch apart horizontally along the ribbing. Thread the elastic thread in your tapestry needle. Turn the piece so that the inside is facing you. Catch the elastic into some of the purl beads along a horizontal line. When all the elastic has been put in place, try the article on and adjust the length of the elastic threads. Then tie a knot in each length of elastic at exactly the same spot. Cut off the excess.

Finishing work is a very important part of knitting. I don't think that there is a knitting instructor alive that did not want to cry in anguish when she saw an exquisitely knitted garment botched by an ugly finishing job. There is no reason for less than perfect finishing. A little time, patience, doing, and redoing will make you an expert at it.

26
BLOCKING IS NOT A CURE-ALL

Blocking: *The infusion of a knitted piece with steam to stretch, shrink, or smooth it. A procedure used in finishing off a completed project.*

That blocking can finish off a completed project is a massive understatement. As a knitting instructor, I have had the unhappy experience of seeing too many finished-off and ruined projects. More often than not, improper and inappropriate blocking was the cause of their ruination and demise.

One day a woman brought in a once-lovely charcoal gray acrylic sweater that she had knitted for her grown son's birthday. With wet eyes she said, "I didn't have time to take it to a professional blocker, so I did it myself. I supposed blocking was pressing with a steam iron and that's what I did."

She had used an ironing board and a steam iron. One sleeve stretched one and one half inches, the other five. The body was now four inches too wide. There were ugly fat shiny spots here and there all over it. She had done what she supposed was blocking and had finished off a once-beautiful garment.

Blocking is the infustion of steam into a knitted fabric that causes the strands of the fiber to relax so they can be reshaped.

When the strands of fiber are in such a very relaxed condition, they have a tendency to stretch when the piece is not supported by a flat surface.

Hot steamy knitted fabric must lie flat until it is cool AND dry.

When you understand the definition of blocking, you naturally understand that hot, steamy knitted fabric hanging off the end of an ironing board is going to stretch because of its own weight.

Another day an angry woman stormed into the store. She told me that I obviously knew nothing about knitting. She demanded that my boss fire me and that the money she had spent for yarn be refunded. In a very loud voice her own words were, "This dress fit beautifully before I blocked it. Now it's way too tight and almost six inches too long! And you call yourself a knitting instructor."

When I cautiously asked her *how* she had blocked it, she confidently replied, "The way I treat all wash-and-wear things. I washed it by hand, then hung it on a plastic hanger to drip dry." My boss did not fire me; the customer's money was not refunded.

Knitted fabric does not usually stretch in both directions at the same time. What you gain in length, you may loose in width and vice versa.

BLOCKING AND SOIL

I, personally, have never been able to follow the admonition to "always keep your work wrapped in a clean white towel to avoid getting it dirty." Neither have I been able to "always wash your hands before picking up your work." How can I wash my hands when I find fifteen minutes in the car after doing the grocery shopping while waiting for Little League practice to be over?

Moreover, when I do wash my hands before I pick up my knitting, I often have to cream them to prevent snagging the wool. My "creamed" hands are then not really "clean" hands at all. Experts with all-encompassing admonitions don't always know what real life is about.

But even when all the admonitions about cleanliness and care are carried out, the work may still appear soiled when finished, especially if it's a light color. This is because we all have a natural oil and acid secretion on our hands. If we didn't have these secretions, our hands would crack and peel and bleed and we would fall prey to every pathogen floating around. The secretions are not bad; they are just a fact of life to be reckoned with.

I don't think that I have ever seen a piece that for some reason or other has had to be ripped back and the yarn reused that didn't have a soiled and smudged area delineating the twice-used yarn. Think about it—the yarn ran through the fingers once to knit it, another time to rip it, and a third time to reknit it. One of my favorite patrons has a discolored streak across the back of a lovely white wool sweater where it had been ripped back and reworked. That streak will never disappear because it was set in permanently by steam blocking.

Never block a soiled piece. Blocking will seal in any soil, dirt, oil, or acid on the piece.

When you have an article with an area that is soiled and smudgy, be sure to mark that spot with a basting thread so that it can receive special attention in the washing or dry cleaning *before* it is blocked. (I've had good luck removing this kind of soil with presoak enzymes.)

WHEN TO BLOCK

Right here and now I need to state emphatically that I do not believe in blocking individual pieces before joining or seaming the garment. Let me tell you my reasons, and soil is only one of them.

Consider the worst possibility, a raglan sweater made in separate pieces. The areas where the front and back join the sleeves must be *exactly* the same length, and these are diagonal measurements. It is an understatement to say that it is difficult to get all eight edges even in length, unstretched and unshrunk, before they are joined together.

Another reason is that one of the best effects that good blocking produces is to smooth out seams, joinings, and areas where stitches have been picked up. These areas cannot be blocked until the garment is woven, joined, picked up, and finished. Why bother to block twice when once will do? Why waste time and effort and take a chance on getting a single area out of shape by blocking individual pieces when the effect of blocking the entire completed project is so much more satisfactory?

(There may be an exception to the rule of not blocking individual pieces before they are woven together. That exception may be pieces of a coat or jacket that is intended to be lined. Sometimes it is difficult to lay the pieces out flat to measure and to use for a lining pattern before they are seamed. But then I'm not fond of cloth-lined hand-knit things. Better to use a pattern stitch, firm gauge, or a combination of fibers to achieve a firm fabric than to hope that the lining will keep it from sagging.)

I get much better results joining and completing a piece and then *hand washing it before blocking.* Then blocking with steam is usually not necessary. Blocking with steam is almost *never* necessary when the article is made with good-quality yarn, following well-thought-out directions and knitted to gauge.

BLOCKING DIFFERENT YARNS

Some yarns should never go anywhere near hot steam. I recall a fluffy mauve mohair coverup that I designed for a patron. Together we created it—I the directions, she the stitches. I checked and corrected during the process and approved a beautiful bit of fluff as it was completed.

Alas, my patron was so proud of it that she wanted to gild the lily and she steam-blocked it by herself alone at home to "finish it off." She returned to the store with a stiff, matted wad of ugly fiber.

Many fluffy yarns will felt, mat, and harden, and some manmade fibers will expand in all directions if steam is applied to them.

Hand-wash blocking is a better solution for garments made of these and most other yarns. Allow me to rave on about the wonderful things hand-wash blocking can do for any washable handknit. Of course, it removes soil accumulated during the knitting process. It gives a fresh smell to the newly completed project. It evens up and smooths the knitted fabric, softening it and restoring the natural "loft" of the yarn.

Wash blocking leaves no harsh, knife like edges that sometimes occur in home steam blocking. Moreover, intricate and lovely pattern stitches are not flattened. (You chose the pattern stitch for its elegant texture—don't defeat your purpose.) No hard, shiny spots can be left by hand-wash blocking because no heat or pressure is applied.

PROFESSIONAL STEAM BLOCKING

I will not give you instructions for home steam blocking of individual pieces because I don't believe in it. Good professional blockers already know how to do their job; they don't need instructions, but I will explain to you what they do.

Good professional steam blockers will have you try the garment on in front of them. (A tape measure is a useful tool, but it cannot understand the true nature of the knitted fabric. Tape measures don't necessarily lie, but they cannot always tell the whole story and trying on is "proof of the pudding.")

The blocker *and* you then decide where and how many changes need to be made, if any. The garment is taken to a steam table or body form where it is infused with steam from underneath or inside, without a cover or using the top half of the steam table. The relaxed fibers are reshaped at the desired locations. *With the top half of the steam table still in an open position,* the steam is removed by *vacuum* from the garment before it is moved. The vacuuming cools and dries the garment and sets the shaping. The blocker will again have you try the garment on. If it suits you, you'll pay him and go home. If it doesn't suit you, he'll take it back to the steam table and try again. The advantage the professional blocker has over the home steam iron or pressing cloths is that he can vacuum out the hot steam immediately, permanently setting in the reshaping exactly where you want it.

Remember, the professional blocker can work wonders, but knitted fabric does have its limitations as to how much it can stretch or shrink.

HAND-WASH BLOCKING

Please give my hand-wash blocking a try. (I didn't invent the idea, I just propound it.) You'll need:

- A completed garment with all the seams woven and loose ends worked in

- A colander (or dish-drying rack) to set the garment into to drain

- Gobs of clean dry, towels, beach towels, or those super-big towels sometimes called "bath sheets," if you have them

- One of the enzyme presoak powders if the garment has lots of soil worked into it

- One of the specialty cold-water, hand-wash cleaners

- A clean kitchen sink or a large dishpan

- A flat airy place to lay the garment undisturbed while it is drying

- A plastic trash bag to protect the surface of the drying area

- About an hour's time

- And a happy loving attitude (inanimate things *do* reflect our attitude).

Try the garment on the intended wearer *and* measure it. Make a note of the present measurements *and* the desired measurements. Mark any badly soiled areas with basting thread. If you plan to use the pre soak enzyme, dissolve it in a small amount of warm water and then add it to a sink or basin full of *cold* water, mixing it with a stroke or two of your hand. Immerse the garment for fifteen or twenty minutes and check the soiled areas you outlined. If necessary, squeeze them a bit to help the enzyme carry away the soil. Then wash as follows.

If you are not planning to presoak, fill the basin with cold water and add the proper amount of specialty cold-water cleaner, mixing it gently with your hand. (You don't want to create a lot of suds.) Immerse the garment for ten or fifteen minutes.

When the soaking time is up, roll up your sleeves and slosh the sweater around a bit. Have the colander handy. With your two hands scoop up the garment from the soaking water and lift it up from underneath to the colander to drain. Let the dirty soak water out of the basin, rinse it, and fill it with cold rinse water.

Press down firmly on the garment as it rests in the drainer to remove excess water. Then, from the colander, dump it into the cold rinse water. Slosh the sweater around a bit and remove it from the rinse as you did before.

Do two more rinse baths in the same manner until the rinse water is clean, clear, and free of suds. Then dump the garment into the colander to drain while you lay out clean dry towels, either one beach or bath-sheet size or two of regular size.

Press down on the sweater several times as it rests in the colander to remove as much water as possible and then dump it into the towel. Arrange the sweater flat and cover it with another towel. Fold the edges of the towel toward the center and then very firmly roll the towels up. Bang it a couple of times on the edge of the sink and then let it rest for about fifteen minutes.

Unroll the towels, remove the sweater and place it in another dry towel roll, and let it rest again. When you unroll the garment this time you will have to make a decision, a value judgment as to whether or not most of the moisture has been removed from the sweater. It can't hurt to roll it in dry towels one more time. (I hope there is a clothes dryer handy. The towels won't need to be washed, but it sure would be nice to be able to get them dry in a hurry!)

Now I use my guest room bed to spread the sweater out to dry. Before I had a guest room I used my dining room table. Before I had a dining room table I used my bed. Select and use wherever is a good, safe, airy (but not outdoor) place where children, kittens, puppies, bugs, and sunshine cannot reach.

But whatever flat surface you choose to use, it is wise to protect it from moisture with a plastic trash bag. Then spread out a layer of towels, one or two deep depending on the thickness of the towels and the sweater.

Remove the sweater from its last towel wrapping and arrange it *lovingly* on the towel, working with your gentle hands those areas that need a bit of evening up or stretching or compressing. Gently pull first across the garment from side to side and then up and down to "seat" the stitches and enhance the pattern relief and texture.

Get out your tape measure and notes and tenderly adjust the sweater as you please to the size you desire. Minor adjustments in width and length can easily be made. Let it dry untouched, un-disturbed, with the windows open or a fan blowing.

Come back in an hour or so and change the towel(s) under the garment. Flip the garment over to the opposite side and remeasure to assure yourself that it is the size you desire. (See now why the list of materials said *gobs* of towels?)

Repeat the dry towel-flipping maneuver until the sweater is dry.

Now aren't you proud of yourself? The garment is clean and fresh, smooth and evened up, the ribbing lies flat, the seams are invisible, and *it fits*. You should be proud of yourself. Usually that's all your garment will ever need.

Blocking is not a cure-all, but, correctly done, it can work wonders, finishing off to perfection handmade knitted projects.

27
ALTERING IS AN ALTERNATIVE

Because needs alter as lifestyles evolve, fashions change, children grow, people gain or lose weight, and catastrophic misadventures in knitting do occur, it would be unfair to write a knitting book without adding a chapter on altering handknits.

While hemlines bounce like a kitten chasing a butterfly, handknits last almost forever. If a dress or skirt is flattering and comfortable, adjust the hemline. If you love your handknitted coat, but now need a jacket, do something about it. If the long-sleeved sweater you loved when you lived in Minnesota is a bother now that you live in Georgia, remove the sleeves, machine-stitch it, cut it open, and make it a vest. Weight watching and the lack thereof have caused many a much-loved handknit to become unwearable. Has someone lost weight? Block the garment longer and narrower and rip off the extra length. If someone has gained weight, block it wider, remove the bottom edge, and add a pattern or stripes to gain extra length.

Has Johnny grown three inches this summer? Is wrist length now elbow length? Lengthen it! Great-Grandma knew this dire necessity: that taxes would be due and that children would lengthen faster then they would widen. She made the children raglan sweaters knit in one piece from the top down, and early every fall she gathered the children together with their sweaters for an altering session. What could be lengthened, what would have to be passed on to whom, and what was to be redone was decided. She didn't have time to reknit everything. Not everything was worth reknitting.

After the fitting session, Grandma began to rip. She ripped off cuffs; she ripped off bottoms. She picked up the stitches; she added length. Mostly she added the length in varied colored stripes because either she didn't have more yarn of the same kind or the sweater had faded and an addition of the original wouldn't be the same color.

Not only was Grandma thrifty, she was aesthetic, too. Sometimes the additional length was done in a Fair Isle pattern so it wouldn't look added on. Sometimes she would change the whole appearance of the sweater by knitting or crocheting collars and edgings.

Thrift and poverty no longer drive us to salvage everything. Most youngsters and adults have never heard the admonition, "Use it up. Wear it out. Make it do. Or do without!" We don't have to. Still, some knits do deserve a second chance.

Do you have a favorite sweater you wish were a few inches longer so it would look better with your new pair of slacks? Or does the man in your life have a sweater in his drawer instead of on his back because it is too short and leaves an area open to drafts above his waistband?

I'm not saying that you have to alter handknits. I'm saying the decision is yours. Just don't let me hear you say, "I didn't know it could be done."

WAYS OF ALTERING

There are a number of ways to alter garments. Keep an open mind as you read the following paragraphs and let your imagination lead you to solutions for your unique altering problems.

THE GUSSET

Once upon a time, back in the dark ages before I stumbled into what gauge is all about and after I had discovered invisible seam weaving, I made a sweater that was too narrow. The body wasn't wide enough and the sleeves weren't either. I loved the sweater and I had intended it for myself, but myself was too wide. The length was okay, the color was right, and the yoke detail was flattering, but the sweater was unwearable.

My solution was to knit two three-inch-wide gussets that fitted under the arms from the bottom of the body up and then out along the underside of the sleeves. I made the gussets each three inches wide because my tape measure told me that was the difference between the sweater and the desired width. The gussets were complete with ribbing on both ends to match the sweater, and when woven in by the invisible method, no one but I ever knew that they were there. The once "unwearable" garment became a joy and a treasure.

CHANGING PICK-UP STITCH LINE

Another way of changing handknits is to slightly but significantly move the place from which stitches are picked up. Let me tell you of three instances in which I have used this technique, so you can use it to your own advantage.

I was making an Irish fisherman sweater for my lovely, dark-haired daughter-in-law. It was to be her first Christmas gift from me since becoming a member of the family, and I wanted it to be perfect. I didn't think I had the time or energy to create the design and pattern myself *and* be able to get the thing finished between the wedding and Christmas, so I used a design from a pattern leaflet. As I was doing the final neck ribbing, I was aware that it puckered and did not lie in an attractive way. Sure that I had made a mistake, I ripped it out, picked up the stitches again, and reworked the whole neckline ribbing.

The second time around I was sure that I had not made a mistake, and still it puckered and looked ugly. It was unacceptable. On the third try I hand basted a guideline of cotton crochet thread to mark where the neckline *ought to be* and then picked up the stitches along that basting line. The finished effect was perfect. Especially so since I made a rolled ribbing twice as long as I wanted the finished length to be. The excess fabric was simply left inside the fold-under ribbing.

(Knit fabric tends to scooch and move when you pick it up to manipulate it. A hand-sewn, loose, running stitch, called *basting*, through the top layer only of the knitted fabric will give your eyes a correct line to follow.)

Back in the days when I was just learning to chart and design, before I became aware from a drafting standpoint of how square and broad my own shoulders were, I made a boat-necked pullover. The front neck rubbed my chin. The sweater was uncomfortable to wear. It made me look and feel like I was strangled. I was ready to give it away to someone who had elegant swanlike shoulders when I stumbled upon Ida Riley Duncan's book on charting, and came across the solution of folding down and to the inside a neck-line that was too high.

I took another look at my boat-necked pullover. It didn't take me long to remove the neck ribbing band, baste a guideline where it needed to be fitted to my body, and to pick up new stitches an inch and a half *below* the original edge. Thereafter I was comfortable boating in my boat-necked sweater!

More recently I was making a knit-in-one-piece-from-the-top-down V-neck pullover for a very dear and special friend. Doing more talking to my guests than paying attention to my project, I made the neckline increases at too frequent intervals. I didn't leave enough space or rows between the increased stitches on the V. I ended up with the center front neck joining almost an inch too high. Remembering the daughter-in-law's sweater and the change in the pick-up line, I basted a thread where I wanted the neckline to be. And that is where I picked up the stitches for the ribbing. On this occasion I did not use a fold-under type of ribbing, and still no one was ever the wiser.

CHANGE THE DESIGN

You do not have to pick up stitches for added trim along the EDGE of the garment.

There is not a rule in any knitting book that says you have to!

Lower a neckline, scoop it out; make an opening appear to be wider. Pick up stitches wherever you want them picked up. It is a method of altering that won't create vast changes, but it can really affect the fit and wearing comfort of a garment.

ALTERING BY BLOCKING

Remember when we discussed steam blocking that I said a few yarns are expansive and will move both up and down and crosswise when steam is applied? However, most yarns can be blocked in one direction or the other, but not usually both. What you gain in length, you may lose in width.

Why not use this characteristic to your advantage? If the wearer has lost weight, or if the new wearer is smaller than the one the piece was knit for, a professional blocker may be able to lengthen the piece and thereby make it narrower. After the blocker is through with it, you may remove the excess length. It is unwise to remove the length before blocking because it is difficult to tell just how much there will be.

THE ART OF LENGTHENING

We have already talked about the fact that children always have and always will increase in length faster than they increase in girth. This is no reason to discard a handknit sweater. It is much easier to add some length than to knit a whole new garment. Unless, of course you have a hangup about remaking and would prefer to create a new special surprise for a child.

REMOVING THE EDGE FINISHING

You must *get rid of the existing edge finishing* in order to either lengthen or shorten. There are two ways to remove edge finishing from an article. Which way will work best for a particular item will depend on a number of factors—from which direction it was knitted, whether it is all one piece or more than one, and how many individual pieces are involved. How you remove the edge finishing will also depend upon how you intend to refinish the article after that length is removed.

The simplest example of all is the case of a garment knit all in one piece from the top down.

> Mark the spot 1 row above where the change is to be made by catching one-half of each of 3 adjacent stitches with a small safety pin. (The carefully placed safety pin will stop the unraveling process.) Grab up a circular needle, small in size, but long in length. Simply find the last bound-off stitch, clip the strand or pull it through and the thing will start to unravel. Follow the instructions in chapter 24 on mistakes for ripping back.

You may refinish the altered piece in any way you choose. You may reknit the old yarn or you may prefer to add new yarn of different colors to form stripes or patterns.

If the piece has been made in separate parts from the bottom up, the procedure is a little different. (Keep in mind that because you are going to be picking up and working from the *opposite* direction, you will be one-half stitch off the original knitting since you're picking up the bottom half of the knit loop instead of the customary top half. I want to tell you about it now before you find it out for yourself and faint or throw this book away. The half stitch won't make any difference! Particularly if you are using Great-Grandma's technique of changing color and pattern, no one but you and I will ever know about the half-stitch difference.)

Grab up a long small size circular needle and secure the nonworking end. Mark the spot 1 row below where you want to reknit with a safety pin on all the separate parts. Clip one strand of yarn 3 or 4 inches away from a side edge so you are not stuck with a ½-inch-long tail end to bother with. Pull firmly but gently on each end of the cut strand to see where its path lies. Using a metal yarn needle or a short double-pointed knitting needle as a pick, follow the path of the stitch, freeing it from its neighbors above and below and sliding it onto the circular needle.

Making sure that you leave a 6-inch tail end on the side edge of the piece, you may clip this row of the unraveling yarn as often as you please as you work the stitches free. Continue until all of the unwanted length has been freed from all of the pieces.

Depending on the type of garment and your preference, you may adjust the length of each piece separately or of the garment as a whole. You may work ribbing, garter stitch, patterns, stripes, or you may crochet for a few rows.

REUSING YARN: IS IT WORTH IT?

Any chapter in altering handknits deserves some words to the would-be-wise about reusing yarn rescued from disasters or altered projects. Some people think that it is smart and thrifty to reuse yarn.

I don't! I'll tell you how to prepare the yarn for reuse and then I'll tell you why I don't do it.

How you prepare once-used yarn for reknitting will depend on the type of yarn, whether or not it has been steam blocked, if the original stitches sat in their crinkled position for a short or long time, and if the yarn has been subjected to daily abuse like children, sunshine, dirt, and dust or occasional torture like moths or silverfish.

Undo any seams, rip and remove any added on things like neck ribbing or collars. Carefully rip the piece, forming hanks about twelve inches in diameter. Be careful not to stretch the yarn and, every time you come to a joining in the yarn or to an end piece, make a new hank. Your hanks should be fastened gently in several places to keep them intact during the uncrinkling process.

When all the hanks are complete, prepare yourself for a long day because they must all be lovingly hand washed in the hopes that the crinkles will fall out. Go through the same routine for cleaning and drying as described in "hand-wash blocking" in chapter 26.

When all of the hanks are thoroughly air dried, wind *one* hank into a soft ball, get out your knitting needles and give it a try. How does the yarn work up? Are you happy with it?

I never have been pleased with it and have always had to go on to the next step, a steam air bath. Though the washing step is absolutely vital and necessary, it has never been sufficient to get all of the crinkles out of the yarns I have tried to reuse.

When you have another big block of undisturbed free time at home alone, give the yarn a steam bath. Get out your largest soup kettle and a colander that fits over the top of it without tipping into the pot. (I actually went out and bought a colander just for this purpose and used it once. Once was enough.)

Make sure that the water level is about four inches below the bottom of the colander as it rests over the soup kettle. (This step alone can take some fancy measuring and experimenting. Best to do it before the water comes to a good rolling boil!)

Be certain that you are prepared with gobs of towels, a pair of longhandled tongs (yep, I bought them, too), a minute timer, and some lined waterproof gloves.

When the water is rapidly boiling and filling the kitchen with steam, place a hank of the yarn in the colander and set it over the pot. Set the timer for five minutes.

At the end of that time, remove the colander or the yarn or both with the tongs, being ever so careful not to burn yourself. Slip your gloved and protected hands into the hank and gently spread your hands apart to put some firm but tender tension on the hanked yarn. Rotate the hank ninety degrees, that is a quarter turn, and spread your hands again. Are the crinkles gone? Does the yarn need to go back to the steam bath for more time? If so, make a note of the amount of time for the rest of the stuff.

Now lay the decrinkled yarn on a towel to dry in a safe place out of the sunlight until completely dry.

That's all there is to it! Simply repeat the process with each and every hank.

I did it once, and once was enough. I figured that I didn't have to do it, that yarn was cheap enough and my time and energy dear enough that I would just leave the glory of being Creative and Thrifty Mother Earth to someone else.

Now that word to the would-be-wise that I promised you. A gift is always for the giver. Accept with profuse thanks a gift of any yarn or knitted project offered you. Smile sweetly and say something like, "How lovely," or at least, "How thoughtful of you," when your mother-in-law says, "It's lovely stuff, dearie. Since you're learning to knit you can just rip it out and reuse it."

Just as soon as you get home, put it into one of those wonderful dark colored, can't-see-thru plastic trash bags which may be one of the greatest inventions of the twentieth century. No one, no nosy neighbor, or vicious person can tell what you are throwing away with the trash.

The next time you are out on errands, alone and preferably in a strange neighborhood, lose the can't-see-thru plastic bag and with it someone else's problem project.

And when your mother-in-law has the very bad manners to ask what you did with the yarn, you can smile sweetly and honestly say, "I just have no idea what became of it. I can't find it anywhere!" knowing the whole time that if reusing the yarn was delightful and pleasurable, the giver would have reused it herself. Add to your list of proverbs, right after "Beware of Greeks bearing gifts; remember the Trojan Horse," this one, "Beware of givers of once- or half-used yarn, as they want you to get all balled up."

28
DELIGHTFUL LITTLE GOODIES

A pom-pom to top off a stocking cap, a fringe to feather the edge of a shawl, tassels to define the points of an afghan, these are just a few of the delightful little goodies that enhance handknit things.

Though they aren't really knitted, they're included here because these special finishing elements emphasize the handmadeness of fine knit articles.

POM-POMS

Many knitting and craft supply stores have handy dandy commercial pom-pom forms for sale that minimize the normal wastage of yarn, and produce uniform-size puff balls that are added for emphasis on hats, slippers, and such.

If you are going to be making many pom-poms, I recommend you purchase such a device.

If you make a pom-pom only once in a blue moon, this is the way it is done:

Have handy long scissors or shears and a wastebasket. If you are going to make more than one matching pom-pom, have a pencil and paper to take notes.

Cut 4 strands of yarn about 18 inches long to use as ties. Take a piece of stiff cardboard about 4 × 6 inches and wrap it round and round on the shorter side with yarn—perhaps about 25 times. Remember to count the wraps so that you will know for next time.

Pull the yarn together at the top and bottom of the cardboard and tie each of the two bundles of yarn with a doubled tie-strand.

With scissors, cut the wrapped yarn between the ties. (Two puff balls will result.) (See drawing # 97.)

If the balls are thin and flimsy, tie them together. If they are puffy enough alone to please you, get ready to trim and "groom" them. Grab a pair of long shears and a wastebasket to catch the mess. Holding on to the long tie-strands which will be used to attach the pom-poms, begin trimming the uneven ends to make a round and uniform ball.

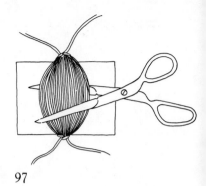

97

I wish I could give you more exact instructions, telling you exactly how many times to wrap around exactly the right size of cardboard. Alas, yarns vary in density and loft (fullness); human beings vary in how tightly they wrap and stretch the yarn. You'll just have to experiment with each different yarn to determine the number of wraps and the size of the cardboard.

FRINGE

As with pompons, the exact instructions for making fringe will vary with the yarn, its density and loft, and the human element of tightness of wrap and stretch. But there is something else to consider in fringe making. That is what you want the final effect of the completed article to be. Fringe can be long, wispy, and romantic, or short, fluffy, and fuzzy. Either way, the procedure to make the fringe is the same. It is the length of the individual strands, the number of them that are put together in one spot, and how closely those spots are located to one another that will make the difference.

I always have to experiment with three or four different lengths of strands and with the closeness of the spots in which they are placed before I can make a final decision about which fringe I like best for a particular article.

The only general rule of thumb that I can give you is that the strands should be cut approximately the finished length you desire *plus* two inches *times* two. For instance, if you want a six-inch-long finished fringe, add two inches to the six and then multiply by two ($6'' + 2'' = 8'' \times 2 = 16''$).

You'll need:

- Yarn
- Long scissors or shears
- A wastebasket to catch the mess
- A hardback book that measures however many inches around that the strands need to be cut

- A crochet hook large enough to hold all of the strands, but small enough to push through the base fabric

To make a six-strand fringe six inches long:

Select a book that measures approximately 16 inches around. Beginning at an open edge of the book, loosely wrap the yarn around the book about 30 times. Cut the yarn along the open edge of the book.

Select 3 strands of the yarn. Hold them together to align them and then fold them in half. With the inside, the private side, of the article facing you, insert a crochet hook through the article close to the edge. Catching the fold of the strands with the crochet hook, pull them back through the hole an inch or so.

Spread the fold open and pull the ends of the strands through the loop that is created. Pull the ends gently until the fringe is securely seated against the garment.

Repeat this procedure as often as specified or as you please, stopping to wrap and cut yarn as needed. When you are finished, grab the wastebasket to catch the mess as you trim the ends. Using the index and second fingers of your left hand as guides, trim the ragged ends of the fringe so that they are even.

The nice thing about fringe is that you *can* experiment with it. If you don't like the overall effect, take it out and try again. There are no hard and fast rules about fringing.

TASSELS

Tassels are simple and easy to make. Wherever added weight is desired to make an article hang properly, they provide an attractive eye teaser.

The supplies you will need are:

- Yarn

- Shears or long scissors

- A piece of stiff cardboard one inch longer than the desired finished length of the tassel

- A wastebasket

To make the tassel:

Cut 2 strands of yarn about 20 inches long to use as ties. Wrap the yarn around the cardboard until you have a nice tidy bundle of it.

Run a doubled strand of the tie-yarn under the bundle at the top of the cardboard and tie it securely. (You will use this tie-strand to fasten the tassel in place.) Cut the yarn at the bottom of the cardboard.

Take the other tie-strand and wrap it around the bundle ½ to 1 inch below the gathering point. Tie this strand securely, wrap it around several times more, and then tie it again. (The knots will just disappear by themselves.) Comb the loose ends smooth with your fingers.

Using the index and second finger of your left hand as a guide, trim up the ragged ends. (See drawing # 98.)

98   CUT

MONK'S CORD

Sometimes a twisted rope belt will add just the right finishing touch to a garment. I've used them on lace dresses, ponchos, and for necktie strings. They look specially handsome in knubby yarns and are the simplest kind of a rope or strong cord known to man. (*See drawing # 99.*)

I hate to say it all the time, but again, experimenting with the number of strands and tightness of the twisting put into them is the only way to achieve exactly the right effect you're after.

You'll need:

- Lots of yarn

- A tape measure and scissors

- An area to work in that is three times as long as you want the finished cord to be

- A door knob or a strong fastening point at the other end of the area in which you are working

To make a cord six feet long:

Cut 10 strands of yarn 18 feet long. Tie the ends together to form a large loop. Thread a small piece of yarn through the loop and fasten it to the door knob or strong fastening point.

Slip a pencil or a small dowel into the opposite end of the loop and twist the pencil round and round in the same direction until the yarn gets tightly twisted. Lay a heavy object on your end of the twisted loop and another half way to the door knob.

Walk to the other end of the area and detach the yarn from the knob. Carry it back to the other end of the room to fold the twisted strands in half.

Remove the books and allow the torque of the strands to twist them-

99

selves together around each other to form a rope. Tie a simple knot about 4 inches from each end to secure the strands.

Cut and unravel these knotted ends, comb them out with your fingers, and trim the ragged ends with scissors.

Back in the "olden days" when I was a Brownie and a Girl Scout, everybody had hand egg beaters or hand drills around the house. They were great little tools to help with the twisting of the yarn. In these modern times, I have in my house an electric mixer, a blender, a wire whisk, and a power-drive drill. None of those seem to work very well for the twisting of the yarn; their speed makes it difficult to control the amount of twist. I now use a good old pencil and do the twisting by hand. Such is a comment on modern American life.

KNITTED CORD

There are times when a twisted monk's cord is too heavy and bulky for an item that needs some kind of a tie piece. If you don't want to resort to cloth, a leather thong, or a shoe string, why don't you consider a knitted cord? It's a little more time consuming to make, but it has its rewards.

You'll need two short, double-pointed needles and something unimportant to occupy your mind while your fingers do the repetitive work.

1. Cast on 4 stitches.

2. Knit these 4 stitches. Do NOT turn the work around.

3. Put the needle that has the stitches on it back into your left hand. Push the stitches toward the tip.

4. Drawing the yarn firmly from the opposite end of the work, knit these 4 stitches. Do NOT turn the work around.

Repeat steps 3 and 4. As the piece grows in length, tug on it occasionally. (The yarn that has been pulled across will "jump" into place and you will have a round, hollow-centered knitted tube.) Continue the procedure until the cord is the appropriate length. If desired, attach a tassel to each end of the cord.

YARN BUTTONS

I've seen three kinds of yarn buttons used to fasten knitted garments: crocheted stuffed ball buttons, crochet-covered "bone" ring buttons, and the commercial sewing notion button forms covered with flat knitted fabric.

I can't say that I have a preference between the ball and the "bone" ring buttons. I like them equally well and use them both frequently. As to deciding which to use, I make up one of each and let the sweater tell me which it likes the best. I do have a distaste for the form covered buttons, and I'll tell you why later.

There are two important things you need to be told about the making of either ball or "bone" ring covered buttons. The first is that it is imperative that you remember what you do on the first one, so that you make all the buttons for one garment identically. (My pencil comes in handy here, because if I don't write it down, sure as phone calls in the shower, I'll get interrupted before I can make three identical buttons.)

Both ball and "bone" ring covered buttons need to be firm and very tight. Therefore, it is necessary to use a crochet hook that is several sizes smaller than would normally be used for a particular yarn.

If you need to refresh your memory about crochet instructions and abbreviations, please see the glossary at the end of this book.

CROCHETED ROUND BALL BUTTONS

These are worked tightly in rounds without turning with a smaller than normal hook.

Make a slip loop 18 inches from the end of the yarn. Chain 2, join to first ch with a slip stitch, ch 1.

Round 1: Make 8 single crochet into ring, join with sl st, ch 1.

Round 2: Sc into sl st, * sc in next st, 2 sc into next st, * repeat between *s around, Join with sl st, ch 1. (12 sc remain.)

Round 3: (optional) Work one round of sc even, join with sl st, ch 1.

Round 4: Decrease 2 sts into 1 around as follows: * Insert hook into next st, yarn over, draw up a loop, insert hook into next st, y o, draw up a loop, y o, go through 3 loops on hook, * rpt bet *s around.

Cut yarn 18 inches long. Fasten off. Stuff ball with as much of the beginning 18-inch piece as possible. Thread ending yarn on a tapestry needle and use doubled to fasten button closed and to sew to the garment.

CROCHET-COVERED "BONE" RING BUTTONS

Note: You can experiment with different size rings to suit the weight of the yarn and finished size of the button.

Work tightly with a smaller than normal hook.

Make a slip loop 18 inches from the end of the yarn. Working through the center of the ring, make as many single crochet sts around the ring as possible, crowding them tightly, but not overlapping them. Join with the slip stitch.

Cut yarn 18 inches long and pull through sl st. Thread both ends of yarn on a blunt pointed needle. Going through the outer loop only of every other sc, run a basting thread to gather sts together. Pull firmly on back side to fill in middle of ring. Make a few darning sts across center to secure.

Use remaining strands of yarn to sew button to garment.

The appearance of covered "bone" ring buttons can be changed by pulling the basting stitch to the *front* instead of to the back. Also, four-leafed clovers can be made by omitting the basting thread and making darning stitches across the circumference of the outside edge of the single crochet stitches in two places at right angles to each other.

KNIT-COVERED COMMERCIAL FORM BUTTONS

I told you that I didn't like them, and now I'll tell you why. It is almost impossible for hand knitters to knit a piece of flat stockinette-stitch fabric tightly and firmly enough to withstand the pressure and stretching that is necessary to securely put into place the back part of the button form. Machine knitters have no problem with this. They simply turn the tension knob way down tight and produce however much fabric they need. I've tried and tried to get my hand tension firm enough to make a good-looking button, but I can't do it. I've only seen a few hand knitters who can.

It would appear that well-made covered form buttons can only be achieved with machine knitting, which is fine, but why dress up your fine hand knit with something that smells of machine knitting?

Be aware—beware of any garment in the fashion magazines or needlework periodicals that has covered form buttons. It was probably designed for and made on a machine. Those instructions do not always transfer well into handknitting directions, and may present you with unexpected problems, like "Decrease every third row." That is fine for machine knitters, but difficult for hand knitters, because usually we only decrease on the knit side every other row.

You don't really need any instructions from me to make covered form buttons. Make your stockinette stitch fabric as firm and as tight as you can and then follow the directions on the button package. And good luck!

IV

LEARNING LESSONS

29
BEGINNERS' LEARNING LESSONS

These are very simple, straightforward, and easy projects that will help beginning knitters perfect the rhythm and motions of making first the knit and then the purl stitch. Take your choice of which of the three to make. All are very lovely to look at and nicely practical to own.

> *Until one's stitches are smooth and uniform and enjoyable to make, it is silly to attempt other more complicated and expensive garments.*

On these three items, stitch gauge is not important. What is important is that your fingers are learning to obey the commands of your mind quickly, easily, and joyfully.

The materials you use are important. I ask my students to use the best-quality wool or fine acrylic yarn they can afford. Don't hinder your progress with stiff, knubby and/or nonresilient yarn. Choose circular needles that have a smooth and easy transition joining from the tips to the cables. They should have neither exceedingly sharp nor blunt points.

GARTER STITCH FRINGED TRIANGULAR SHAWL

This reversible shawl is knit in one piece from the point outward. The exact finished size will depend upon how firmly or loosely the knitter is forming the stitches, but, generally speaking, it will be approximately 29 inches long from the cast-on edge, and 50 inches across the bound-off edge not including fringe.

Materials Needed:

- 3 3½- or 4-ounce skeins of Class C smooth classic knitting worsted yarn

- Size 8 circular needle, 29 inches long

- Tapestry or metal yarn needle

- Size J crochet hook for making fringe

- Scissors

Before starting, first review the two-strand method of casting on in chapter 10, how to form the knit stitch in chapter 11, how to form the purl stitch in chapter 12, and making yarn-over increases in chapter 14.

Note: If you have to cut and join yarn because of knots or imperfections, do it at the end of a row, even if you have to rip back a few stitches.

Cast on 2 stitches.
Row 1: Knit 1 stitch, yarn over, knit every stitch to the end of the row.
Repeat row 1 until one skein of yarn has been used up.
Stop at the end of a row and push all of the stitches to the opposite end of the needle.

At the opposite end of a row from where you stopped, begin with a new yarn.

Row 2: Purl every stitch across the row until one stitch remains on the left-hand needle, yarn over, purl the final stitch.
Repeat row 2 until the second skein of yarn has been used up.
Review binding off in chapter 13.
(Note: The binding off is done in a special way with decreases to tighten up the edge so that the shawl won't slip off the wearer's shoulders.)
**Bind off 3 stitches purlwise, purl the next 2 stitches together as if they were one and bind off that stitch *. Repeat between *'s across the row.*

Weave in any tag ends of yarn.

Review fringe making in chapter 28.

Cut yarn for a 6-strand fringe to finish 6 inches long. Place the first strands in the yarn-over hole at the bottom point and in every third YO hole along the diagonal sides.

Hand-wash block the shawl (see chapter 26).

Wear with a sense of pride and accomplishment, for you are on your way to becoming an accomplished knitter.

HOODED GARTER-STITCH SCARF WITH FRINGED ENDS

This reversible cold weather coverup is made in two pieces. The scarf and hood are made separately and whipstitched together. The fringe is added later. The exact finished size will depend upon how firmly or loosely the knitter is forming the stitches.

Materials Needed:
- 2 3½- or 4-ounce skeins of Class C smooth classic knitting worsted yarn.

- Size 8 circular needle, 24 or 29 inches long

- An extra circular needle of any size

- Tapestry needle or metal yarn needle

- Size J crochet hook for making fringe

- Scissors

Review the two-strand method of casting on in chapter 10, how to form the knit stitch in chapter 11, how to form the purl stitch in chapter 12, and binding off in chapter 13.

Note: If you have to cut and join yarn because of knots or imperfections, do it at the end of a row, even if you have to rip back a few stitches.

Scarf directions: *Cast on 30 stitches. Knit every stitch of every row until the piece measures approximately 50 inches long overall from cast-on edge. Loosely bind off as if to knit.*

Hood directions: *Cast on 80 stitches.*

Purl every stitch of every row until the piece measures 11 inches long overall from the cast-on edge.

As if to purl, slip the first 40 stitches to an extra circular needle. Fold the hood in half so that the two circular needles, each holding 40 stitches, are lying parallel to each other.

Review binding off two pieces together at the same time to form a seam as described in chapter 13.

Bind off both sides of the hood to form a seam.

Finishing:
Mark the lengthwise center of the scarf with a safety pin. Mark the center of the cast-on edge of the hood with a safety pin. Fasten the two pins together. Mark a spot along the same edge of the scarf 8 inches in each

direction from the attached safety pins. Pin each edge of the hood to those spots. With a tapestry needle and matching yarn, whipstitch the hood in place, easing in any fullness. Weave in loose tag ends of yarn.
Review fringe making in chapter 28.

Cut yarn for a 6-strand fringe to finish 6 inches long. Place fringe in every other stitch at each end of the scarf.

Hand-wash block the scarf (see chapter 26).

Wear with a sense of pride and accomplishment. You have learned to make something attractive and useful.

LACY SHOULDER CAPELET

The lacy effect of this simple garter-stitch coverup is achieved by deliberately dropping selected stitches on the final bind-off row. The finished size will vary according to the stitch size of the individual knitter, but will be approximately 12 inches long and 50 inches around.

Materials Needed:
- 2 3½- or 4-ounce skeins of Class C smooth classic knitting worsted yarn.

- Size 8 circular needle, 29 inches long

- Tapestry needle or metal yarn needle

- 60 inches of purchased ribbon for tie at neck.

Review casting on with a two strand method in chapter 10, how to form the knit stitch in chapter 11, and how to form the purl stitch in chapter 12.

Note: If you have to cut and join yarn because of knots or imperfections, do it at the end of a row, even if you have to rip back some stitches.

Cast on 200 stitches. Knit every stitch of every row until half of the yarn has been used and the piece is 6 inches long overall from the cast-on edge. Stop at the end of a row.

Starting at the OPPOSITE *end of the row from where you stopped, add new yarn. Purl every stitch of every row until the remainder of the yarn is nearly used, but making sure that you leave a length 4 times the width of the piece for binding off.*

At the beginning of the next row, loosely, as if to purl, bind off 4 stitches. Drop the next stitch off the needle. Stretch the piece a bit to cause the dropped stitch to fall down and become unworked. *Bind off the next 4 stitches. Drop the next stitch off the needle*. Repeat between the *s across the row. Gently manipulate the piece to make all of the dropped stitches come undone all the way back to the cast-on edge. Weave a ribbon drawstring through the open spaces made by the dropped stitches.

Weave in any tag ends of yarn.

Hand-wash block the capelet (see chapter 26).

Enjoy your first hand-knitted project!

30
LEARNING LESSONS
FOR INTERMEDIATES

These three learning lessons will take you step by step once you are proficient at making the basic knit and purl stitches to reading and understanding abbreviated knitting instructions in order to make more complicated garments. Once you are past kindergarten you are promoted into first grade. Once you have perfected making the basic stitches, you are ready to learn to follow directions and make garments and pattern stitches.

I have used these three learning lessons over and over for years in the teaching of my classes. They didn't happen just by accident. I stayed awake nights thinking about all of the problems my students would encounter in their ordinary knitting lives and incorporating the solutions to these problems into small items that could each be easily and inexpensively completed in a class session of five or six weeks.

Before I devised these learning lessons, I used to let my students choose their own projects to make. Some chose projects that were much too complicated; others chose projects that did not give them an opportunity to learn enough. Some students knitted faster than others and invariably the class period would be over and important things left untaught.

Now I force my students to make these three baby garments. That's right, hand-knitted tiny garments that a newborn might wear, not because either they or I are fond of making baby things, or have any use for them, but rather because they *are* small and yet contain *all the essentials of making any size garment.*

I don't care what you do with these baby things when you have learned all you can from them. And I don't pretend that they are things of beauty, but they are filled with learning experiences. What you do with the silly things after the learning is over is your business. One student gave them to a granddaughter for her doll. Another gave them to the Salvation Army. One young lady gave the sweater to a little boy for his dog. What you do with them isn't important. That you learn from them *is!*

Let me explain how these instructions work. They are broken up into sections separated by a wavy line. Within each section you will be told how to do something in three different manners:

1. In plain English

2. *In Standard Simplified Instructions*

3. IN SHORT ABBREVIATED DIRECTIONS.

They will all say the same thing in different words. Please read all the way through to the next wavy line before you begin to do anything. I want you to understand what you are doing and why you are doing it. And I want you to be able to do it from any kind of instructions.

When you have finished with these learning lessons, you will understand why my students have fondly called two of the articles "The Dumb Baby Sweater" and "The Stupid Baby Bonnet." When you are finished, you won't be afraid to tackle *any* project.

THE DUMB BABY SWEATER

Materials Needed:

- 1 3½- or 4-ounce skein of fine-quality Class C heavy-weight smooth classic worsted wool or acrylic yarn

- Size 8 circular knitting needle, 24 or 29 inches long

- 3 smaller-size circular needles to use as stitch holders (16 inches long if possible)

- 8 rubber needle point protectors

- Small safety pins

- Very thin plastic ring markers

- A small amount of heavy cotton crochet thread or ⅛-inch-wide knitting ribbon

- A large tapestry or small metal yarn needle

● 4 small purchased buttons ⁷⁄₁₆ inch in diameter

〰〰〰〰〰〰〰〰〰〰〰〰〰〰〰〰〰〰〰〰〰

All knitting patterns and instructions worth following begin with a statement about *gauge* or *tension*. Both words refer to how many stitches and how many rows there are in a 1-inch square or in a 4-inch square.

The *assumed* gauge for this baby sweater is 5 stitches per 1 inch on size 8 needles in stockinette stitch.

Gauge: 5 sts = 1 ″ in St st
Tension: 20 st = 4 ″ or 10 cm

5 sᴛ = 1ɪɴ

I do not usually make my students work a gauge swatch for this project. The best lesson about gauge they will ever learn will be to compare the differences in the sizes of the various students' sweaters all following the same instructions with the same number of stitches.

〰〰〰〰〰〰〰〰〰〰〰〰〰〰〰〰〰〰〰〰〰

Determine which way the "nap" of the yarn flows and use the yarn from either the inside or the outside of the ball (see chapter 3).

Use the rule of thumb of three to determine where to put the slip loop (see chapter 10). Divide the total number of stitches by the gauge. 57 divided by 5 = 12 (roughly). 3 × 12 = 36. 36 + 6 = 42.
Place a slip loop on the right-hand needle 42 inches from the end of the yarn.
Using a double strand method and placing ring markers after every 20 sts to make counting easier, cast on 57 stitches. Wrap the tail end of surplus yarn around your finger and secure it with a safety pin so you don't accidentally start to make the first row with the wrong end.

On #8 needle cast on 57.

c o 57.

〰〰〰〰〰〰〰〰〰〰〰〰〰〰〰〰〰〰〰〰〰

Remember that in chapter 22 we said that unless some other pattern stitch or trim is used along the top, bottom, and edges of stockinette-stitch fabric, it will roll and curl. The main body of this little garment will be made of stockinette stitch, and its necessary trim will be seed stitch. If you need to, review the sections on these stitches in chapter 22.

Work *even* in seed-stitch pattern for ½ inch, discarding the markers on the first row as you work along. The word *even* means without making any increases or decreases.

*Row 1) * K 1, P 1 *, repeat between *s across, ending K 1.*
Row 2) Rpt row 1.
Rpt these 2 rows once.

WORK SEED ST ½ IN.

~~~~~~~~~~~~~~~~~~~~~~~~~~

Have you thought about how we are going to make this silly sweater stay on our mythical baby? We could tie a ribbon bow under our baby's chin, but *real* babies drool on bows and ribbons wilt. Let's learn to make buttonholes.

But, alas buttonholes in seed stitch take a little forethought and planning. Also, unfortunately, this baby sweater is to be made before our mythical baby is born; before we know if it is a boy or a girl. Society has dictated that boys' buttonholes are made on the left side and that girls' buttonholes are made on the right side.

To cover either possibility (boy or girl), we are going to make buttonholes on *both* sides. When we know the sex of the child, we can sew over the unwanted buttonholes as we fasten on the buttons.

Work the first 2 stitches in the ordinary way according to the seed-stitch pattern. Stop, and determine how, according to the pattern. the *second* stitch on the left-hand needle should be made. Take the yarn between the tips of the needles to the correct side of the work to make that second stitch. Without inserting the right-hand needle into the next stitch, scoop up or wrap the yarn around the right-hand needle as if you were making that stitch. This will form an extra "yarn-over" loop on the right-hand needle. Now work the next 2 stitches together-as-if-they-were-one in whatever way that second stitch should be made. (This will decrease 1 stitch and compensate for the yarn over and its hole which is what we want for our button.) Work across the row in pattern stitch until 3 stitches remain, yarn over, work the next 2 stitches together in the pattern that the next-to-last-stitch should be, work the last remaining stitch in pattern.

*Next row) K 1, P 1, Y O, P 2 tog, * K 1, P 1 *, rpt bet *s across, until*
  5 sts remain, end K 1, Y O, P 2 tog, K 1, P 1.

WORK EYELET BUTTONHOLE AT BEG & END OF NEXT ROW.

Don't let it confuse you; it all means the same thing.

~~~~~~~~~~~~~~~~~~~~~~~~~~

If you need to review how to measure, see chapter 21.

Work even ½ inch more. (The piece measures 1 inch overall from cast on edge and 57 stitches remain.)

Repeat rows 1 & 2 twice more.

WORK EVEN ½ IN.

~~~~~~~~~~~~~~~~~~~~~~~~~~~~~~~~~~~~

Usually in Standard Simplified Knit and Crochet Instructions, the first time a word is used, it is spelled out in full. Thereafter it is often abbreviated *without* a period. Typesetting and paper and printing and shipping and storage are all expensive. Abbreviations are used to make it possible for you to purchase instructions at a reasonable price. I know, at first they seem terrifying and impossible, but they are really not. If you will read instructions *out loud* to yourself using the whole word, the full term intended, you will usually understand them in a flash. Just try it in the next paragraph of simplified instructions and substitute the whole word, the full term intended—that is, for M say out loud to yourself, "Place a marker on the right-hand needle."

Set ring markers to define front bands and raglan increase points as follows:

Work seed-stitch pattern across the first 4 stitches (to mark off the right front band), place a marker on the right-hand needle, purl 8 stitches (for the right front), place another marker, purl 7 (for right sleeve), marker, purl 19 (for back), marker, purl 7 (left sleeve), marker, purl 8 (left front), marker, work across the remaining 4 stitches in seed-stitch pattern (for left front band).

Six markers have been placed in the work. The first and the last markers separate the 4 edge stitches, which will *always* be worked even in seed-stitch pattern and will *never* be increased or decreased. The other 4 markers indicate the raglan increase points.

Work 4 Seed St, M, P 8, M, P 7, M, P 19, M , P 7, M, P 8, M,
    work 4 Seed St.

~~~~~~~~~~~~~~~~~~~~~~~~~~~~~~~~~~~~

Remember the definition of stockinette stitch is to alternate rows of all knit stitches with rows of all purl stitches. On this sweater we have just begun with a purl row.

The type of increase that I want you to use next for this raglan sweater is called *knitting in the front and the back of a stitch* (if you need to review it, see chapter 14). This increase leaves a purl-like bead on the knit side of the fabric and will add a decorative element to the raglan design.

On the flat-knit side of the stockinette-stitch fabric that we are using to make the center parts of this baby sweater, *we are going to add one stitch before and one stitch after each raglan increase point*. The all-purl rows on the reverse side of the stockinette stitch will be worked even and have no added or increased stitches.

Another way of saying it is:

Keeping right and left front seed-stitch bands even, increase one stitch before and after each raglan marker every other row. Since there are 4 raglan increase point markers and we are making extra stitches before and after them, it follows that we will be making 8 more sts on every k row. Continue in this manner until the piece measures 2 inches from the buttonhole row.

Begin raglan increase rows.
Row 1) *Work 4 edge sts in seed st pat, slip marker, * K to within 1 st of next marker, increase, sl M, inc in next st *, rpt bet *s 3 times, ending K to within 1 st of last M, sl M, work 4 edge sts in seed st pat as established. (65 sts remain.)*
Row 2) *P even bet bands.*
Rpt rows 1 & 2 until piece measures 2 " from last buttonhole.

Once you understand the basic idea of a raglan cardigan—of adding one stitch to the first half of the front, two stitches to the first sleeve, two stitches to the back, two sts to the next sleeve, and one stitch to the remaining front—it is easy as making pie. But trying to write it out in either Standard Simplified Instructions or in plain English is difficult, to say the least. Perhaps the difficulty in explaining the simple techniques is the reason why so few made-in-one-piece-from-the-top-down patterns are written.

~~~~~~~~~~~~~~~~~~~~~~~~~~~~~

Stop frequently and admire your work and yourself. You are making something out of nothing and you should be proud of what you are doing and proud of yourself for doing it!

Continue in this same manner, increasing on the knit rows and purling even between the front bands. The basic idea behind a knit-in-one-piece-from-the-top-down raglan sweater is to make a carefully calculated rectangle that grows bigger every other row and keeps the same proportions until that rectangle is large enough to be divided up into separate sleeves and body.

The piece should look like this:

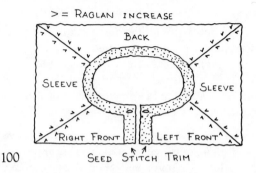

I expect you to finish this project whether you like the garment or not because it is a learning lesson. If, however, at this point on any other garment, you are not happy with the way it looks, do not continue. Don't put more time and effort into something that does not please you. Change it; get help; rip it out. Both the process and the product of knitting should be joy.

〰〰〰〰〰〰〰〰〰〰〰〰〰

Continue to work in this same manner, making a buttonhole on this row and every 2 inches thereafter, *until* there are 47 stitches on the back and the piece measures 3½ inches from the end of the neck band. (169 sts remain and the piece measures 4½ inches overall from cast-on at center back.)

Work as established until 47 sts on back and piece measures 4½".

WORK AS ESTABLISHED 4½ IN.

〰〰〰〰〰〰〰〰〰〰〰〰〰

Stop again! Check the work! Try the garment on! If you can, find a doll or a teddy bear or even a real live baby. If you cannot find a good model, use a small pillow or a rolled-up towel.

This is the key to all perfect-fit raglans made in one piece from the top down. Remember this procedure! Cut a forty-inch long length of size 8 crochet thread or ⅛-inch-wide knitting ribbon. Tie a button or a "bone" ring to one end of this thread or ribbon. Thread a tapestry needle on the other end. Now, one at a time, as if to purl, slip each of the stitches from the working knitting needle to the thread or ribbon. Pin the armholes together at the raglan increase points. *Try the garment on.*

Look at the sweater:

1. If you are pleased, you may continue.

2. If the garment is too small (narrow) *and* too short, continue in the same manner until it is long and wide enough.

3. If the garment is too big (wide) and/or too long, rip back a few rows.

4. If the garment is wide enough, but not long enough, work a few more rows even.

5. If the garment is long enough, but not wide enough, you will need to cast on extra sts for the sleeve and body width at the underarm division point.

After the sweater has been tried on, it will need to be returned to the regular needles in stages.

Using a smaller-size circular knitting needle secured at the opposite end with a rubber point protector, slip all of the stitches one at a time as if to purl to the extra needle. You may either work the stitches off the smaller needle onto the regular one, or you may slip them from one to the other.

~~~~~~~~~~~~~~~~~~~~~~~~~~~~~~~~~~~

When the desired length to the underarm has been reached, it is time to divide the work. The sleeves are going to be separated from the body.

(The first time you do this you will want to follow the instructions *exactly*—perhaps even having someone else reading them to you aloud while doing what it says. It is just different and new. After you've done it once, it won't bother or worry you at all.)

Divide the row:

Work across the left front band and the left front. Remove the marker and place these stitches on an extra circular needle and secure both ends of that needle with rubber point protectors. These stitches will be worked later. Work across the left sleeve. Slip the marker. Drop the ball of yarn you have been using. Do not cut it off; just leave it hanging there. Add new yarn and work across the back. Place these back stitches on an extra circular needle as before. Slip the marker and work across the last (right) sleeve. Remove the marker and place the remaining right front and right front band stitches on an extra circular needle as before. (*See drawing # 101 on following page.*)

The right front is purposely left unworked so that you will not have to join and conceal ends of yarn on the front edge band. The "old" yarn is left hanging so that both sleeves can be worked on the

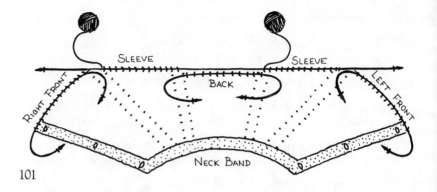

101

same needle at the same time with different yarn *to make sure that both sleeves will be the same.*

> *Work across front, place sts on holder. Work across sleeve, add new yarn. Work across back, place sts on holder. Work across sleeve, place rem front sts on holder.*

Always work the sleeves for a few inches before working the body to avoid stretching the underarms.

One of the reasons that I like knit-in-one-piece-from-the-top-down-for-perfect-fit sweaters is that it is almost impossible to run out of yarn. The sleeve and body lengths can be determined by the amount of yarn I have on hand. If I don't have enough for long sleeves, I can make three-quarter length sleeves. Or I can make the body an inch or two shorter than I had originally planned. On the flip side of the coin, if I have lots of yarn, I can make the sweater extra long or the sleeves extra full.

On future knit-from-the-top-down garments, you may not want to completely finish the sleeves before you resume work on the body. And you don't have to! Just be sure that you *do* work at least a couple of inches on the sleeves before you do the body.

~~~~~~~~~~~~~~~~~~~~~~

Because there is not extra yarn to work with and because there are only a few stitches involved at the underarms, you will be asked to use the simple single-strand, under-the-thumb cast-on method. If you need to review it, see chapter 10.

Since you will be narrowing and tapering the sleeves, you will not get a true measure of length along the edges. The edges will be longer than the center. In order to get an accurate length you need to place a marker in the center of the sleeve. You may also want to review how to place a horizontal thread marker in chapter 7.

When you are working two pieces of a garment on the same

needle at the same time, it could be easy to get confused about which piece should be worked next, especially if you have to put it down between the two pieces. To avoid confusion, with a scrap piece of yarn, tie one edge of one sleeve to one edge of the other so that you can't accidentally forget to work across both pieces.

Working on both sleeves at the same time on the same needle with separate yarn, cast on 2 stitches at each edge of each sleeve and place a horizontal thread marker in the middle of the row.

~~~~~~~~~~~~~~~~~~~~~~~~~~~~~~~

Work the sleeves even in stockinette stitch for ½ inch.

Work sleeves even in St st ½".

work sleeves ½ in.

~~~~~~~~~~~~~~~~~~~~~~~~~~~~~~~

Before you begin to shape and narrow the sleeves, please re-member what was said in chapter 14 about keeping track of in-creases and decreases with safety pins.

You are going to make full-fashioned decreases 2 stitches in from each edge of each sleeve. In order for the grain of the fabric to remain straight up and down, it will be necessary to use a type of decrease near the beginning of the row different from the type that you will use near the end of the row. Near the beginning of the row you will make a SSK decrease and near the end you will make a K 2 together decrease. You are to make these decreases every ½ inch 5 times.

Dec row. On K side, K 2, SSK, K to within 4 sts of end, K 2 tog, K 2.
Rpt every ½" 4 times.

dec i st each side every ½ in 5 times.

~~~~~~~~~~~~~~~~~~~~~~~~~~~~~~~

The sleeves should now measure 3 inches long from the horizon-tal thread marker.

Work even in seed stitch 1 inch (to match neckband).

Note: If you have accidentally gained or lost an extra stitch Standard Instructions may cause you to make ribbing instead of seed st (see chapter 22).

*Row 1) * K 1, P 1 *, rpt bet * s, end K 1.*
Row 2) Repeat row 1.
Rpt these 2 rows for 1".

WORK SEED ST 1 IN.

~~~~~~~~~~~~~~~~~~~~~~~~~~

If you need to review, binding off both knitwise and purlwise are explained in chapter 13. It is important that you retain the seed-stitch pattern as you bind off.

Maintaining pattern stitch as established, bind off all stitches. Be sure to form the stitches knitwise or purlwise as they should be for this final row as you bind off. Before you cut off the yarn, stop and think about it for a moment. You are going to have to put together the edges of the sleeves. I want you to weave the seam. Be sure to clip the yarn long enough to begin to make that seam. Even if you don't want to do the seam right away, you can use the technique of wrapping the yarn around your forefinger to form a loop and fastening it to the work with a small safety pin until you are ready for it.

Bind off all sts.

B O.

~~~~~~~~~~~~~~~~~~~~~~~~~~

In chapter 25 on finishing techniques, you will find the instructions to weave a "row-to-row" seam. Reread it if you need to. Make the sleeve seam.

~~~~~~~~~~~~~~~~~~~~~~~~~~

You are now ready to resume work on the body of the garment. Review, if you choose, chapter 18 about picking up and knitting new stitches.

Beginning at the underarm edge of the left front where the stitches were left unworked, add new yarn. Pick up 3 stitches from the sleeve cast-on.

Stop and think a moment. You cast on 2 stitches at each side of each sleeve. 2 + 2 = 4. Why are you now told to pick up 3 stitches over the underarm cast-on? Because you used half of each edge stitch to form the seam! 4 − 1 = 3, or one less than the total that you cast on for the sleeves.

In picking up stitches, work as closely to the edge as possible. Don't be afraid of picking up the stitches in the very outside loop. The back side of the pick-up row will fill in a lot of holes and spaces.

Work across the remaining left-front stitches from the holder. Turn. Work back across this front and the picked-up stitches. Work across the back stitches from the holder. Pick up 3 more stitches over the sleeve underarm cast-on. Work across the remaining right front stitches from the holder.

Stop! Check your gauge and your work. The piece should look like this:

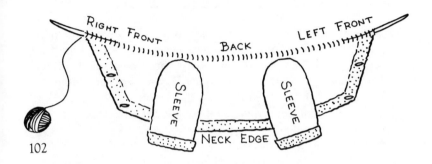

102

With the whole body now as one piece, work even in stockinette stitch 1 inch. Stop and try the sweater on again to double-check that it is just as you want it to be.

Work across rem front. Work across front, C O 3 sts at underarm, work across back, C O 3 at U A, work across front. Work even 1".

RESUME WORK ON BODY 1 IN.

~~~~~~~~~~~~~~~~~~~~~~~~~~~~

All the babies that I know wear diapers. We want this little baby sweater to flare out to cover the diapers. It will not be nipped in at the waist or hips as many other types of garments are. Also, we do want this sweater to hang straight at the front and do not want the fronts to separate to leave the poor baby's tummy exposed to the cold. The best way to accomplish both of these fitting techniques is to increase at the *center back.* (This applies for knitted coats and jackets of all sizes.)

An occasional increase in the body of a garment that will allow extra ease and width should be both invisible and cause the fabric grain to move neither to the right nor to the left. A *blind stockinette stitch increase* will work very well here. You may review it in chapter 14.

To position the increase, place a ring marker in the center back. Remember to place buttonholes in the front bands 2 inches apart.

Now increase *before* the marker. Work even for ¾ inch and then increase *after* the marker. Continue to increase in this manner until the piece measures 4 inches long at the underarms, or 1 inch less than the desired finished length.

Work in St st 4″ inc'ing 1 st at center back every ¾″.

INC'ING 1 ST AT CTR BACK EVERY ¾ IN, WORK IN ST ST 4 IN.

〜〜〜〜〜〜〜〜〜〜〜〜〜〜〜〜〜

Work even in seed-stitch pattern again for 1 inch to match the neck edge and front bands. You may have to juggle and "fudge" 1 stitch to make the seed-stitch pattern come out right. Stop about 3 stitches before you get to the final front border. Count backwards from the border to see if you are coming out with the correct sequence of k 1, p 1. If it won't come out right, simply work 2 stitches together.

Standard Simplified Instructions could cause a problem here depending upon whether you begin the border after completing a k or a p row, and upon how many times you inc'd, rendering an odd or an even number of sts. You will have no trouble at all, however, if you have learned the definition of seed-stitch pattern.

WORK IN SEED ST 1 IN.

〜〜〜〜〜〜〜〜〜〜〜〜〜〜〜〜〜

Again, maintaining the pattern st, bind off all stitches.

B o all sts.

BO.

〜〜〜〜〜〜〜〜〜〜〜〜〜〜〜〜〜

Securely weave in all loose ends of yarn. You may want to work a duplicate stitch over the stitches at the underarm division point which normally have become stretched.

Hopefully, we now know the sex of the mythical child and can attach the commercially purchased buttons over the unwanted buttonholes.

Hand-wash block the sweater (see chapter 26). No steam blocking should be necessary because this garment was knitted to fit properly.

I hope that you have enjoyed making this learning project. I never said that it was a thing of beauty or that it was easy to do. What you choose to do with it now is your business. But it was my business that you have had an opportunity to learn and do, and to learn why you are doing it. The Dumb Baby Sweater may well go its own way, but I hope that the essentials that I have taught you will stay with you.

THE STUPID BABY BONNET

Note: These instructions follow the same format as the baby sweater above. Be sure that you read the introductory remarks that are printed for both these projects.

Materials Needed:

- 1 3½- or 4-ounce skein of fine-quality Class C heavy weight worsted wool or acrylic yarn

- Size 8 knitting needles any length, straight or circular (or any size needles that will give the correct gauge)

- Very thin plastic ring markers

- Slip-on ring markers

- Heavy cotton crochet thread for horizontal marker

- A small-size double-pointed "sock" needle

- An extra-small-size circular needle (to pick up stitches)

- Rubber needle point protectors

- Small safety pins

- A large tapestry or small metal yarn needle

- 1 yard of ¾-inch-wide purchased ribbon for tie

Determine nap of the yarn (chapter 3.)

~~~~~~~~~~~~~~~~~~~~~~

The gauge or tension for this garment is four and one half sts per one inch. (All of the following say the same thing.)

Gauge: *4½ sts = 1" in stockinette st*
9 sts = 2" in stockinette st
18 sts = 4" or 10 cm in stockinette st
Tension: *18 sts = 10 cm in stockinette st*

GAUGE: 4½ STS = 1 IN

Please review the chapter on gauge if you need to.

To save time take time to determine gauge before starting.

~~~~~~~~~~~~~~~~~~~~~~~~~~~~~~~~~~~~~

Follow the rule of thumb of three to determine where the slip loop should be placed to begin your casting on (see chapter 10).

~~~~~~~~~~~~~~~~~~~~~~~~~~~~~~~~~~~~~

Using a double strand method, placing ring markers after every 20 sts to make the counting easier, cast on 50 sts.

On # 8 needles cast on 50 sts.

C O 50.

Wind any remaining surplus yarn around your finger and fasten it with a small safety pin to keep it out of your way.

~~~~~~~~~~~~~~~~~~~~~~~~~~~~~~~~~~~~~

Work means "do." *Even* means "without any increases or decreases." Remember, or review the definition of seed stitch from chapter 22 and the preceding learning lesson. There will be a difference in the way that Standard Instructions read according to whether there are an odd or an even number of stitches.

Work even in seed stitch 1 inch.

*Row 1) * K 1, P 1 *, repeat between *s.*
Row 2) Rpt row 1.
Rpt rows 1 & 2 3 times.

WORK EVEN IN SEED STITCH 1 IN.

~~~~~~~~~~~~~~~~~~~~~~~~~~~~~~~~~~~~~

Knit one row to form a purl-ridge definition row.

Next row) K.

K 1 ROW.

~~~~~~~~~~~~~~~~~~~~~~~~~~~~~~~~~~~~~

Review the discussion of stockinette stitch in chapter 22; review the blind stockinette stitch increase in chapter 14.

On the next row increase 5 stitches evenly across as follows: Knit 1, * increase, knit 12 *. Repeat between *s 4 times, ending knit 1. (55 stitches remain.)

*Next row) K inc'ing 5 as follows: K 5, * inc, K 10, *, rpt btn *s across,
ending K 5. (55 sts rem.)*

WORKING IN ST ST INC 5 STS EVENLY ACROSS THE NEXT ROW.

You'll be doing two things in this section, establishing stockinette
stitch and increasing across the row.

After knitting to make the purl ridge on the last row, by making
the knit stitch on this row you begin the first row of stockinette
stitch and establish that this is the outside, the public side, of the
bonnet. Of course, stockinette stitch can begin with either a knit or
a purl row. I have chosen to start with a knit row on this project.

Sometimes instructions will give you specific directions concerning the spacing between increases. More often, though, instructions will leave it up to you to figure out how many stitches
there ought to be between increase points. Often it is just as well to
guess, or to randomly place slip-on ring markers across the row
before you begin, and then increase at the markers. Just *please* do
not bunch them all up in one place or put them in at the edge
stitches.

~~~~~~~~~~~~~~~~~~~~~~~~~~~~~~~~~

Work even in stockinette stitch 1 inch more until the piece measures
2 inches overall from cast-on.

Work even 1".

WORK EVEN 1 *in.*

If you need reminding about how to measure, see chapter 21.

~~~~~~~~~~~~~~~~~~~~~~~~~~~~~~~~~

The crown of the head of our mythical baby needs extra room and
this gives us an excellent opportunity to learn to make short rows.
They are discussed fully in chapter 19. I won't take the space here to
lead you through the 9 steps again. Simply follow them, making 6
rows 8 stitches shorter every time.

Hold 8 sts in waiting at end of next 6 rows.

SHORT ROW 8 STS 6 TIMES.

When you have completed the short-rowing, stop and admire it.
From the outside, you shouldn't be able to see a thing, but the
middle of the bonnet will be longer than the outside edges to fit
over the baby's head.

Since the center of the bonnet is now longer than the outside edges, we need to place a horizontal thread marker to have an accurate place from which to measure. Reread chapter 7 if you don't remember how to do it.

~~~~~~~~~~~~~~~~~~~~~~~~~~~~

Work even in stockinette stitch as established 2 inches more until the piece measures 4 inches long overall, measured at the side edges. End with a purl row.

Work even in St st 2"

WORK EVEN 2 IN.

Work even in pattern stitch as established is another one of those catch-all phrases that knitting designers use. It means that once you have gotten the pattern going merrily along and you can see what you are doing, keep on doing it.

End with a p row means to stop after completing a purl row.

~~~~~~~~~~~~~~~~~~~~~~~~~~~~

Now it is time to quit working on the sides of the bonnet and continue only with the back flap.

Review binding-off in chapter 13.

Place a slip-on ring marker 18 stitches in from each edge of the piece. *Bind off loosely, as if to knit, at the beginning of the row, the first 17 stitches. (One loop will remain on the right-hand needle.) Remove the ring marker. Place the loop that is on the right-hand needle onto the left-hand needle. Through the fronts of the stitches, work that loop and the adjacent stitch together as if they were one. Work even across *. At the beginning of the next row, repeat the directions between the *s. (You should then have 19 stitches remaining.) Purl across these remaining stitches.

At the beg of the next 2 rows, bind off 18 sts.

B O 18 STS AT BEG OF NEXT 2 ROWS.

After you have bound off about 3 stitches, stop and check to make sure that they as loose and elastic as the rest of the knitted fabric. If they are not, rip them out and do it over again. If they are, you may continue.

~~~~~~~~~~~~~~~~~~~~~~~~~~~~

We need to taper this back flap because the baby's neck is narrower than the back of its head. We are going to do that with matched decreases. Ordinary instructions will *not* give you matching decreases. Review chapter 14 so that you understand the problem and realize that *you* can do a better than ordinary job.

Let's take this opportunity to learn to do the two different matching sets of full-fashioned decreases. Making them and viewing the finished project will allow you to choose in the future which set you prefer. (Remember to have your tiny safety pins handy to keep track of the dec's.)

> *First set of decreases:* *Knit 2, SKP, knit to within 4 stitches of end, knit 1, with the left-hand needle, lift this stitch off the right-hand needle and put it *back* onto the left-hand needle, lift as if to purl the third stitch from the end up and over the fourth stitch and off the left-hand needle. As if to knit, move the closest stitch on the left-hand needle to the right-hand needle. Knit the remaining 2 stitches. Work 3 rows even in stockinette stitch.* Repeat between the *s 3 times.
>
> *Second set of decreases:* *Knit 2, SSK, knit to within 4 stitches of end, knit 2 together, Knit 2. Purl across the next row *. Repeat between the *s one time more. (7 stitches remain.)

> *K 2, SKP, K to within 4 sts of end, K 2 tog, K 2 *. Rpt bet *s every 4th row 3 times, then every other row 2 times. (7 sts rem.)* (Of course, you know from chapter 14 that these decreases don't really match.)

DEC 1 ST EACH END EVERY 4TH ROW 4 TIMES THEN EVERY OTHER ROW 2 TIMES.

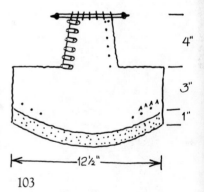

103

Notice how the flap neatly tapers in and the edge three stitches appear to be raised. The decreases add a decorative design element to the flap.

Hang in there! You're almost done. And look at how much you are learning. The stupid bonnet should look like this: (*see drawing # 103*).

There should be seven stitches remaining. The back flap would now measure four inches long. It should be the same length as the bound-off stitches. Fold the two edges together and find out.

If the flap is a bit too short, you may work a couple of rows of stockinette stitches without making more decreases.

~~~~~~~~~~~~~~~~~~~~

Chapter 12 tells you how to move stitches from one needle to another.

Slip as if to purl these 7 remaining sts to a small-size double-pointed sock needle. Secure both ends of the needle with rubber point protectors.

Put back flap sts on holder.

PLACE REM STS ON HOLDER.

~~~~~~~~~~~~~~~~~~~~~~~~~~~~~~~~~

Review invisible seam weaving in chapter 25 on finishing. Our problem here is to weave bound-off stitches to a vertical edge of rows. Remember that there may be more rows than there are bound-off stitches, and some juggling may be necessary.

Go ahead and weave the seam.

Sew side of back flap to BO sts.

MAKE SEAMS.

~~~~~~~~~~~~~~~~~~~~~~~~~~~~~~~~~

Review the section in chapter 18 about picking up and knitting new stitches. Have tiny safety pins handy to divide each of the sides of the bonnet into halves, and have ring markers available. (These things aren't really necessary on this small a piece, but it is a good learning experience to use them.)

Mark the center of each 4-inch edge with a safety pin. With your left hand, hold the bonnet edge up. Make sure that the outside, the public side is facing you. Put the unstoppered end of a small-size circular needle in your right hand. Starting at the seed-stitch end, along the very edge, insert the needle into the first stitch. Pick up a ball of yarn. Leaving a tail end that is at least 6 inches long, knit a stitch.

Work as close to the edge as possible. Don't be afraid of picking up stitches in the very outside loop. The back side of the pick-up row will fill in a lot of holes and spaces.

In the same way, pick up and knit 6 more stitches to reach the safety pin. Place a ring marker on the needle. Remove the pin. Pick up and knit 8 more stitches to the holder. (There are now 15 stitches on the needle.) Place another ring marker. Knit across the 7 stitches from the holder and place another marker. Now pick up and knit another 8 stitches to the next safety pin to match the other side. Place a ring marker and remove the pin. Pick up and knit 7 more stitches to the outside edge of the seed-stitch front band. There should be 37 stitches picked up and knitted onto the small size circular needle.

Always stop and recount at the ring markers and again at the end of the row. It is easy to pick up or drop one or two extra stitches now if you have made an error. It is difficult to change things at the end of the next row when your pattern may not work out because you have picked up the wrong number of stitches.

With the right side of the garment facing, pick up 15 sts to holder, k 7 from holder, pick up 15 sts to end.

PICK UP FROM HOLDER AND ALONG BOTTOM EDGE 37 STS.

With the private side of the bonnet facing you, change to the regular-size needle and throw up a purl-ridge row by knitting across, discarding the markers as you go.

Review the general definition of ribbing in chapter 22. I always like to work one-by-one ribbing over an odd number of stitches so I end up with the same kind of stitch on the finished edges.

Work even in one-by-one ribbing for ½ inch.

*Row 1) * K 1, P 1. * rpt bet *s across, ending K 1.*
*Row 2) P 1, * K 1, P 1 * rpt bet *s.*
Rpt rows 1 & 2 one time.

WORK ½ IN IN K I, P I RIB.

*Next row, right side facing, K 1, P 1, K 1, * Y O, K 2 tog *, rpt bet *s, ending K 1, P 1, K1.*

NEXT ROW WORK EYELET.

Eyelet row? Yarn-over? She has got to be kidding! Come on, hang in there; it's not that bad!

We need a set of holes in this ribbing to thread a ribbon through in order to tie this stupid bonnet on the baby's head. Yarn-overs make nice holes. But they also add an extra stitch. For every yarn-over we are going to have to make a decrease.

All you are supposed to do is to work the first 3 sts in ribbing as usual. Then make a yarn-over and work the next two stitches together as if they were one all across the row until the three final stitches, which are worked in ribbing.

Work even in ribbing ½ inch more.

Work even in pat as established ½ ".

RIB ½ IN MORE.

~~~~~~~~~~~~~~~~~~~~~~~~~~~~~~~~~~

Review chapter 13 on binding off.

Loosely bind off all stitches, maintaining the ribbing pattern.

Loosely bind off.

B O ALL STS.

~~~~~~~~~~~~~~~~~~~~~~~~~~~~~~~~~~

Review chapter 25 on finishing, particularly the securing of tag ends of yarn.

Finish.

SECURE ENDS OF YARN

~~~~~~~~~~~~~~~~~~~~~~~~~~~~~~~~~~

Hand-wash block the bonnet, placing a rolled-up towel or small pillow inside it for shaping as it finishes drying after being wrapped in towels.

Block.

STEAM.

If you read chapter 25, you will know how I feel about applying steam at home to handknitted articles.

~~~~~~~~~~~~~~~~~~~~~~~~~~~~~~~~~~

Weave purchased ribbon through the eyelets.

ADD RIBBON.

Notice how the ribbon works through the eyelets, ending up on the same side as it went in to give a very finished and professional effect!

Tie a bow in the ribbon and sit back and relax. Admire the bonnet. Admire yourself! You have mastered enough detail to make *any* simple garment. In the future, on other projects, you may encounter directions of either the National Simplified Standards type or the older, more concise ones. It will not matter to you, for you will not be at a loss to understand them. Neither will you be frightened off.

Just for fun, go back through these two learning lessons and read first only the *italicized* instructions, then only the ALL CAPITAL directions. They should now make sense to you. You have learned to read instructions and to follow even skimpy directions. You have made something out of nothing. You have mastered a new hobby and how to be creative with it, doing it all with a sense of humor.

SUZANNE'S BABY BOOTIES
(TO MATCH THE DUMB BABY SWEATER AND THE STUPID BABY BONNET)

One of my students, who was about to become a new grandmother, asked me to design for her a pair of baby booties to match the sweater and bonnet she had made as learning lessons in order to have a complete layette set for her daughter-in-law. That afternoon I quickly scribbled out the simple directions to be made flat with a seam up the back.

But I awoke in the middle of the night with a different thought: What a wonderful opportunity to learn to use four double-pointed needles and experience working in the round. In the morning I wrote out these instructions:

Materials Needed:

- Small amount (about 1 oz) of Class C smooth classic knitting worsted yarn

- One set of 4 double-pointed # 8 knitting needles 7 inches long

- A ring marker

- 4 rubber point protectors

- A tapestry or metal yarn needle

- 1 yard ½-inch-wide purchased ribbon

  Cast on 24 stitches. Evenly divide the stitches in groups of 8 onto three needles. Place a ring marker after the last stitch to mark the beginning of a round. Make sure that the stitches are not twisted and join together, using the fourth needle to work with to form a triangular round. (After you work

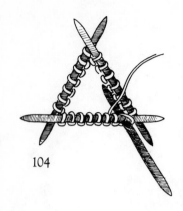

104

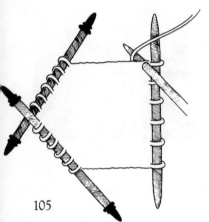

105

across 8 stitches, that needle will then become the empty right-hand needle.) (See drawing # 104.)

Work even in seed stitch for 1 inch.
(Remember, seed stitch is rnd 1),* K 1, P 1 *, rpt bet *s around. Rnd 2) As the sts face you, P the K sts and K the P sts. Rpt these 2 rnds for pat st.)

Maintaining pattern stitch, decrease before and after the ring marker every ½ inch 3 times, until the piece measures 2 ½ inches long from cast-on and 18 stitches remain. Rearrange the stitches so that there are 6 sts on each of three needles. Work an eyelet row of * Y O, K 2 tog *, around. Work 3 rnds of stockinette stitch.
(Remember St st in the round is K every st of every rnd.)

Turn the work around and purl back across the last 6 stitches just knitted.
    Put point protectors on the other two double pointed needles to act as stitch holders while you work on these 6 sts for the instep of the bootie in flat stockinette stitch for 2 inches. End after completing a K row.
    Pick up and K 8 sts along the side of the instep. (See drawing #105.)
    Knit the 6 stitches from the first holder. Knit the 6 stitches from the next holder. Pick up and knit 8 stitches along the other side of the instep.
    Working again in the round, rearrange the stitches equally among the three needles. Work even in stockinette stitch 2 inches.
    Make a decrease round as follows: * K 1, K 2 tog *, rpt bet *s around.
    Rearrange the stitches so that they are distributed evenly on two needles lengthwise of the sole of the bootie. Turn the piece inside out. Holding the two needles parallel, bind off the stitches together to form a seam.
    Weave in all tag ends of yarn. Weave ribbon through the eyelet row for ties.
    Make other bootie to match.

GLOSSARY

General note: In Standard Simplified knit and crochet instructions, abbreviations do *not* have periods.

alt: An abbreviation for "alternate."

approx: An abbreviation for "approximate" or "approximately."

as established: Means to keep on doing what you were doing before you were interrupted. If you were making a fancy pattern stitch before, you may have to start the pattern sequence at some spot other than the beginning of the first repeat.

as if to knit: A term that means to insert the needle from the front to the back of the work.

as if to purl: A term that means to insert the needle from the back to the front of the work.

asterisk: A starlike symbol, *, this is used in knitting and crochet directions to indicate that the instructions that follow are to be repeated.

batwing sleeve: A way of making sleeves as an integral part of the body of the sweater. Usually stitches are cast on at the underarm for the additional width necessary to cover the arms. These stitches will lie crosswise as the garment hangs on the human body.

bauble: A made-on-purpose glob of knitted or crocheted stitches.

bead: The horizontal strand that lies directly across the base of a purl stitch.

bead: To work commercial beads into knitted or crocheted fabric. Before starting the beaded row, use a small tapestry or large darning needle to string the beads on the working yarn. *For knits:* usually done in stockinette stitch fabric with the public side of the fabric facing you, work to the desired spot to place a bead, take the yarn to the front of the work, as if to purl slip the next stitch, slide the bead into place, take the yarn to the back of the work, knit as directed. *For crochets* (Usually done in single crochet). With the public side of the fabric facing you, slide a bead into place, insert the hook into the next stitch and make a single crochet.

beg: An abbreviation for "beginning."

bet: An abbreviation for "between."

bind off: To fasten off the stitches in a secure way and quit working on them.

blind stockinette stitch increase: A type of increase that is almost imperceptible to the casual eye. It is made by picking up the strand before the next stitch and knitting into the back of it. This increase does not cause the grain of the fabric to move either to the right or to the left. It goes straight up.

bobbin: Devices to hold small amounts of yarn. Used in multicolor work, especially Argyles.

brackets: Square marks, [ ]. Symbols used in knitting and crochet directions to indicate that the instructions that follow are to be repeated.

CC: An abbreviation for "contrasting color."

cap: The upper portion of a sleeve where it will join the shoulder of a garment. A sleeve cap.

cable: The name for a whole group of knitting pattern stitches in which some of the stitches are worked out of sequence in a very particular way.

cast off: Means the same thing as "Bind off"; to get rid of stitches in a secure way.

cast on: The name of the procedure for putting the first row of loops on a knitting needle.

ch: An abbreviation for the crochet stitch called a "chain" made by laying the yarn over the hook and drawing it through the loop on the hook.

ch-sp: An abbreviation for the crochet term "chain space."

cm: An abbreviation for "centimeter."

cont: An abbreviation for "continue."

continue in the same manner: Keep on doing what you were doing. If you were decreasing at regular intervals, keep on doing it. If you were increasing in a certain manner at specified spots, continue to do so.

crab stitch: A single crochet stitch made in the opposite direction, that is from left to right across the row. Often used as the final row, it gives a ropelike edging. (The only trick to it is to draw up a *long* loop before you yarn-over and go through two loops.)

dc: An abbreviation for the "double crochet" stitch, which is made by making a yarn-over before inserting the hook into the appropriate stitch and working off the loops on the hook in two steps.

dec: An abbreviation for "decrease."

decrease: To get rid of loops so you won't have to work them again. There are many ways to make decreases. Often your directions will not tell you what type of decrease to use.

dolman sleeve: A type of sleeve that is extra wide at the underarm. Often these sleeves spring from the garment at the waistline. They may cause difficulty when you try to wear a coat or jacket over them.

dpn: An abbreviation for "double-pointed needle."

dropped shoulder sleeve: A type of sleeve that emerges from an exaggeratedly wide-shouldered garment. A style common in ethnic garments.

dtr: An abbreviation for a "double treble" crochet stitch, which is made by making four yarn-overs before inserting the hook in the appropriate stitch and working the loops off the hook in four steps.

duplicate stitch: An embroidery stitch worked over knitted fabric.

even: A term that means "without increasing or decreasing." Work *even* means to work on the same number of stitches.

Fair Isle: The name of certain multicolored patterns in which a few stitches are worked with one color and then the next few stitches are worked with a different color.

fasten off: This means to cut the working yarn, always leaving at least a six-inch tail end, *and* pulling that end up through the last stitch to end the work.

felt: A process (on purpose or by accident) of applying steam to woolen fibers which causes them to mat together and become stiff and firm, as in a felt hat.

foll: An abbreviation for "following."

fisherman: A style of heavy warm sweaters copied from the designs worn by ethnic fishermen, usually from northern Europe. Also wool that is "unscoured" or unwashed, leaving the natural lanolin in it to make it water repellent.

flat knitting: An old phrase for stockinette stitch.

g: An abbreviation for "gram" or "grams."

garter stitch: To make knitted fabric by knitting every stitch of every row when working back and forth on a flat piece, or by knitting and purling alternate rounds when working circular.

gauge: The number of stitches and rows there are in a measured square of knitted fabric. Gauge is sometimes given for one inch, two inches, or four inches (which is ten centimeters). Usually written something like *6 st = 1*, or *22 sts = 10 cm*.

gm: An abbreviation for "gram(s)."

gr(s): An abbreviation for "gram(s)."

grafting: A synonym for the Kitchner stitch. To weave a row of knitting in thin air to join together two pieces of knitting which have free exposed loops.

grp(s): An abbreviation for "group(s)." Sometimes it refers to a cluster of stitches or a multiple of a pattern stitch.

hdc: An abbreviation for the "half double crochet" stitch, which is made by making a yarn-over before the hook is inserted. Unlike a double crochet, all three loops are worked off at one time.

inc: An abbreviation for "increase."

increase: To make an extra loop or stitch that will be worked as a regular stitch on the next row. There are many ways to increase. Often instructions do not tell you which kind of an increase to make.

in the same manner: Means to "do it just like you did it before."

Jacquard: Originally the word meant colored chevron-shaped stripes. Now it is used loosely to mean many kinds of multicolored knitting and crochet.

jersey: An old term for smooth knitted fabric. It also means a simple, classic long-sleeved pullover sweater.

k or K: An abbreviation for "knit," meaning "make a knit stitch."

k 2 tog: An abbreviation for "through the front loops, knit the next two stitches together." It is a type of decrease that slopes to the right.

k, k, y o, psso: A type of decrease that slopes to the left. It means to "knit, knit, yarn over, pass the knitted stitches over the yarn over and off the tip of the needle."

krb: An abbreviation for "knit in the row below."

knit in the front and back: A type of increase.

knitwise: Short for "insert the needle from the front to the back as if to knit."

Kitchner stitch: A special way of manufacturing a row of stitches in thin air between two pieces of knitted fabric that have free exposed loops. Synonomous with "grafting."

LH: An abbreviation for "left hand."

lp(s): An abbreviation for "loop(s)."

m: An abbreviation for "meter" or "meters."

m: Marker.

m 1: An instruction to "make one stitch," which is a type of increase.

MC: An abbreviation for "main color."

make one-English: A type of increase made by knitting under the strand that lies before the next stitch.

make one-European: A type of increase made by picking up the strand that lies before the next stitch and knitting into the back loop of it. It is synonomous with "blind stockinette stitch increase."

mm: An abbreviation for "millimeters."

multiple: The *number* of stitches that comprise a sequence of stitches that will produce a certain pattern effect.

nap: Refers to the direction in which the individual hairs are laid in the spinning of a yarn.

oz: An abbreviation for "ounce."

p or P: An abbreviation for "purl." It means "make a purl stitch."

parenthesis: Curved vertical lines, ( ) . They are used in knit and crochet instructions to indicate a group of directions that will be repeated.

partial knitting: A method of knitting only a certain number of the total stitches on a row. Used to "turn the heel" of a sock.

passover: A knitting technique made with the left-hand needle which lifts the second stitch on the right-hand needle over the first stitch and off the needle.

pat(s): An abbreviation for "pattern" or "patterns." It often means the same as "multiple" or "multiples," and refers to the number of sequences of stitches across a row.

patterns: A term that is often used very sloppily. It can mean the number of multiple repeats across a row. It can mean several different types of textured fabric variations. It can also mean "directions" or "instructions". (Try to figure it out from the context in which it is used.)

picot: A series of bumps along an edge of either knitted or crocheted fabric.

ply: The number of strands that are twisted together to form a single strand of yarn. An example might be four-ply or twelve-ply yarn. In today's world the term is meaningless in trying to figure out how thick a yarn is.

ply: A verb meaning "twist."

popcorn: A cluster of knitted or crocheted stitches.

psso: An abbreviation for "passover."

public-side/private-side: Terms that I invented to keep track of which side of the fabric one is working on. The phrase "right side" can very easily be confused with the "right-hand side" of a garment and on a reversible fabric the words "inside" and "outside" are meaningless.

purl: Means to "make the next stitch a purl stitch."

purlwise: Short for "insert the needle from the back to the front as if to purl."

raglan sleeve: A style of sleeve in which the cap or tip tapers all the way up to the neckline. It is a very satisfactory and flattering kind of sleeve for knitted garments.

rem: An abbreviation for "remain."

remain: A term that means the stitches that are left after you have done something. Often after you have made a series of bind-offs and/or decreases the directions will tell you how many stitches you should have "remaining" to work on.

rep: An abbreviation for "repeat."

repeat: This word can have several meanings. It can mean to "do it over again." Sometimes it refers to how many rows it is necessary to make to achieve a complete pattern stitch design. It is also used in reference to how many multiples there are across a row. (Try to determine its meaning from the context where it is used.)

rev st st: An abbreviation for "reverse stockinette stitch."

reverse stockinette stitch: A name that means fabric made of knitting one row, purling one row, then repeating the sequence, in which the purl side will be used for the public side of the garment. Simply stated, it is stockinette stitch knitting worn inside out.

rib: A verb that means to make "ribbing."

ribbing: The generic name of a type of knitted fabric that is very elastic and does not curl up at the top or bottom. Ribbing is the regular alternation of knit and purl stitches along a row where on the subsequent rows the knit stitches are knitted and the purl stitches are purled. Ribbing can be made K 1, P 1, or K 2, P 2, or any other combination of K and P stitches.

RH: An abbreviation for "right hand."

rpt: An abbreviation for "repeat."

RS: An abbreviation for "right side."

right side: It is often difficult to know whether this means the side that is not the left side or if it means the side that is not the wrong side of an article.

rnd(s): An abbreviation for "round(s)."

round: When knitting a circular tube, the individual rows are usually called "rounds."

saddle sleeve: A type of sleeve in which the cap is extended to fit across the top of the shoulder to the neckline. It is a very wearable and flattering kind of sleeve for knits.

sc: An abbreviation for the "single crochet" stitch. The hook is inserted in the appropriate spot, the yarn is passed over the hook and a new loop drawn up, and the yarn is laid over the hook again and drawn through the two loops on the hook.

seed stitch: The name of a pattern stitch that makes a reversible nonroll fabric. The first row is made K 1, P1. On the second and all following rows as the stitches face you, knit the purl stitches and purl the knit stitches.

selv: An abbreviation for "selvedge" or "selvedge stitch."

selvage: An alternate spelling for "selvedge."

selvedge: A noun that means the outside vertical edge of a fabric.

selvedge stitch: The stitch that is on the outside vertical edge of knitted fabric.

set-in sleeve: An ordinary kind of sleeve. It often looks terrible in knitted garments because the designer planned it wrong.

short-rowing: A way of turning around in the middle of a row without leaving a hole. Synonomous with "partial knitting" and "holding stitches in waiting." It is a useful technique for making darts.

SKP: An abbreviation for "slip, knit, passover."

sl: An abbreviation in knitting for "slip," or in crochet to make a "slip stitch."

sl st: An abbreviation for the crocheted "slip stitch."

slip, knit, passover: A type of decrease that slopes to the left. It means to "slip as-if-to-knit the next stitch, knit the next stitch, with the tip of the left-hand needle pass the slipped stitch up and over the knitted stitch and off the end of the needle."

sl: An abbreviation for "slip."

sl st: An abbreviation for the crocheted "slip stitch."

slip loop: A term that means the beginning loop for both knit and crochet. It counts as one stitch in knitting. It is not counted in crocheting.

slip, slip, knit: A type of decrease that slopes to the left. It means to "one at a time, as-if-to-knit, slip the next two stitches to the right hand needle. Into the fronts of these two stitches, insert the tip of the left-hand needle and knit these two stitches together as if they were one."

slip stitch: The name of a crochet stitch made by inserting the hook into the appropriate place, yarn over and draw up a loop, pull that loop through the original stitch.

sp(s): An abbreviation for "space(s)."

ssk: An abbreviation for "slip, slip, knit."

st: An abbreviation for "stitch."

stitches in waiting: This term has two meanings. It can mean the remaining stitches that are not used for short-rowing. It can also mean stitches that are sitting on a stitch holder.

st st: An abbreviation for "stockinette stitch."

stockinette stitch: The name of a type of knitted fabric that is made by knitting one row and purling back on the next when working on a flat piece. In circular knitting, it is made by knitting every stitch of every round. It is the most common type of knitting. One side of the fabric is flat and smooth. The other side of the fabric is covered with pearllike beads. Older instruction books may call it "flat knitting," "jersey," or "tricot."

tapestry needle: The name of a kind of sewing needle that has a blunt tip. It may be of any size.

tension: A term that has two meanings. Tension is synonomous for "gauge" in many Europoean instruction books. The word also means "flow" or "finished appearance," as in, "It has an uneven tension."

t-ch: An abbreviation used in crocheting that means "the turning chain."

tbl: An abbreviation for "through the back loop."

tog: An abbreviation for "together."

tr: An abbreviation for the "triple" crochet stitch in which there are two yarn-overs before inserting the hook into the next stitch and the loops are worked off in three steps.

wb: An abbreviation for "take the yarn between the tips of the needles to the back of the work."

wf: An abbreviation for "take the yarn between the tips of the needles to the front of the work."

wl bk: An abbreviation for "between the tips of the needles take the wool to the back of the work."

wl fwd: An abbreviation for "between the tips of the needles take the wool to the front of the work."

work: An overworked word that just means "do." It saves the writer thought, time, effort, and energy in writing instructions.

WS: An abbreviation for "wrong side."

wrn: An abbreviation for "wrap the wool around the needle." It means the same as "yarn-over."

wyib: An abbreviation for "with the yarn at the back of the work."

wyif: An abbreviation for "with the yarn at the front of the work."

y b: An abbreviation for "take the yarn between the tips of the needles to the back of the work."

yarn-over: A kind of increase made by wrapping the yarn around the right-hand needle before inserting it into the next stitch. On the next row the wrap is worked as an ordinary stitch. This increase leaves a hole in the work.

yd(s): An abbreviation for "yard(s)."

y fwd: An abbreviation for "bring the yarn between the tips of the needles to the front of the work."

y o, yo, Y O, or YO: They are all just abbreviations for "yarn-over."

yon: An abbreviation for "yarn over the needle."

INDEX

Gauge
    and circular knitting needle,
        26–27
    as factor in neck-down one-
        piece garments, 35–36
    of garter stitch, 96
    measuring and, 10–11, 125,
        150
    problems with, 11–13
    term defined, 9
    test swatch for, 10–13
    width and, 12–13
    on yarn label, 21, 22
"Getting lost," solutions for,
    160–161
Grafting, types of, for joining,
    120–21
Grain. See Nap
Graphs, term defined, 127
Gusset, as way to alter, 185–186

Hand-washing
    for blocking, 181–183
    for used yarns, 189–91
Heavy-weight yarn, described, 17
Holders for yarn, types of, 44
Hooded garter stitch scarf with
    fringed ends, directions for,
    203–204
Horizontal buttonhole, method
    for, 102–103
Horizontal markers, function of,
    37–38

"Idiot tags," as markers, 40, 113
Increasing
    full-fashioned, 85–86
    functions of, 83–84
    keeping track of, 84–85
    methods for, 86–90
    see also Decreasing
Instructions
    copy of, as item for knitting
        bag, 43
"Intermediate Knitting" (video
    tape), 86

Intermediates, projects for, 206–
    228
Irish fisherman sweaters, 75
Irish moss stitch, method for,
    135–136

Jackets, knitted, flared, method
    for, 217–218
Jersey. See Stockinette stitch
Joining yarn, methods for, 96–99
Judgment, importance of, in
    knitting, 3–8

Kitchner stitch, for grafting, 120
Knit stitch
    American method for, 64, 65,
        66–67, 68, 74, 110
    Arabic method for, 64, 65
    binding off in, 77
    direction of, 68
    English method for, 64, 66–67
    European Pic method for, 64,
        65–66, 68, 74
    Continental method for, 65–
        66, 68, 110
    for garter stitch, 128
    increasing and decreasing in,
        84
    and purl, alternating, binding
        off in, 78
    vs. purl stitch, 63–64
    and yarnovers, 87
Knitted cord, directions for, 197
Knit-covered commercial form
    buttons, 198
Knitting
    bag, and equipment for, 41–48
    on circular vs. straight needles,
        25–27
    flat. See Stockinette stitch
    instructor, function of, 3
    judgment in, importance of, 3–
        8
    machines, commercial patterns
        and, 31–32
    needles. See Knitting needles

on. See Knitting on
    partial. See Short rows
    periodicals, evaluating, 3–8
    in round, amount of yarn and,
        214
    see also Knit stitch
Knitting, Creative Use of Leisure
    Time, 30
Knitting needles
    circular. See Circular needles
    double-pointed, using, 27, 47,
        155, 227–228
    gauge and, 10
    history of, 23–24
    as item for knitting bag, 42, 47
    matching yarn and, 27–28
    size. See Size, knitting needle
    sizing of, converting, 28
    tip shapes of, 27
    see also Protectors, needle-tip
Knitting on
    double strand, 56–58
    two-needle, 59–60
    see also Casting on

Labels, yarn, information listed
    on, 20–22
Lace
    eyelet, raised, method for, 140
    feather and fan, method for,
        141–142
    patterns, getting lost in, 160–
        161
    snowdrop or tulip, method for,
        142–143
    yarn ends in, tidying up, 172
Lacy shoulder capelet, directions
    for, 204–205
Length
    of armhole, measuring, 125
    measuring, 37–38, 150
    of yarn, on yarn label, 21
Lengthening, procedure for, 188–
    189
Linen yarn, characteristics of, 15
Loose stitches, to finish, 171